T&T Clark Reader in John Webster

T&T Clark Reader in John Webster

Edited by
Michael Allen

t&tclark

LONDON · NEW YORK · OXFORD · NEW DELHI · SYDNEY

T&T CLARK
Bloomsbury Publishing Plc
50 Bedford Square, London, WC1B 3DP, UK
1385 Broadway, New York, NY 10018, USA

BLOOMSBURY, T&T CLARK and the T&T Clark logo are trademarks of
Bloomsbury Publishing Plc

First published in Great Britain 2020

Cover design: Terry Woodley
Cover image © Keith Taylor/Alamy Stock Photo

A catalogue record for this book is available from the British Library.

Library of Congress Control Number: 2020938313

ISBN: HB: 978-0-5676-8751-7
PB: 978-0-5676-8750-0
ePDF: 978-0-5676-8753-1
eBook: 978-0-5676-8752-4

Typeset by Newgen KnowledgeWorks Pvt. Ltd. Chennai, India

To find out more about our authors and books visit www.bloomsbury.com
and sign up for our newsletters.

In memoriam John Webster

Contents

Reading John Webster: An introduction 1

1 **Theological theology** 21

2 **Biblical reasoning** 43

3 **The immensity and ubiquity of God** 65

4 **The place of Christology in systematic theology** 85

5 *Non ex aequo*: **God's relation to creatures** 105

6 **'It was the will of the Lord to bruise him': Soteriology and the doctrine of God** 121

7 **Eschatology and anthropology** 141

8 **Christ, church and reconciliation** 163

9 **Evangelical freedom** 181

10 **Intellectual patience** 195

John B. Webster – Chronology of publications 213

Index 223

Reading John Webster: An introduction

Michael Allen

We misread theology regularly and in various ways. Misreadings can come through textual narrowing, that is, excerpting and foreshortening a corpus. Perhaps nothing tops the way in which Thomas Aquinas's *Summa Theologiae* was excised and gutted immediately upon his death. In so doing, his attempt at reforming medieval pastoral theology and practice was largely missed for years. Misreadings can emerge through allowing parallels with extra-biblical philosophy to overdetermine the content of a theologian. In this regard, Thomas again serves as an object of misreading, for many continue to treat him as an Aristotelian (downplaying his Platonic influence and missing his even deeper commitment to exegesis of Holy Scripture). Given these and other pathways to misreading, we do well always to ask whether we read a given theologian (or other writer) well.

Such dangers do not exist only when dealing with theologians from long bygone eras. Modern theologians can similarly be mis-engaged, either owing to what is (not) read or how it is (mis-)read. For instance, the German Lutheran theologian Eberhard Jüngel was regularly viewed by English-speaking theologians who had heard of him as a student and interpreter of Karl Barth and, further, one engaged in critical engagement of modern philosophy (what is regularly deemed the 'interrogative' mood of reflection). John Webster introduced him afresh to the English world, perhaps surprisingly as someone engaged with classic theological problems latent in a much deeper tradition of reflection and with penning 'positive' doctrinal texts as much as with any 'interrogative' or 'critical' procedures.[1] Or consider the way in which Karl Barth's corpus has been engaged at great length and by many at this point. But engagement with the corpus is not the same as catching the structural framework of the project. Again, John Webster worked feverishly to demonstrate that assumptions that Barth's dogmatics held no space for human moral agency or Christian ethics were indefensible.[2] While Barth did seek to offer a rather extreme version of christocentrism throughout his dogmatics (whether successful or not), he maintained a vigorous and consistent place for an ethics of response. In both cases, Webster sought to read patiently and broadly and to allow the witness of a theologian to express itself in distinctly theological terms.

We might ask a related question then: What would it mean to read John Webster well? He has not written as widely, perhaps, as Barth or Jüngel, though his imprint on Christian theology today has had similar influence. Indeed because of the combination of his own theological genius and his investment to the institutions of the guild, he may well have more significant concrete influence in years to come. Yet his theology is often engaged piecemeal or perceived by means of extraneous principles and procedures. In what ways can we get a sense of his witness as a whole? And in what practices or protocols can we see him exemplifying the theological task? In brief, how do we read Webster well? This introductory chapter seeks to answer that question by identifying three key elements of his own theological witness. The nature of his testimony defines the shape of its proper reception. Yet Webster's principles themselves highlight the value of reading Christian classics for theological formation and, thus, introductory matters ought not overburden or delay engagement of his corpus as such. This introduction, then, will highlight and orient, but it will do so largely by way of exposition of his specific texts (itself a Websterian mode of reflection).

To introduce his primary concerns, we'll explore the practice of theology which takes the form of engaged readings of the classics of the Christian tradition, not only Holy Scripture but also the significant witnesses to the gospel found therein. Webster's work manifested a concern to mandate and to model careful readings of theological classics as a mode of practising holy theology today. The chapter will analyse three oft-overlooked essays of Webster. First, it will describe his programmatic manifesto 'Reading Theology' as an orienting project over against the dominant modes of modern academic theology. Second, it will turn to his 'Resurrection and Scripture' which raises questions of divine agency and speech. Third, it will look to the last essay written before his death, 'Theology and the Order of Love', which brings out the character of created relationships within which theological practice and intellectual virtue (like human life more generally) take shape. Observing broad patterns and principles from these three essays will help prime us to engage this reader fittingly and, hopefully, then to range more widely through the wider corpus. Before turning to those expositions, however, we do well to ask why one would even bother to read John Webster.

1. Why read Webster?

'Of making many books there is no end, and much study is a weariness of the flesh' (Eccl. 12.12). The preacher could not have imagined Amazon.com, yet the principle remains the same: the available resources in the world of letters are overwhelming and incessant. Even a subject area as defined as that of Christian theology finds an unimaginably large set of current publications in any given database search. Of all available Christian theology from the past and among the many resources which continue to be produced each and every year, why read the writings of John Webster? It's a worthy question to ask of any thinker. To be sure, the proof is in the pudding, and the only truly satisfactory answer comes by way of beginning to read and to find confirmation in the value of doing so. But an anticipatory answer should be given.

At the time of his death in May 2016, John Webster was regularly noted as perhaps the greatest living theologian writing in the English language. He had begun his career by studying the texts of modern Protestant divinity. He wrote a dissertation, translated numerous works and organized an essay collection that introduced the German Protestant theologian Eberhard Jüngel to the English-speaking world and began the process of his reception.[3] Then he turned and spent the better part of a decade working on the writings of the figure behind Jüngel, that is, the Swiss dogmatician Karl Barth.[4] At the same time, he worked with a colleague in Toronto to lead seminars and to address in varied outlets the ongoing project known as postliberalism, perhaps the most significant theological movement of the 1980s and 1990s to claim Barth as a primogenitor.[5]

Webster partnered with Colin Gunton to found the *International Journal of Systematic Theology* (*IJST*), which quickly garnered a reputation as the leading periodical in the field of constructive Christian theology. Having taught in Durham, he spent a decade at Wycliffe College in Toronto, eventually holding their Armitage Chair of Systematic Theology. Then he was appointed Rowan Williams's successor in occupying the Lady Margaret Chair of Divinity at Oxford University. After a number of years in that prestigious post, he moved northward to the Chair of Systematic Theology at the University of Aberdeen. Eventually he moved to a Chair of Divinity at the University of St Andrews. He supervised many doctoral students who have gone on to make significant contributions themselves to the practice of Christian systematic theology.

While Webster continued to provide stability and guidance to the discipline through his role as editor of *IJST* for almost two decades, he also served in various other roles at particular junctures that helped mark the development of the field. He served as editor or advisory board member for a range of book series. He helped shape the 'Barth Studies' and 'Great Theologians' series for Ashgate in the early 2000s. Later he would contribute to the 'Studies in Theological Interpretation' series for Baker Academic and help give direction to the 'New Studies in Dogmatics' series for Zondervan Academic. One can see his fingerprints, then, in notable projects devoted to studying Barth, attending to major theologians across the tradition, in attending to the theological interpretation of Scripture and in the practice of Reformed dogmatics. With Kathryn Tanner and Iain Torrance, he would edit *The Oxford Handbook of*

Systematic Theology, a major reference work that serves as something of a bellwether of the discipline's viability in the mid-2000s.[6]

At the time of his death, his readers were anticipating projects yet to come. For years he had noted an intent to publish the volume on Ephesians for the Brazos Theological Commentary on the Bible series. While he had lectured occasionally on the text and referenced it often in other writings, he hadn't yet written the text. He was hoping to bring two major lecture series to print form: the Kantzer Lectures given in 2007 at Trinity Evangelical Divinity School in Deerfield, Illinois, under the title 'Perfection and Presence: "God with Us" according to the Christian Confession', which was something of a small-scale systematics in its own right, and the Hayward Lectures delivered in 2009 at Acadia Divinity School on the theme of Creation. Whether or not print versions are made available in the future, these lecture cycles are already available in audio and video format online, respectively. His productivity and range was broad, then, with significant new ventures (into biblical commentary, into a small-scale systematics and into the doctrines of creation and providence) ongoing at the time of his death. The crown jewel of theological readers' hopes, however, was a projected multivolume systematic theology, the first volume of which he had begun drafting prior to his death.

At this time of his death, he was not best known for his distinguished historical work, nor even as an aspiring constructive theologian whose significance was merely projected for some arrival date yet to come. He had already published seven significant volumes of systematic theology in the final decade and a half of his life, feverishly writing working papers in the course of preparing to write that magnum opus. *Word and Church, Confessing God, The Domain of the Word* and the two-volume *God without Measure* were each significant essay collections in their own right.[7] *Holy Scripture* and *Holiness* were both major lecture series that have played a distinctive and abiding role with respect to the topics of Scripture and holiness, respectively.[8] Another lecture series from the late 1990s, the Burns Lectures given in 1997 at the University of Otago, was released in the journal *Stimulus* and has been published anew as a small book titled *The Culture of Theology*.[9] Many more reviews, articles and essays appeared in a variety of places, and some of his most notable works are substantive review essays on major texts over a range of topics (i.e. canon, salvation, the doctrine of God, ethics).[10]

Reading John Webster proves worthwhile because he models a particular set of theological principles and protocols, which themselves aid one in reading across not only the terrain of modern divinity but also the whole Christian tradition. By studying Webster, not only do we learn of some solo performance of the truths of the gospel, but we glean how more faithfully and productively to take in the full chorus of theological confession. In what follows, we will consider three essays wherein Webster reframes our thinking about reading theology, about grace in doing theology and about the kind of moral community involved in the theological task.

In each case, we'll seek to follow closely the course of a particular essay, so that his principles and his argumentative procedures can be traced and understood, for the two are not ultimately separable.

2. Why read theology at all?

If John Webster is worth reading, one reason is that he helps us see why theology itself is worth engaging. Indeed, given the distinct ambivalence of the overwhelming majority of the global population to the enterprise of Christian systematic theology, this is no small question. Why engage in theology? More specifically, why bother reading significant texts in Christian theology? John Webster's first inaugural lecture, 'Reading Theology', has been almost entirely overlooked in accounts of his theology, yet it lays out a genealogical, theological and practical sketch of his theological programme with unsurpassed candour (even if his handle on the resources of the doctrinal tradition was underdeveloped at this point). In this first section, I will identify ways in which he identifies the maladies of modern Protestant divinity, before assessing the way in which he offers what he here first calls a theological account of theology, concluding with a sketch of practical implications for the practice of theological study.

On 29 November 1995, John Webster delivered an inaugural lecture entitled 'Reading Theology' upon his appointment, ultimately to be brief, as the Ramsey Armitage Professor of Systematic Theology at Wycliffe College in Toronto. I say brief in as much as Webster would soon thereafter move back to the United Kingdom to take up the Lady Margaret Professorship at Oxford. The lecture was published in the *Toronto Journal of Theology* in 1997, though it has hardly gained any notice in the wider literature then or now.[11] The lecture warrants exposition, however, inasmuch as it both illustrates major tendencies in Webster's writings as well as includes topics that gain further formal and material development in years to come. Thus, it serves as a useful lens for identifying that which remains continuous throughout his writings and also that which develops and changes over time.

'Here I want to try to make a theological case for giving high profile to texts in the intellectual life of the Church.'[12] Why would such a case ever need to be presented? Webster turns immediately to the approach of Rene Descartes in commending the 'unschooled self' in the early portions of his *Discourse on Method*. Descartes identifies texts, the study of letters, as being hindrances to thought. He narrates his own quest to move texts to the safety of an arm's length, such that he can turn to the world of reason within himself. What burden of proof does this cast upon the scholar who turns to letters as a help? Webster then turns to Hegel's *Lectures on the History of Philosophy* and charts his account of philosophy as an inherently traditional enterprise, by which he means that reason is always occurring within a conversation that predates a thinker's own agency. The summary? '[T]exts and the conventions of schooling for which they are associated are for Hegel a shape for the mind, whereas for Descartes they are an obstacle, an invasion of that pure inwardness which for him is the ground of true science and which later generations will associate with spontaneous freedom.'[13]

Those genealogical comments serve to orient and to locate the ensuing argument that Webster will develop in this lecture. However, Webster will not remain long in the realm of the general. He will speak of texts in an ongoing intellectual conversation, but he observes almost immediately that Christians do so by talking of 'tradition' for they exist within 'God's history with humanity, for whose description the language of revelation, spirit, faith and church is irreducible.'[14] Broader categories – conversation, dialectic, traditioned inquiry – may well inform the self-understanding of theology's engagement of the letters or texts that mark its history, but it cannot define that self-understanding. 'Put somewhat differently, in theological usage tradition is an ecclesiological concept and not simply a variant of a more general affirmation that knowing and reflecting are inescapably bound up with belonging.'[15] To parse out the specifically Christian and distinctly theological principles of engaging tradition, Webster develops two theses throughout the remainder of the lecture.

'A first proposal is this: *Theology serves the Word of God by assisting the Church to remain faithful to the gospel as it is manifest in Holy Scripture*.'[16] This kind of assistance defers – always defers – transparently to the claims of the Bible if it is to listen before speaking, hearing prior to confessing. 'Conceived in this way, theology serves the need of the Christian tradition to specify itself … through which the tradition retains its determinancy as this particular stream of life.'[17] The task of explication and retrospective depiction looms large in his account, whereas critical analysis of the possibilities of such material claims fades into the background. This thesis surely sounds like unto what most persons conjure up in thinking of tradition, namely, a concern for fidelity to a given and enduring standard. Webster speaks of a 'localizing' function wherein theology is the 'Church's attempt faithfully to elucidate that to which its life is a response.'[18] He dismisses the notion that fidelity is guaranteed by the mere exercise of theological reason; no, any such assistance owes only to the grace of God's acts. Theology's role in helping to commend the 'faith once for all delivered to the saints' (Jude 3) manifests action by grace, not by nature.

Webster concludes this section by noting not merely that efficacy comes from without, by God's agency and involvement by Word and Spirit, but also that the human work of theology is implicated in the vagaries of earthly political and moral life. 'Especially in their quasi-catechetical functions vis-à-vis orthodoxy, theological texts are a political reality, moving along lines of power and constituting a potentially repressive social imaginary.'[19] He does not paper over the dangers of theological sin. But, ironically, 'it is just this potential which makes a theological account of theology imperative, precisely because, properly construed, such an account does not *legitimate* theological texts, but *relativizes* them'.[20] Knowing that theology owes its life and function to God, for it owes its very being and perfection unto God, puts theologians in their place. It gives hope, but only with a strong dash of humility. It fosters faith, though only that which begins and ever grounds itself in the fear of the LORD.

To that localizing role, a second function for theology is added. 'A second proposal is this: *Theology serves the Word of God by assisting the Church to remain alert to the challenge of the gospel as it is manifest in Holy Scripture*.'[21] Webster sounds apocalyptic in tone here (as regularly in his writings in the 1990s): 'God's Word divides, breaking up the continuity of the structures of human life and culture by exposing us to that which is other and new. And it does all this because it is the living voice of God.'[22] Jesus is the living Lord of the church, and he speaks to address his people. His speech brings judgement and hope, killing and making alive.

This second thesis likely strikes a more discordant note relative to expectations about traditioned inquiry in theology, inasmuch as it suggests that a theology attuned to classic texts will be capable – indeed, more so – of assisting in resisting the sinful *status quo*.

> Crucially, as the Church undertakes this kind of self-critique, it does not do so either by seeking to occupy some absolute space from which to judge its own activities or by abandoning itself to the judgment of worlds of discourse other than its own. On the contrary, the Church counters its own capacity for entrenchment by reading the Bible against itself.[23]

Whereas the wider academy has tended to employ critical theology with its suspicions registered from outside the material contents of any given discipline, Webster suggests that reading the Bible (not merely in the task of exegesis but also the mode of dogmatic analysis) occurs 'against itself'. In other words, the most promising mechanism for judging the status quo where it falls short of the new creation will be the ever-living word of the risen Christ.

The lecture ends somewhat abruptly. He returns to note the way the wider culture of North American theological education runs: 'Perhaps one of the most distinctive features of much mainstream Protestant Christianity in North America is the fact that it has very few distinctively Christian ideas, and so often has to make shift with a rather thin collection of borrowings from the largely bankrupt culture of liberal pluralism.'[24] His claim that attention to theological texts which aid us in hearing the Word of God more faithfully and more repentantly is meant to prompt 'growing into and maintaining an unanxious non-conformity'.[25]

On 28 October 1997, Webster would give a far more famous inaugural lecture entitled 'Theological Theology' upon his professorial appointment in Oxford. A number of similarities mark that well-known essay. First, genealogical work marks the argument, and he begins again by ranging observation regarding the place of theological inquiry among the contemporary academy. In this case close readings of Descartes and Hegel on the role of letters in the life of the scholar have expanded into a reading of the marginalization of theology in modern intellectual culture.[26] Second, the practice of theology demands careful definition of the task of theology, that is, the nature and function of the enterprise and its subject matter provide a Northstar by which we can find guidance unto that definition. Third, a polemical concern manifests itself, evidencing and at times eschewing practices of theology which cannot be described as 'theological theology' but which take their cues for the nature and function of theology from external disciplines or principles.[27] Thus, he identifies the crisis of modern theology as much owing to disorder within doctrine as to any external threats; inappropriate moves regarding the doctrines of revelation and of the resurrection of Jesus come in for particular analysis here.[28] Fourth, routines and postures of theology befit its nature, over against the tendencies of modern intellectual life, such that citation and commentary appropriately mark the receptive character of theology before the divine word.[29] Fifth and finally, 'the distinctiveness of Christian theology lies … not simply in its persistence in raising questions of ultimacy, but rather in its invocation of God as agent in the intellectual practice of theology'.[30] In both lectures theology is described as a positive science, ultimately defined as being receptive and responsive before bearing any creative and constructive or interrogative and critical capacity.

3. With what grace do we read?

We have seen why Webster believed theological texts worth reading, namely, because classics of the Christian theological tradition help pass on the faith and also assist in challenging us with the faith. Thus, they extend the tradition but they also take us through the epistemological turbulence of the life-giving Word of God. In this next section, a later essay of Webster's will be examined to see how he furthered these concerns as he developed.

The essay 'Resurrection and Scripture', written almost a decade after 'Reading Theology' and 'Theological Theology', illustrates the principles of that earlier programmatic piece and develops them further. First, this essay illustrates a relocation of theology and theological method within the categories of theology itself, in this case thinking through the doctrine of Scripture in light of the presence of the risen Jesus. Second, this account furthers and refines Webster's earlier writing, thereby manifesting his two formal principles regarding theology, namely, that it locates the church or furthers a church, on the one hand, and that it serves as a critical register for ongoing discipleship, on the other hand.

First, Webster begins what will be an essay on Holy Scripture by addressing its redemptive setting and its metaphysical context. 'Scripture and its interpreters have their being within the compass of this all-embracing reality; acts of interpretation are undertakings within the history of reconciling and revealing grace over which the exalted Christ presides.'[31] The economy of God's grace marks not merely 'content' for theology but also the 'context' within which theology occurs.[32] He calls then for a metaphysics of Scripture – its nature and its use – over against those who would rest satisfied with an aesthetics or ethics or, perhaps more common in the early twenty-first-century academy, a politics of Scripture. To provide such a metaphysics he turns to this notion of the divine economy, not merely the narrative of God's works but the way in which those works are narrated, that is, as free actions of the perfect God.

He focuses upon the claim that Jesus has risen from the dead in laying out that divine economy. He begins by reflecting on the resurrection as a reality within that economy. In so doing he moves beyond attesting the event; he shows how the event bespeaks something true of reality itself.

> Jesus Christ *lives*. Whatever further claims may be made about the resurrection of Jesus, and whatever consequences it may be necessary to draw from the primitive Christian confession that 'God raised him from the dead' (Rom. 10.9), they can only be a repetition, expansion or confirmation of the primary reality, namely that Jesus Christ is 'the living one' (Rev. 1.18). As the living one, Jesus Christ is alive with divine life.[33]

Observe here that the scriptural text from Romans 10 speaks of God performing an action – resurrecting Jesus – though Webster's insistent language falls upon the consequent reality: Jesus lives and is the living one. Resurrection is not merely a statement of occurrence, indeed not so much a statement of occurrence as a statement of existence, reality and being. 'As the living one', he says, indeed perhaps what he really means in context is closer to 'As the *resurrected* one, Jesus Christ is alive with divine life' (note the substitution of the adjective therein).

Hence Webster moves seamlessly between resurrection itself and exaltation. 'Resurrection, ascension, and heavenly session together constitute the declaration or manifestation of the lordship of Jesus Christ.'[34] His exaltation in these three actions relates not only to his lordship but also, perhaps in a counterintuitive manner, to his omnipresence. 'The risen one is no longer present in the flesh, but exalted in such a way that in his divine majesty he is ubiquitous.'[35] His divine life engages and encounters all in a singular way. Thus he moves into a reflection on how absence and presence are not polar opposites in this case; physically absent, he is now newly and freshly present spiritually. His presence in this newly absent manner comes through what are still truly communicative instruments. 'He is present, not simply as an inert or silent *substratum*, but as the king of glory: resplendent, outgoing, and therefore eloquent.'[36]

Webster thinks backward and forward with regard to this new presence of the risen Son. First, he thinks backward by relating resurrected glory to the aseity of the Son. He will use the language of 'manifestation' and 'vindication' rather than 'acquisition' to describe this 'enthronement'.[37] Further, the resurrection manifests not merely something of the Son but also something of the 'material definition of God's aseity'. The language here offers nothing really to relate the exalted Son's aseity and that of the *logos incarnandus*, that is, the eternal Son prior to his incarnational assumption of human flesh, though the prior passage gestures in such a direction and seems to affirm such a doctrine. Webster also thinks forward by talking about how the risen one serves as the space for created being metaphysically. 'Created being and history are thus not that in terms of which the resurrection of Jesus is to be placed, but rather the opposite: he is axiomatically real and true, having his being of himself and of himself bearing witness to himself'.[38] This discussion of resurrected being concludes by using the imagery of the transfiguration to describe the way in which the exalted Son's relation to humanity has spiritual significance: 'Created being is being in this divine act of transfiguration, being in the miracle to which Paul points with such wonder: ἰδοὺ γέγονεν καινά' (2 Cor. 5.17).[39]

In the remainder of the essay, then, Webster will develop three lines of argument that relate to this exposition of the significance of the resurrection of Jesus for created being.

> Giving an account of the nature of Scripture and of its interpreters, and of the acts required of those interpreters, involves developing three related claims: (1) Holy Scripture is a divinely constituted sign in the new order of being established at the resurrection of the Son of God and now at work through the Holy Spirit; (2) Christian readers of Holy Scripture are part of the same order of being, that is, of the eschatological order of regeneration; (3) Christian interpretative acts are fitting insofar as they exhibit conformity to this order of being in which both Scripture and its readers exist.[40]

He will go on to identify his project here as an effort in developing not merely a metaphysics of created being (as earlier in the essay) but 'offering a theological explication of "hermeneutical ontology"'.[41] In this regard Webster offers a parallel to what he had analysed in Barth's dogmatics, namely, a 'moral ontology' wherein basic Christian doctrines provided the deep structure and framing for an account of the moral life.[42] In many ways, he was pressuring the theologians around him to pause and not simply assume that various terms and categories can be brought undisturbed into the construction of a theological hermeneutics or ethics. 'In theological hermeneutics we need to start much further back than we customarily suppose, with a theological metaphysics of communicative agents and communicative action.'[43]

In this essay on hermeneutics and Scripture, then, he addresses Scripture's nature, its location and our appropriate activity with regard to it. In other essays, he would consider the pertinent metaphysical questions that help us 'start much further back than we customarily suppose' in considering the university or peace in the church or the act of mercy. On display in this one essay is a working methodology that served as something of a pattern for his constructive writing over the course of several years and a wide range of topics. It is plain here that dogmatics has a unique but limited role, and it is incumbent upon the dogmatician to make sure that they hearken back to first principles (of Scripture primarily and other classical Christian texts secondarily) in seeking to locate or frame that topic or question appropriately in a Christian manner.

Now the retort to such a dogmatic approach may well be that it sets one up for a sect-like narrowing of one's attention span. Perhaps it could be argued that it has a colloquial bent and will fail to keep its ear to the ground for knowledge found beyond the pale of the ecclesial conversation. Webster was attuned still to the danger of non-theological theology (as in the language of his earlier manifestos, 'Reading Theology' and especially 'Theological Theology') and yet patient reading shows that his writings of this period were anything but sectarian. He engages repeatedly with postmodern approaches to anthropology or to cutting-edge work on linguistic philosophy, and his varied writings on the culture of theology range patiently over classics of the modern intellectual culture with which he is at times doing battle. His relativizing such resources within the task of dogmatics, then, is hard won and not trite. They are the signs of a participant in a field pushing back on expansive claims regarding its impact. And yet he does push back, *repeatedly*.

The task of dogmatics is not to say everything that might be said about hermeneutics or morals or anything else. But it is to say one thing, namely, how the presence of the perfect God frames and defines our consideration of anything and everything we might wish to think about. Later Webster will come to put it this way: '[F]or all its scope, Christian theology is an exercise in concentration, required to fix its eyes not on everything but on the ways of God (Ps. 119.15); only in assent to this restriction will theology find itself having something to say about everything.'[44] An example might be instructive here; in this essay under consideration, when Webster comes to discussing the location of the Scriptures, he reflects on time and space in two distinct ways: 'The historical location of Scripture is the eschatological present; its social location is the communion of saints.'[45] He compares his eschatological sense of time to the historicist bent of much modern biblical scholarship. While he warns against a docetic understanding of the risen Christ's eschatological speech as the enduring temporal location for Scripture, he nonetheless suggests that this is the primary chronological location.[46] These are not the only possible locations in which one might consider Scripture, but he is here 'deploying a distinctively and directly theological category' in this task of dogmatics.[47]

The preface to *Holiness* offers something of a judgement regarding why such dogmatic backbone is necessary now:

> [T]he kind of theology attempted here … more naturally thinks of its host culture, not as Athens, but as Babylon. It is acutely conscious of the menace of wickedness in the life of the mind. And it is intensive before it is extensive. That is, its work is focused upon a quite restricted range of texts (the biblical canon) as they have been read and struggled with in the complex though unified reality which we call the tradition of the Church. Yet although it is intensive in this way, it is not stable or settled. The persistence with which it returns to its singular theme is an attempt to face the reality of the gospel as a permanent source of unsettlement, discomfiture and renewal of vocation. The intensity of this kind of theology is not the internally-directed energy of an achieved, separated world of ideas, but that of a way of thinking which might be called eschatological – always, that is, emerging from its own dissolution and reconstitution by the presence of the holy God.[48]

Intensive reasoning that fixes upon Scripture and the church's attempt to listen to that Word of God befits dogmatics. Extensive or conversational reasoning only follows thereafter; put otherwise, theological catechesis is necessary because the practitioners of theology have been malformed in Babylon and demand the sanctification of their minds now.[49]

It is crucial, then, to catch his second emphasis in this paragraph: intensive reflection provides an intellectual fit with the eschatological epoch in which we do theology; in point of fact, it fits snugly with our need to be unsettled by nothing less than God's own Word. So intensive reasoning is not a return to the status quo; as in 'Reading Theology', it also serves as a canonical or ruled measure by which God continues to confront us. In many ways Webster's fixation or attentiveness to the defined resources of Christian theology prompts him, like an Israelite prophet, to continue returning again and again the Torah or instruction of God as the most pertinent, timely and pointed means of rebuking contemporary failings. Time and again, Webster's own patient analysis of more conversational approaches to theology showed them to be rather enamoured with the fascinations of the current ideological climate and far less likely to be called to account in Christian terms. Essays in this collection address that tendency with regard to ecclesiology's temptation to draw too heavily (as in postliberalism) on ethnography or general approaches to community and traditioned reasoning, or even for anthropology to assume notions of selfhood that fail to reckon with the Bible's emphasis upon creatureliness (perhaps through too unconstrained investment in theologies of vocation or work, where the image of God is cut loose from the broader doctrine of creation).[50] By tending to the self-presentation of the risen Christ, and derivatively to the doctrinal categories developed through the long-won history of exegesis (in the genres of both biblical commentary and dogmatics), Webster says we will be formed not only for faithfulness but also for the journey of intellectual repentance and theological asceticism.[51]

4. In what kind of moral community do we read theology?

We should examine one final essay, again one not found in this collection, to observe tendencies in Webster's writing. In this case we turn to the final essay he wrote before his death in 2016, entitled 'Theology and the Order of Love'. It is instructive not merely because it represents his final days and most mature thought but also because it illustrates two new developments in his later writings: a concern to address moral theology with greater concreteness and also a turn to reflect on human relationships or communities anew. Here issues of gratitude and generosity are paired with a sense of belonging and location with certain intellectual relationships (both *coram Deo* ['before God'] and among fellow humans in the *communio sanctorum* ['communion of saints']).

His outline can be identified rather easily. 'Pursuit, enjoyment and communication of the intellectual goods of theology cannot be done in solitude, but only in a necessary double relation.' 'The first and principal relation is relation to God, who is both the *res* of theological inquiry and the one by whom this inquiry is prompted and kept in motion.' 'Alongside this is a second relation, derivative but no less necessary, which arises from the fact that pursuit of theology requires participation in intellectual society with other creatures.'[52] The essay addresses that metaphysical and relational/covenantal context for intellectual life as well as parsing its implications for intellectual virtue. If 'Resurrection and Scripture' offers something of a 'hermeneutical ontology', then this essay sketches what we might call an 'intellectual ontology'. But the essay also presses a bit further than the final section of 'Resurrection and Scripture' does in sketching the virtues of that domain with greater concreteness and specificity.[53]

Moral demands run in two directions. Looking backward, we must observe: 'Theological inquiry is indebted to those who exemplify fitting and fruitful ways of seeking out intellectual goods, and from whose communication of those goods theological inquirers have benefitted and continue to draw.' A forward look also alerts us: 'And theological inquiry is obligated to those with whom it is called by apostolic mandate to share the intellectual goods to which it has been afforded access and which it has been moved to love.'[54] These obligations flow because this is an 'order of love', with that term 'order' being employed specifically to speak not merely of happenstance relationships or connections of affinity but further of obligated and structured relationships. Webster acknowledges that these relations do 'assume cultural form' and yet their assumption flows from a more permanent 'created condition'.[55]

Webster turns not only to creation but also to providence to speak of how God upholds this order of loving relations. It is 'moved, directed, preserved and brought to perfection by God in his work of nature and his work of grace'.[56] God acts in both nature and in grace, because his work of nature is assaulted by the disorder of sin and demands a work of new birth or regeneration.[57] Baptism marks out that work of renewal, which 'separates' and 'initiates' a new order of the mind – 'initiates' in this distinct or separate order because 'the order of love in which Christian theology takes place is full of promise, but not yet devoid of affliction'.[58]

Webster turned from this sketch of sin and grace to describe how regenerate intelligence 'requires possession, formation and deployment of intellectual powers – faculties, talents and skills – and of intellectual virtues'.[59] Here he identifies love of knowledge as the 'supreme intellectual virtue' and, perhaps more notably, 'the root of the others', among which he names studiousness, docility, benevolence, patience and two virtues which receive lengthier analysis here: gratitude and generosity.[60] In so doing he addresses the call to gratitude unto God himself and then unto our fellow saints in the fellowship of the church; he then concludes by addressing the way in which 'in the order of love, intellectual gratitude gives rise to and is reinforced by intellectual generosity, in which that order is displayed and extended'.[61]

In many ways, this essay's topic does not sit at the centre of Webster's corpus. Its significance flows from just that point, namely, that even in addressing a topic such as intellectual relationships, he brings to bear a number of principles and protocols. In so doing this is one of many essays in his later years that focused upon the tasks of intellect and virtue; his final essay collection (*God Without Measure*) contained an entire second volume subtitled *Intellect and Virtue*. These moral essays are disciplined by the material judgements of theological principle: for instance, this reflection on intellectual generosity chastens how we might speak of humans as teachers, thereby serving as a 'ministerial (creaturely) agent' working under the providential and redemptive instrumentality of the 'principal (divine) … agent'.[62] In so doing, the human teacher is located and limited, though also freed and sent on their way with a word. Any number of contemporary intellectual realities are challenged herein: the free-ranging guru mentality of the (public) intellectual, the *poietic* or self-creative styling of intellectual work, the reduction of intellectual validation to identity politics and the like.

5. Beginnings to reading Webster

If Webster is right, then we ought to read deeply in the Christian tradition. If he is accurate, then we ought to read anticipating to have our expectations upset and prejudices disarmed. If he is legitimately on to something here, then the best word is that we do not read alone, for the living and true God of the gospel reigns and speaks from heaven high. Perhaps the best proof may be getting on with the task of reading him, then, to see if doing so leaves us undisturbed or if, ironically enough, the most challenging theology is precisely the most exegetical theology. In so doing,

I wager that the diligent reader will find Webster to help them contemplate God more deeply, understand their creatureliness more fully and more powerfully appreciate the gracious reality of the fellowship God has with creatures in nature, grace and glory.

This reader is designed to help introduce and guide novices in engaging Webster's writings. Essays representative of each of these three areas of Webster's work can be found therein: 'Theological Theology' expands on what we saw in 'Reading Theology', 'Biblical Reasoning' widens the material from 'Resurrection and Scripture' and 'Intellectual Patience' pairs with 'Theology and the Order of Love'. Hopefully reflecting on parallels helps situate each of those essays and enhances the reading of them.

The reader includes many essays besides those three, however, and the patterns and principles discussed so far prove illuminating in considering the full span of texts found here. Indeed, Webster's work is notable not least for the fact that its principles manifest themselves time after time, whatever the topic or text at hand. The essays represent his constructive work temporally and topically, providing opportunities to see these foundational principles and fundamental protocols at work across the range of Christian theology. The range of chapters included can be appreciated temporally and topically, introducing readers to texts from the full extent of years in which he wrote constructively and also providing teasers of his work in a range of subject areas.

Temporally speaking, there are inclusions from each essay collection. Two essays from *Word and Church* appear: 'Christ, Church, and Reconciliation' and 'Eschatology and Anthropology'. Three essays from *Confessing God* are included: 'Theological Theology', 'The Immensity and Ubiquity of God' and 'Evangelical Freedom'. *Domain of the Word* provides 'Biblical Reasoning'. Several essays from *God without Measure* appear as well: 'The Place of Christology in Systematic Theology', '*Non ex aequo*', '"It Was the Will of the Lord to Bruise Him"' and 'Intellectual Patience'. In terms of topics, the material also represents his major concerns (though, admittedly, not every area into which he ventured): on scripture and reason, 'Biblical Reasoning'; on theological principles, 'Theological Theology'; on the doctrine of the triune God, 'The Immensity and Ubiquity of God' and 'The Place of Christology in Systematic Theology'; on creatureliness, 'Eschatology and Anthropology'; on covenant fellowship, '*Non ex aequo*'; on salvation, 'It Was the Will of the Lord to Bruise Him'; on church, 'Christ, Church, and Reconciliation'; on ethics, 'Evangelical Freedom' and 'Intellectual Patience'.

Each chapter includes a brief introduction wherein I will sketch its main concerns and arguments, pointing to its relevance in his wider corpus, the field at present and the Christian tradition at large. I include footnotes throughout the essays that provide explanatory comments or observe connections to other portions of his writings. The goal is to give just enough guidance that readers can grow in their competence and develop deeper confidence in turning to his texts by themselves. This reader is not the place for critical analysis of his corpus, a necessary task that shows respect to his significance, manifests commitment to his own principles and helps draw his contribution into the ongoing witness to the gospel that is the Christian doctrinal tradition. Thankfully, other projects are beginning to offer both detailed exposition as well as the beginnings of critical analysis with his theological project.[63]

John Webster remains worthy of attentiveness, not merely of reading. He sought to reframe our metaphysics, epistemology and ethics by locating each in light of the perfect, triune God of the gospel. In so doing, however, he turned not merely to the divine economy (which has been fairly common in recent debates of Trinitarian theology) but more deeply to the doctrine of divine perfection and its various pairings (i.e. aseity). Also interesting was the fact that his reframing was that of one calling theologians back to reengaging Holy Scripture, first, and the classics of the Christian tradition, second. Relative to those who reform by drawing on (or abdicating unto?) non-native discourses (i.e. critical theory, cultural theory, literary theory, analytic philosophy), his was a regular call for 'straight systematics' and 'intensive' immersion or catechesis in the practice of Christian doctrine. And yet his retrieval methodology was not a manifesto for bolstering the status quo, for it was always inflected by a reminder that the most sanctifying theology was a scriptural theology. In all this, his project leaned upon this claim: 'God is not summoned into the presence of reason; reason is summoned before the presence of God.'[64] Let us answer that summons and begin reading.

Notes

1   John Webster, *Eberhard Jüngel: An Introduction to His Theology* (Cambridge: Cambridge University Press, 1986), 3.

2   John Webster, *Barth's Ethics of Reconciliation* (Cambridge: Cambridge University Press, 1995); John Webster, *Barth's Moral Theology: Human Action in Barth's Thought* (Edinburgh: T&T Clark, 1998).

3   Webster, *Eberhard Jüngel: An Introduction to His Theology*; Eberhard Jüngel, *Theological Essays I*, ed. and trans. John Webster, 2nd edn (Edinburgh: T&T Clark, 1991); John Webster, ed., *The Possibilities of Theology: Studies in the Theology of Eberhard Jüngel in his 60th Year* (Edinburgh: T&T Clark, 1994); Eberhard Jüngel, *Theological Essays II*, ed. and trans. John Webster (Edinburgh: T&T Clark, 1995); Eberhard Jüngel, *God's Being is in Becoming: The Trinitarian Being of God in the Theology of Karl Barth*, ed. and trans. John Webster (Edinburgh: T&T Clark, 2001); John Webster, 'Introduction', in Eberhard Jüngel, *Justification: The Heart of the Christian Faith*, trans. Jeffrey F. Cayzer (London: T&T Clark, 2001), vii–xvii.

4   Webster, *Barth's Ethics of Reconciliation*; Webster, *Barth's Moral Thought*; John Webster, *Barth* (London: Continuum, 2000); John Webster, ed., *The Cambridge*

Companion to Karl Barth (Cambridge: Cambridge University Press, 2000); John Webster, *Barth's Earlier Theology* (London: T&T Clark, 2005).

5 John Webster and George Schner, eds, *Theology after Liberalism: A Reader* (Oxford: Blackwell, 1999).

6 John Webster, Kathryn Tanner and Iain Torrance, eds, *The Oxford Handbook to Systematic Theology* (Oxford: Oxford University Press, 2007).

7 John Webster, *Word and Church: Essays in Christian Dogmatics* (Edinburgh: T&T Clark, 2001); John Webster, *Confessing God: Essays in Christian Dogmatics II* (London: T&T Clark, 2005); John Webster, *The Domain of the Word: Scripture and Theological Reason* (London: T&T Clark, 2012); John Webster, *God without Measure: Working Papers in Christian Theology.* Volume 1: *God and the Works of God* (London: T&T Clark, 2015); *God without Measure: Working Papers in Christian Theology.* Volume 2: *Virtue and Intellect* (London: T&T Clark, 2016).

8 John Webster, *Holy Scripture: A Dogmatic Sketch* (Cambridge: Cambridge University Press, 2003); John Webster, *Holiness* (Grand Rapids: Eerdmans, 2003).

9 *The Culture of Theology* (ed. and intro. Ivor J. Davidson and Alden McCray; Grand Rapids: Baker Academic, 2019).

10 A bibliography can be found in a *festschrift* volume marking his sixtieth birthday: R. David Nelson, Darren Sarisky and Justin Stratis, eds, *Theological Theology: Essays in Honour of John Webster* (London: T&T Clark, 2015), 349–58. Though not completely exhaustive, it includes virtually all his writings.

11 John Webster, 'Reading Theology', *Toronto Journal of Theology* 13, no. 1 (1997), 53–63. So far as I am aware, the only analysis in print is Michael Allen, 'Toward Theological Theology: Tracing the Methodological Principles of John Webster', *Themelios* 41, no. 2 (2016), 220–4 (217–37).

12 Webster, 'Reading Theology', 53.

13 Webster, 'Reading Theology', 55.

14 Webster, 'Reading Theology', 55.

15 Webster, 'Reading Theology', 56.

16 Webster, 'Reading Theology', 56 (italics original).

17 Webster, 'Reading Theology', 57.

18 Webster, 'Reading Theology', 58.

19 Webster, 'Reading Theology', 59.

20 Webster, 'Reading Theology', 59 (italics original).

21 Webster, 'Reading Theology', 59 (italics original).

22 Webster, 'Reading Theology', 59.

23 Webster, 'Reading Theology', 60.

24 Webster, 'Reading Theology', 61.

25 Webster, 'Reading Theology', 61.

26 John Webster, 'Theological Theology', in *Confessing God*, 12–16.

27 If Webster sounds fervent in his pitch at just this point, it is no doubt largely because he had previously advanced such claims himself. Two early essays highlighted the need for and purported to illustrate the practice of a theology done conversationally by taking up resources from non-theological disciplines.

For instances of an earlier fascination with conversation and dependence on non-theological sources, see 'Locality and Catholicity: Reflections on Theology and the Church', *Scottish Journal of Theology* 45 (1992), 1–17 (esp. 6 and 16, where he will say that ' "conversation" with publics other than our own is, then, a Christological imperative'); John Webster, 'The Church as Theological Community', *Anglican Theological Review* 75, no. 1 (1993), 102–15 (esp. 103 fn. 4, where he admits that 'My tiny sketch of "tradition" is informed less by theological sources and more by work in philosophy … and in the human sciences'). While such reference to and engagement of non-theological sources continued (even in 'Reading Theology' and 'Theological Theology'), it tended to arise more as a foil and less as a principle or even a principal source for his own constructive case. This shift fits snugly alongside his growing frustration with postliberalism as a project in the 1990s, a judgement hard-won through teaching seminars in Toronto alongside Yale-trained Roman Catholic theologian, George Schner. The two colleagues edited *Theology After Liberalism* (Blackwell Readings in Modern Theology; Oxford: Blackwell, 2000).

28 Webster, 'Theological Theology', 18–20.

29 Webster, 'Theological Theology', 21.

30 Webster, 'Theological Theology', 25.

31 John Webster, 'Resurrection and Scripture', in *The Domain of the Word*, 32.

32 On the economy as 'content' and 'context', see especially John Webster, 'The Holiness of Theology', in *Holiness* (Grand Rapids: Eerdmans, 2003), 12.

33 Webster, 'Resurrection and Scripture', 139 (italics original).

34 Webster, 'Resurrection and Scripture', 139.

35 Webster, 'Resurrection and Scripture', 140.

36 Webster, 'Resurrection and Scripture', 141.

37 Webster, 'Resurrection and Scripture', 139–40.

38 Webster, 'Resurrection and Scripture', 141–2.

39 Webster, 'Resurrection and Scripture', 142.

40 Webster, 'Resurrection and Scripture', 143.

41 Webster, 'Resurrection and Scripture', 143. It is not clear why he placed quotation marks around the phrase 'hermeneutical ontology'.

42 See especially John Webster, *Barth's Ethics of Reconciliation* (Cambridge: Cambridge University Press, 1995), 215. In using the language of moral ontology, he explicitly draws upon the work of Charles Taylor, *Sources of the Self: The Making of Modern Identity* (Cambridge: Harvard University Press, 1989), 8.

43 Webster, 'Resurrection and Scripture', 143.

44 John Webster, 'What Makes Theology Theological'? in *God without Measure*, vol. 1: *God and the Works of God* (London: T&T Clark, 2015), 223.

45 Webster, 'Resurrection and Scripture', 147.

46 For comparison with 'critical historians of biblical literature', see Webster, 'Resurrection and Scripture', 147–8; for warnings against a docetically malformed sense of eschatology, see 148.

47 Webster, 'Resurrection and Scripture', 149.

48 John Webster, *Holiness* (Grand Rapids: Eerdmans, 2003), 4–5.

49 For perhaps the most pointed reflections upon 'conversational theology' in Webster's corpus, see John Webster, 'Article Review; David F. Ford, Self and Salvation', *Scottish Journal of Theology* 54, no. 4 (2001): 548–59.

50 See 'Church, Church, and Reconciliation' and 'Eschatology and Anthropology', respectively.

51 For a comparison of the approach to theological asceticism in Webster with that of Sarah Coakley, see Michael Allen, 'Dogmatics as Ascetics', in *The Task of Dogmatics* (ed. Oliver D. Crisp and Fred Sanders; Grand Rapids: Zondervan, 2017), 189–209.

52 John Webster, 'Theology and the Order of Love', in *Rationalität Im Gespräch – Rationality in Conversation* (ed. Christina Drobe et al.; Marburger Theologische Studien 126; Leipzig: Evangelische Verlagsanstalt, 2016), 175–85.

53 While 'Resurrection and Scripture' does address 'The Interpretation of Scripture', it restricts its focus to addressing 'the persons of interpreters and the ends of their action' without also moving forward to speak of the shape, manner, form, and discipline of their activity. While 'Theology and the Order of Love' similarly begins with persons and ends (what we might deem creation and eschatology), it moves on towards material specificity in a fuller manner. Parallels can be seen in an incomplete, four-part series of expositions on the fruit of the Spirit (from Gal. 5.22–23) which appeared on the blog Reformation21 in 2015, offering an introduction and analyses of love, joy and peace.

54 Webster, 'Theology and the Order of Love', 175.

55 Webster, 'Theology and the Order of Love', 176.

56 Webster, 'Theology and the Order of Love', 176.

57 Webster, 'Theology and the Order of Love', 176, 177.

58 Webster, 'Theology and the Order of Love', 177.

59 Webster, 'Theology and the Order of Love', 177.

60 Webster, 'Theology and the Order of Love', 177.

61 Webster, 'Theology and the Order of Love', 178–80 on gratitude to God, 181–3 on gratitude to the saints, and then 183–5 on generosity among our fellow image-bearers (whom he calls 'a double object: the baptised, and those who are as yet *extra ecclesiam*' [183]).

62 Webster, 'Theology and the Order of Love', 184.

63 See especially Michael Allen and R. David Nelson, eds, *A Companion to the Theology of John Webster* (Grand Rapids: Eerdmans, forthcoming). Several doctoral dissertations are also in progress regarding various areas of Webster's theology.

64 Webster, *Holiness*, 17.

Theological theology[1]

EDITOR'S INTRODUCTION

'Theological theology' was delivered originally as an inaugural lecture as Lady Margaret Professor of Divinity at the University of Oxford on 28 October 1997. John Webster begins by describing the way in which theology plays a marginal role in the modern university, for reasons external and internal to theology itself. Then he will offer a programmatic sketch of how theology might otherwise serve the university at large more fruitfully by tending to its theological task more faithfully.

To offer a brief anatomy of the situation in the university, he charts the development of a modern 'anthropology of enquiry' which prizes 'inwardness' rather than 'participation in a particular tradition', which undertakes the task of *Wissenschaft* (technical competence in science) rather than *Bildung* (moral formation), and which sits uncomfortably with 'appeal to texts' as a mode of intellectual discourse. But Webster does not rest satisfied sketching a genealogy of wider intellectual disorder; rather, he also speaks of problems within the house of divinity itself. 'Far from ensuring the survival of Christian theology in the face of challenges to its plausibility, the relinquishment of specifically Christian doctrine in favour of generic theism in fact hastened its demise.' He gives two case studies, showing how in the post-Reformation era, 'construed epistemologically, revelation becomes predoctrinal, prolegomenal, the ground of doctrine which is itself explicable in relative isolation from (for example) Christology or pneumatology'. Secondly, he laments the shift of resurrection to an almost entirely apologetic frame of reference, whereby it 'shifts from being an *object* of belief to being a *ground* of belief'.

Just so, Webster gives a textured account of the malaise of divinity in the modern university. However, he also goes on to note that the protocols of the university are being challenged by postmodern thinkers and critical theorists. 'Oddly enough, then, the very high premium on critical activity in the university may make us insufficiently aware that the university is a customary institution as much as a reflective one: indeed, its critical practices are customary in character.' Webster raises the question, then, how may theology serve the university in such a situation where even critical thinking is being critiqued? He argues that theology needs to do more than provide moral motivation or a panged conscience, rather theology needs to speak of God and God's actions.

Providing that distinctly theological frame of reference, Webster turns to Johannes Wollebius's description of the principles of theology: 'The principle of the being of theology is God; the principle by which it is known is the Word of God.' He highlights the fact that God is not merely the object of enquiry but also the agent who makes himself known. As he parses this quotation, he shows that this involves theology in a determinate or bounded field of enquiry, seeking to know God specifically. Further, theology listens to the Word of God, what Webster calls the 'eschatological self-presence of God in Jesus Christ through the power of the Holy Spirit'.

Interestingly, this essay does argue by citation, though more so with regard to the genealogical accounts of modernity and the paradigmatic texts which he seeks to probe. A range of other essays and articles from this time period similarly manifest remarkable command of this literature (i.e. Eberhard Jüngel, Michael Buckley, Alasdair MacIntyre, Martha Nussbaum, Charles Taylor on the one hand and various postmoderns on the other hand, such as Calvin Schrag, Mark C. Taylor, Michel Foucault). He would soon begin working by citation and exposition, however, of classic Christian texts (i.e. biblical texts such as 2 Cor. 5.18 or patristic voices such as Clement of Alexandria); in this essay, such citation is meagre (limited to brief engagement of Johannes Wollebius's textbook of Reformed dogmatics). A rather different rhetoric and set of resources marks his 2015 redux (entitled 'What Makes Theology Theological'?).

Webster itemizes a range of topics which would need to be explored in vivifying intellectual life with a reinvigorated theological contribution to the university: 'Filling out this picture of the academy would require us to say much more: about teaching as the engendering of the habits of man of particular traditions (including their habits of self-critique); about the role to be played by awed reading of classical texts; about the need to deregulate the genres of scholarship.' In many ways his Burns Lectures on 'The Culture of Theology' in 1998 filled out these subthemes with greater texture and specificity. The renewed protocols, though, depend upon a new intellectual ontology and anthropology which is itself attentive to and disciplined by the definitive presence and activity of the triune God.

> [W]hat is needed is a renewed 'conflict of the faculties', though not one driven by 'the quest for commensuration', but by a confident sense of the importance of non-conformity. And, crucially, what such conflict requires is not just a better epistemology, but a changed anthropology of enquiry and politics of intellectual exchange, so that differences can be seen not as a curse but as the given condition for the university's life.

While 'Theological theology' was a manifesto delivered with verve, it was not yet a mirror depicting a fully formed Christian theologian. It continues to serve as a useful entryway to Webster's working papers in Christian doctrine and is still likely his most widely known and broadly impactful essay.

Suggested readings

The Culture of Theology (ed. Ivor J. Davidson and Alden C. McCray; Grand Rapids: Baker, 2019). Originally published as six articles in the journal *Stimulus*: 'Culture: The Shape of Theological Practice', *Stimulus* 6, no. 4 (1998): 2–9; 'Texts: Scripture, Reading and the Rhetoric of Theology', *Stimulus* 6, no. 4 (1998): 10–16; 'Traditions: Theology and the Public Covenant', *Stimulus* 6, no. 4 (1998): 17–23; 'Conversations: Engaging Difference', *Stimulus* 7, no. 1 (1999): 2–8; 'Criticism: Revelation and Disturbance', *Stimulus* 7, no. 1 (1999): 9–14; 'Habits: Cultivating the Theologian's Soul', *Stimulus* 7, no. 1 (1999): 15–20. Ivor Davidson's introduction (in the book form) is a stellar and incisive guide to the place of the lectures in Webster's development.

'What Makes Theology Theological?', *Journal of Analytic Theology* 3 (May 2015) 17–28; repr. in GWM 1: 213–24.

'*Sub ratione Dei*: Zum Verhältnis von Theologie und Universität', *Communio. Internationale Katholische Zeitschrift* 42 (2013): 151–69 = 'God, Theology, Universities', in D. Nelson (ed.), *Indicative of Grace – Imperative of Freedom. Essays in Honour of Eberhard Jüngel in his Eightieth Year* (London: T&T Clark, 2014), 241–54; repr. in GWM 2: 157–72.

Martin Westerholm, 'The University', in *A Companion to John Webster's Theology* (ed. Michael Allen and R. David Nelson; Grand Rapids, MI: Eerdmans, forthcoming).

Michael Allen, 'Toward Theological Theology: Tracing the Methodological Principles of John Webster', *Themelios* 41, no. 2 (2016): 217–37; repr. in *A Companion to John Webster's Theology* (ed. Michael Allen and R. David Nelson; Grand Rapids: Eerdmans, forthcoming).

THEOLOGICAL THEOLOGY

One of the signs of the health of a university discipline is its ability to sustain lively self-critical disagreement about its intellectual processes. It is no doubt true that, in academia as much as in politics or marriage, endless procedural debate usually does nothing more than defer the hour of decision. But universities (like parliaments and marriages) are supposed to be places of contained conflict, conflict which unearths fundamental intellectual and spiritual ideals and holds them up for correction and reformulation. No less than others, theologians ought to be busy about this kind of dispute, both among themselves and in their extra-mural conversations. Among the many gifts which my immediate predecessor brought to the study of theology in Oxford and beyond was a conviction that theology is and ought to be disturbing, for at its heart lie those events in which, according to Christian faith, human life and thought are entirely transfigured. Rowan Williams' intellectual temper – energetic and courteous at the same time, suspicious both of premature resolution and of mere ironic detachment, genuinely hospitable, above all, *prayerful* – sets an extraordinarily high standard for us, above all by its seemingly inexhaustible suggestiveness, its sheerly provocative effect. And so it is fitting that the new occupant of this ancient chair should continue to devote attention to the task of clarifying what the discipline of Christian theology is about, provoking the kind of disturbance of usual business which the recently arrived are permitted to make, if only for a little while.

That being said, it is worth bearing in mind that, in its very first years, the Lady Margaret professorship could hardly have been less provocative. The first of Margaret Beaufort's divinity readers in Oxford was one Dr Wilsford, who gave a set of lectures in the first term on the entirely predictable topic of Duns Scotus' *Quaestiones Quodlibetales*, at the ungodly hour of seven in the morning. We do not know what the good doctor told his audience at that early hour, but from the subject we may surmise that it was in keeping with the faculty conventions of the time, and hardly likely to kindle debate about the basic self-understanding of the discipline.[2] For something really provocative, one would have gone to hear John Colet, back in Oxford from Europe, lecturing on the Pauline epistles with startling originality and turning the discipline inside out.

But if nowadays one were to follow Colet's lead and to try to reconfigure the discipline of Christian theology, the problem would be simply this: hardly anybody would notice. For Christian theology is not taken very seriously in modern Western universities: sometimes encouraged, occasionally attacked, it is most often treated with a benign indifference, so that if one day theology were simply to absent itself, the university's pursuit of its ideals would in no way be imperilled. Above all, Christian theology is not a serious factor to contend with in thinking about the university's intellectual agenda and its modes of enquiry. Why is this? Why is it that Christian theology has for at least two hundred years played so slender a role in establishing the intellectual culture of the modern research university? Two clusters of reasons come to mind. First, the history of the modern research university and its ethos of scholarship has had as one of its major corollaries the marginalization of moral and religious conviction, and thus the discouragement of theological enquiry. Second, most traditions of modern Christian theology in the West have very deeply internalized the models of enquiry which have become normative in modern academic institutions, and so have found themselves increasingly alienated from the subject matters and the cultural and intellectual processes of the Christian religion.* This confluence of external and internal factors has had a twofold effect. On the one hand, it has meant that Christian theology has by and large retained its prestige in the university only by taking on the colouring of its environment – by becoming *wissenschaftlich*. On the other hand, it has meant that the more theology invokes theological doctrine to articulate its nature and procedures, the more precarious has been its tenure in the dominant institutions of intellectual enquiry. What is it about those institutions of intellectual enquiry which has rendered them a generally inhospitable environment for the practice of Christian theological reflection?

Universities work with conventions about what constitutes learning and what are appropriate methods of enquiry. Although we may not necessarily be reflectively aware of these conventions at all times, they are ubiquitous, constituting a shared set of assumptions about what responsible intellectual activity will look like, encouraging certain practices and disapproving of others. The routine invisibility of these conventions ought, of course, to alert us to their ideological potential; conventions which are not regularly subject to inspection and dispute quickly assume an air of necessity and their conventional character is eclipsed. This is not, of course, to suggest that the modern university's conventions of enquiry are *simply* arbitrary, or that their prestige is merely social or political. Modern conventions of intellectual enquiry have acquired their prestige largely because, in a number of culturally dominant fields (notably natural and social science and, to a lesser degree, history), they have consistently displayed extraordinary explanatory power. Nevertheless, we would be unwise to be mesmerized by this state of affairs into thinking that conventions which have proved themselves locally successful can claim universal applicability or normativity. Above all, we need to grasp that '[l]earning is not some eternal essence that happens to enter history at particular times and places, but a long-enduring social practice whose goals, methods, standards of excellence, and legitimating and orienting frameworks of conviction change drastically over time and are often deeply

---

*Webster will begin his analysis with external threats but turn and linger more patiently over internal disarray in the discipline of theology itself. Surely his judgement of priorities follows the length of his analysis rather than the sequence of it.

contested'.[3] Taking the point seriously will involve us in coming to terms with the fact that, although the university may often believe itself in pursuit of the permanent essence of scholarship, '[w]hat it is actually doing is lending institutional support and preference to just some versions of that malleable, often-changing, long-enduring social practice that is learning – and excluding others'.[4] What conventions are being referred to here?

The modern research university conducts its business on the basis of a particular 'anthropology of enquiry'. That is to say, underlying its specific practices and preferred modes of research, its norms of acceptability and its structures of evaluation, is an account of the intellectual life, of what intellectual selfhood ought to look like. That anthropology, largely implicit but nevertheless possessed of enormous authority, is bound up with some of the most potent moral and spiritual ideals of modernity. Above all, it is an extension of the ideal of freedom from determination by situation, which is one of the deep foundations of liberal culture.

To give consent to the ideals of the university is to envisage one's intellectual practice as a reiteration of these ideals. Prominent amongst them is the principle that learning is a generic human enterprise. What is of greatest interest in describing the operations of the intellect can be isolated from any contingent, secondary characteristics which happen to be true of particular enquirers in particular fields. No *background* is needed; indeed, if the intellectual life is to proceed properly, then the enquirer has to leave all particular convictions at the portal of the university before stepping inside, since such convictions have to be factored out from the very beginning. For the practice of intellectual enquiry ought to be as unaffected by the specificities of culture, personality, or political and religious conviction as is the functioning of the bodily organs. And so, when theologians routinely admonish first-year students to 'forget everything you have learned so far', they are doing much more than cleaning out the lumber of inherited prejudice; they are as likely as not initiating students into one of the most tenacious conventions of modern intellectual life.

Within that convention lies hidden the notion that what is most basic to responsible selfhood is to be identified, not with the specificities of background, custom or training, nor with the habits of mind and spirit which are acquired from participation in a particular tradition, but with *inwardness*. What is most basic is interiority, and the most characteristic activity of interiority is that of making representations of the world. My most basic act as a reflective self is that act in which I summon the world into my presence, as it were commanding it to appear before me by making a representation of it, interrogating it and making judgements about it.* In this model of the practice of reasoned enquiry, the enquiring self is considered to be what the great Canadian philosopher, George Grant, called a 'transcending

---

*The essay 'Eschatology and Anthropology' will later unfurl Webster's anthropology over against the individualist and expressivist depictions that dominate the wider intellectual climate.

summonser'.[5] Reason, that is, is instrumental, in two senses. First, its essential task is that of getting hold of the world, objectifying it so that it becomes something of which I can formulate a picture. Second, reason is instrumental in that it is considered a tool, quite unaffected by a particular context in which I might deploy it or any convictions I may have as its user. In short: the anthropology of enquiry of the modern research university is dominated by ideals of procedural rationality, context- and conviction-independence, and representation and judgement. The effect of this anthropology is to isolate and then privilege an ideal of rational competence: 'human rationality is such and the methods and procedures which it has devised and in which it has embodied itself are such that, if freed from external constraints and most notably from the constraints imposed by religious and moral tests, it will produce not only progress in enquiry but also agreement among all rational persons as to what the rationally justified conclusions of such enquiry are'.[6]

This anthropology of enquiry has been formative of the culture of the modern university in at least two interconnected ways. First, it has been a major factor in the decline of *Bildung*, formation, as an ideal of schooling, and its replacement by *Wissenschaft*. When education is understood as *Bildung*, the goal of schooling is the cultivation of a particular kind of person who has acquired certain habits of mind and will, a certain cast or temper of the soul, and so is oriented to what is considered to be the good and the true. Schooling is transformation, and involves the eradication of defects and limitations, as well as the fostering of skills which are learned through engagement in common intellectual practices (of speech and argument) in which the skills are inculcated and refined. Schooling in this mode both depends upon and gives authoritative expression to a particular version of the human good; to be schooled is to be educated into reflective appropriation of the roles and practices of a specific moral and intellectual world.[*]

The ideal of *Wissenschaft* differs from this in a number of ways. Its anthropological ideals exclude any concern with schooling as transformation, precisely because the activities of enquiry are standard to any rational person. Unlike *Bildung*, it does not perceive itself as tradition-specific, for reason is independent of contexts; hence *Wissenschaft* is concerned with intellectual practices which transcend all localities and instead summon those localities for review. And, moreover, *Wissenschaft* is by its very nature anti-authoritarian: given versions of the good and the true, especially when embodied in authoritative traditions, are not there as arrangements to which we must assimilate ourselves, but as matters into which we are obligated to enquire.

---

[*]A number of Webster's essays on Holy Scripture would look back to the notion of formation as a key element in need of recovery (see, e.g., *HS*, ch. 3 on the importance of grace and character or *WC*, ch. 3 on Barth and Bonhoeffer's examples in this respect). 'Biblical Reasoning' will pick up these emphases in its discussion of reason within the economy of the gospel.

This leads to a second way in which the modern university is shaped by its underlying anthropology of enquiry. That anthropology is partly responsible for a shift in the status of texts in university schooling. Though books are omnipresent in the modern university, our relation to them has a distinctly modern cast. The *Bildung* model of education was in large part sustained by agreement about a canon, and flourished within a culture which had as one of its governing instruments a set of interrelated texts, ordered in such a way that at the centre lay Scripture, around which other texts, secular or sacred, were ranged as nearer or more distant commentary, paraphrase or extension. Within this model, learning is by and large a matter of reading: absorbing and reiterating the textual bearers of the culture, and mapping the intellectual terrain with their aid. Argument within this model is very often a matter of citation – not through wooden repetition of proof texts, but through a respectful conversation with the canon, animated by a reverent sense of its richness, depth and catholic applicability. In citation, a present argument is concerned to identify and apply the resources of a textual tradition, rather than to find out what happens if we abandon texts and inquire *de novo*. Yet it is just this – the rejection of citation in favour of enquiry – which has become the hallmark of the *wissenschaftlich* university of modernity. There the decline of citation as a mode of argument, and the more general decline of appeal to texts, is related to a repudiation of authority as a vehicle of rational persuasion. In the university, we tell ourselves, we argue not *from* but *towards* authority, and do so only as free enquirers.[7]

This anthropology, centred on reason as the power of representation and embodied in intellectual and educational practices, has proved very barren soil for theological enquiry informed by Christian conviction. Substantively, its account of the human self has – despite all manner of attempted syntheses or correlations – proved itself largely incompatible with Christian understandings of the human creature. Procedurally, the method of enquiry has excluded *ab ovo* the modes of reflective activity which have been most commonly deployed in the traditions of Christian theology. And yet, strange as it may seem, Christian theology has – like most other disciplines in the universe of humane letters – experienced considerable difficulty in formulating critical judgements about this barren intellectual context. This in itself is an indication of how successfully the research university has been able to represent itself as definitive of rational practice *tout court*. But more is involved: a certain failure of theological nerve. The nature and extent of that failure of theological nerve can only, I believe, be demonstrated historically, by giving a lengthy account of the fate of Christian self-description since the later Middle Ages (something which, you will be relieved to know, I am not going to attempt on this occasion). In unfolding that history, it is of capital importance that we break free of one of the grandest myths of modernity: the myth that intellectual history is to be read progressively as the gradual reduction of 'obstacles to general enlightenment or the release of self-imposed tutelage'.[8] Freed from that constriction, we may be able to see that the history of modern theology can also be read as its steady alienation from its own subject matter and procedures.* If this is true, then the intellectual disarray of modern Christian theology owes as much to its loss of confidence in its own habits of mind as it does to the enmity sometimes shown by its cultural context. Schleiermacher's arguments in favour of theology at the new University of Berlin were, in retrospect, just as damaging for theology's survival as were Fichte's arguments against. If theology finds itself on the margins, responsibility may well lie not only with a desacralized culture but 'within the field of theology itself.[9]

Tracing the history of that alienation of theology from its own habits of thought would mean identifying how it came about that Christian theology began to argue for its own possibility without appeal to any specific Christian content.† In his quite wonderful study *At the Origins of Modern Atheism*, Michael Buckley suggests that the alienation of theology begins in the very early modern period, when theology left its own ground in order to debate with natural philosophy over the existence of God. He argues that '[i]n the absence of a rich and comprehensive Christology and a Pneumatology of religious experience Christianity entered into the defence of the existence of the Christian god without appeal to anything Christian'.[10] The result of this concession, Buckley suggests, was the production of 'an emancipated philosophy which eventually negated all religion'.[11] And so, '[a]s theology generated apologetic philosophy and philosophy generated Universal Mathematics and Universal Mechanics, and as these in their turn co-opted theology to become foundations of theistic assertions, theology itself became a *disciplina otiosa* in the justification and establishment of its own subject matter'.[12] A companionable account, this time focused on Descartes and the German idealist tradition, is suggested by Eberhard Jüngel in his slightly earlier study *God as the Mystery of the World*. Here, in a series of sweeps through the history of the relations of modern theology and metaphysics, Jüngel builds up a portrait of the decline of the theological culture within which Christian claims had their home. Like Buckley, Jüngel is concerned above all to delineate the ways in which theology's failure to construe the concept of God in positive Christological and trinitarian terms left it mortally exposed to failure in the face of its philosophical critics. Far from ensuring the survival of Christian theology in the face of challenges to its plausibility, the relinquishing of specifically Christian doctrine in favour of generic theism in fact hastened its demise.‡

---

*Webster's insistence (from this essay all the way through to its later adaptation – 'What Makes Theology Theological?' in GWM 1) on theology as about God and all things in God is meant to curtail this self-alienation of modern theology. It also marks his most polemical moments: for example, his critique of David Ford's *Self and Salvation* as turning exclusively to the mode of conversational theology ('Article Review: David F. Ford, *Self and Salvation*', *Scottish Journal of Theology* 54 [2001], pp. 548–59).
†One might be hard pressed to find a more apt description of the secularization of theology.
‡Webster later shows even less interest in genealogical accounts in 'What Makes Theology Theological?', preferring instead to focus upon specific doctrinal malformations.

If these historical accounts are substantially correct, they demonstrate that the decline of 'theological theology' has a great deal to do with the disorder within Christian dogmatics and the hesitancy of theology to field theological claims. A couple of examples may reinforce the point.

The first is the rise to prominence of the doctrine of revelation in modern Protestant theology. In its full-dress epistemological form, the doctrine of revelation is a fairly modern invention. It is not to be found, for example, in the magisterial Reformers, who generally remain content to handle the question of how it is that we know God, not by the elaboration of a theory of knowledge or consciousness, but by pointing to a feature of Christian teaching about God, namely, God's prevenience. If God is prevenient in all things, then God is prevenient in our acts of knowing, and so our knowledge of God is rooted in God's self-manifestation. If there is such a thing as a doctrine of revelation in the theology of Calvin, for instance (and it is doubtful if his thought can be folded into that shape), it is only as a corollary of a much more basic conviction about divine grace: in the noetic sphere, too, all is to be ordered towards the glorification of the *magnalia dei*. The shift away from this in post-Reformation dogmatics – a shift described by Ronald Thiemann as one 'from assumption to argument'[13] – is not simply a matter of making explicit basic principles of Reformation thought. Quite the opposite: it often takes the form of the replacement of a doctrine of God by an epistemology.[*] Moreover, construed epistemologically, revelation becomes predoctrinal, prolegomenal, the ground of doctrine which is itself explicable in relative isolation from (for example) Christology or pneumatology. Accordingly, revelation migrates to the beginning of dogmatics, taking up its place before the doctrine of God, acquiring greater and greater epistemological sophistication, but at the same time threatening to sever its ties with the loci that follow: Trinity, Incarnation, Spirit, Church.

A second example of the same process is theological talk of the resurrection of Jesus from the dead. In a fashion similar to what took place in the doctrine of revelation, the resurrection shifts from being an *object* of belief to being a *ground* of belief.[14] That is to say, the resurrection comes to perform a function in an apologetic strategy as part of the endeavour of fundamental theology to defend the possibility of revelation and special divine action. And as its role changes, so also does its content. Extracted from its proper Christological home, it is no longer considered part of the *Credo*. Instead, it is handled evidentially, as furnishing extrinsic grounds for subsequent attachment to the *Credo*. As a result, the more obviously evidential aspects of the resurrection – notably, of course, the empty tomb – come to occupy centre stage, precisely because they can most easily be assigned a job in the search for transcendental foundations for Christian doctrine.

---

[*]Later engagement of historical sources (such as R. Preus and R. Muller) would complicate Webster's account of post-Reformation Protestant theology on this score.

Neither of these moves could have taken place without a certain forgetfulness of the inner structure and dynamic of Christian doctrine, and without the adoption of intellectual procedures which are themselves seriously underdetermined by doctrinal considerations. The effects of this reach deep into theology's self-understanding and practices, and can be seen both in the literary forms of modern theology as well as in the ways in which it has construed itself.

The history of the genres of theological writing is still largely unexplored in any systematic way; yet the importance of such a study for interpreting the situation of theology in modernity can scarcely be over-emphasized.* What happens to styles of theological writing when *Wissenschaft* replaces citation as the dominant mode of enquiry and argument? When citation is in the ascendant, the literary forms of theology are generally governed by the fact that the Christian worlds of meaning are shaped by biblical, credal and doxological texts and by the practices which both carry and are themselves carried by those texts. Theology's literary forms and intellectual architecture, its rhetoric and its modes of argument, are controlled by proximity to these sources. Hence its favoured genres: biblical commentary, exposition of texts which have a heavy presence in the tradition (such as the creeds, the Lord's Prayer or the decalogue), or polemic conducted within an agreed frame of reference supplied by a stable canon of biblical materials and of major voices in the tradition. When they function well, these genres are transparent to that into whose presence they seek to introduce the reader. They are not construed as an improvement upon the canon of Christian texts, organizing it more effectively according to scientific principles, or translating its rough, immediate language into a more sophisticated and reflective idiom. Rather, theology maps out the contents of the canon, or applies them in particular circumstances by extended paraphrase of their content.

As enquiry replaces citation, the genres of theology are steadily assimilated to those of standard rational discourse. The canon gradually shifts from being that on the basis of which theology proceeds to that into whose transcendental conditions theology enquires. This shift involves retiring the rhetoric of commentary, paraphrase and reiteration, for those ways of doing theological work cannot serve the goal of enquiry, which is proof underived from the terms of the tradition itself. They are replaced, therefore, by modes of theological discourse which reflect a quite different set of interests, modes of evaluation and standards of justification, whose key feature is undetermination by the self-representations of the traditions of Christian practice. In the writing of Christian doctrine, this can readily be seen by comparing the style of Calvin's *Institutes* – loose, occasional, very close to the biblical ground – with the dogmatics of Reformed scholasticism. Though initially rather inaccessible to the modern reader, the latter texts are rhetorically a good deal closer to modern scholarly writing than those of the sixteenth-century Reformers, above all because they recast

---

*See further analysis of the rhetoric of the commentary genre in *HS*, 131–43.

their matter by transferring it from the more immediate discourse of faith into an improved, more orderly and better warranted mode of expression. Or compare a modern scholarly biblical commentary with one by Calvin. The difference is not simply the availability to the modern writer of considerably more by way of historical materials, but a changed relation to the text itself and to the act of explication. A modern scholarly commentator has the task of accounting for the text, and a set of tools at her disposal to establish how the text came to be. Calvin's task is at once more modest and more urgent: more modest, because he is simply interested in eliciting the plain sense of the text; more urgent, because his rhetoric positions the reader in such a way as to be accountable to the text, or better, to be called to account by God through the medium of the text. Hence a fundamental criterion for the success of a piece of exegesis is its ability to let the rhetoric of Scripture stand and itself shape the theologian's discourse. If, as often happens, we find this an unilluminating procedure, it is more than likely because modern theology suffers particularly acutely from the effects of the standardization of discourse which has afflicted the humanities in modernity. Reflecting on this standardization in an essay on philosophy and literature, Martha Nussbaum suggests that '[t]here is a mistake made, or at least a carelessness, when one takes a method and style that have proven fruitful for the investigation and description of certain truths – say those of natural science – and applies them without further reflection or argument to a very different sphere of life that may have a different geography and demand a different sort of precision, a different norm of rationality'.[15] And theology, no less than philosophy or literary studies, has not always avoided the mistake.

One consequence of this normalization is that it has made it increasingly difficult for practitioners within the various subdisciplines of theology to state with any clarity what is specifically *theological* about their enquiries. The theological disciplines have, in effect, been 'de-regionalized', that is, they have been pressed to give an account of themselves in terms drawn largely from fields of enquiry other than theology, fields which, according to prevailing criteria of academic propriety, more nearly approximate to ideals of rational activity. And so the content and operations of the constituent parts of the theological curriculum are no longer determined by specifically theological considerations, but by neighbouring disciplines – disciplines which can exercise that controlling function because their lack of determination by theological conviction accords them much greater prestige in the academy. This process of assimilation means that, for example, the study of Scripture, or doctrine, or the history of the church draw their modes of enquiry from Semitics, or the history of religions, or social anthropology, from philosophy, or from general historical studies.*

---

*Webster will later refer to such enterprises as 'theology and …' wherein theology takes up a fascination with objects of study in the frame of another discipline's categories (rather than employing theology's own material categories as lenses for analysis).

Individual scholars or schools have no doubt been able to strike various kinds of local bargains with neighbouring disciplines whilst retaining some of the theological ends of their endeavours. But even such bargains, however carefully brokered, nearly always prolong the assumption that, at the level of actual operations, theological doctrine does not need to be invoked, and may at best enter the picture as an ultimate horizon of processes which it does not immediately affect.

So far, then, I have sketched the decline of a theologically informed account of theology as a mode of intellectual enquiry by pointing to two developments: the steady expansion of certain academic practices, rooted in a universalist anthropology of enquiry and largely detached from particular fields of intellectual work, and the decline of the invocation of theological doctrine in talking about what theology is, as theologians conform their practice to prevalent cultural norms. It is very important, I believe, not to view the problem from one angle only. It is not simply that theology has failed to keep pace with modernity (in one sense, it has kept pace all too well); nor simply that theology was turfed out by rationalism (for theology itself contributed a great deal to its own decline). It is rather a matter of seeing how internal disarray incapacitated theology all the more because it left theologians with such a reduced intellectual capital to draw upon as they sought to make judgements about the ideals, academic and spiritual, which presented themselves for their attention with such institutional force.

Yet those ideals, and the institutions which bear them, are themselves showing signs of strain. Particularly in the world of the humanities, these conventions of enquiry and the understanding of the human situation which undergirds them do not always command immediate assent. A good deal of attention has been devoted in recent years to developing what might be called a critical pragmatics of academic institutions and activities. The work of Foucault, Bourdieu, Guillory and others suggests that what have often been judged to be invariant principles of rational enquiry are in fact customs whose self-evidence has much to do with the plausibility structures which surround them.[16] Oddly enough, then, the very high premium on critical activity in the university may make us insufficiently aware that the university is a customary institution as much as a reflective one: indeed, its critical practices are themselves customary in character. The academy has not always resisted the temptation to idealize itself as a place of total, interest-free reflection, especially in the way it writes the history of its own disciplines. But its reflective practices have sometimes been a good deal less than that. To see this is not just a matter of conceding that the university is sometimes at the mercy of local interests; any member of any university committee knows that. It is more that, in representing itself as a sort of disinterested tribunal, the university may in important respects obscure from itself and others the real character of its operations: its place as regulator and distributor of cultural capital, its proposing of ideals of acceptable intellectual practice, its commitment to determinate moral and political goals. The most sharp analysis along these lines has emerged in materialist social science and in some kinds of literary theory. But the uneasy situation of Christian theology in the academy is another place where some of these protocols break the surface and become visible. If this is so – if the fate of theology in the modern university signals the limitations imposed by compliance with that institution's account of itself – then theology could in fact have some considerable critical significance for the university. Far from being an obstacle to unfettered liberty of enquiry, theology may furnish one of the chief means through which instrumentalist and representational ideologies are opened for inspection and critique. In this way, theology may offer a set of critical tools through which we may plot a different geography of the academy's intellectual life.*

How might Christian theology make this contribution? The immediate temptation is to limit theology's role to one of providing a vaguely moralistic or mysterious tinge to hard-edged intellectual pursuits, by drawing attention to the realm of so-called 'values', or articulating the awe which the researcher feels in face of the unknown. But theology is more than the academy's conscience or its folk religion. Its contribution to the wider culture of reflective institutions will rather be this: by holding fast to its own concerns, pursuing its own goals and fulfilling its own responsibilities by making full use of its own procedures, theology will raise a question about the dominant conventions of enquiry. In effect, its importance for the university will be secured by its being not less theological but *more* theological, by 'exercising theology's right to be exclusively theological'.[17] As a significant contemporary practitioner of this kind of theology has put it, 'the discipline lives by its ability to contribute from Christian sources things that would not otherwise be said'.[18]

It has sometimes been argued on this basis that the signal contribution of Christian theology to the academy is its talk about God.[19] Certainly, talk about God may function iconoclastically, relativizing false disciplinary absolutisms by setting the whole intellectual enterprise in a transcendent context. But such a task could quite adequately be performed by other disciplines – some styles of philosophy or aesthetics or religious studies, for example – in which we are, as it were, nudged into considering an absolute context for ourselves and our endeavours. The distinctiveness of Christian theology lies elsewhere, however: not simply in its persistence in raising questions of ultimacy, but rather in its invocation of God as agent in the intellectual practice of theology. In order to give account of its own operations, that is, Christian theology will talk of God and God's actions. Talk of God not only describes the matter into which theology enquires but also, crucially, informs its portrayal of its own processes of enquiry. In effect, theology is a contrary – eschatological – mode

---

*Analysis of theology's place in the university focuses less on its suffering than on its service, both here in Webster's lecture and in his litany of essays on the intellectual life (several of which are gathered in GWM 2). Part of the reason for his call to theology to maintain its own voice was a belief that such a theological voice would provoke and provide benefit to the intellectual conversations of the wider university.

of intellectual life, taking its rise in God's disruption of the world, and pressing the academy to consider a quite discordant anthropology of enquiry. To try and make some sense of this seemingly perverse point, we may perhaps ponder a proposition which stands near the beginning of an entirely forgotten theological text, Wollebius' *Compendium theologiae christianae*, a brief handbook of Reformed teaching published in 1626, soon after the Synod of Dordt. Wollebius writes: 'The principle of the being of theology is God; the principle by which it is known is the Word of God.'[20] Grasping Wollebius' point involves us in reclaiming two primary convictions which are largely lost to us, one ontological and one noetic. The first is what has been called 'the classical priority of the object of theological study'.[21] Giving priority to the object immediately calls into question any notion that methods of enquiry are set by the subjective conditions of enquirers and not by that to which they direct their loving attention. For theology as Wollebius envisages it, the being of God is not simply an hypothesis into which theology enquires, but rather is the reality which actively constitutes and delimits the field of theological activity.* Talk of God and God's actions will not just describe theology's ultimate horizon, as it were the furthest boundaries of the field, within which theologians go about their business unconstrained. Rather, the field of theology and the activities which theologians perform within that field – its texts, its modes of interpretation, its standards of assessment, its rhetoric and modes of persuasion – will be described by talk of God. What Wollebius calls 'the principle of the being of theology', what we might call its intellectual ontology, has priority over anthropology and epistemology. Theology is simply not a free science.

This leads to the second of Wollebius' points, namely that the noetic principle of theology is the Word of God. His point is not that theology is governed by a doctrine of Scripture or revelation, but something prior to both, namely this: the 'object' to which the theologian's gaze is directed is inalienably *subject*. We would not be far from Wollebius if we were to say that the object of theology is nothing less than the eschatological self-presence of God in Jesus Christ through the power of the Holy Spirit. Theology is oriented to this active presence, and its enquiries are both materially and formally determined, borne along and corrected by that presence. In a very important sense, the notion of the Word of God undertakes here the duty which in later theology will be performed by epistemology and anthropology: it shows how it is that knowledge of God is possible and real. When such language falls away and is replaced by a psychology or metaphysics of the human knower, the object of theological enquiry is itself re-construed as absent, inert or mute. But, as John Macquarrie once remarked, '[t]he subject matter of Christian theology, God in Christ, is not a passive object laid out for our scrutiny … but the transcendent reality which already encompasses us'.[22] To neglect that point, to forget that the intellect

---

*As he says elsewhere, 'God is not summoned into the presence of reason; reason is summoned before the presence of God' (*Holiness*, 17).

must be 'docile to the given',[23] is to shift into a different intellectual ontology which abrogates the connexion within which alone theology's status as *Wissenschaft* is secure: its reference to the work and Word of God.

How on earth does *this* constitute a serious contribution to the life of the academy? In Oxford, at least, the argument since the 1850 University Reform Commission has taken the form that theology's place in the university is to be won by its conformity to an ideal of disengaged reason, an ideal which many theologians have deeply internalized (with the exception of a few crackpots like Pusey, who can safely be dismissed). My suggestion is the opposite: the most fruitful contribution which theology can make to the wider world of learning is by demonstrating a stubborn yet cheerful insistence on what Barth called 'the great epistemological caveat … [T]he way of thought [of theology] … is not secure except in the reality of Jesus Christ and the Holy Spirit'.[24]

But the understanding of theology which I am proposing – theology as the articulation of 'Christian difference'[25] – raises a critical question about the university's self-understanding. For it casts doubt on the combination of pluralism and dogmatism in liberal culture – a pluralism which suspends all strong claims and traditions, and a dogmatism which insists that all such claims and traditions present themselves for inspection before the universal bar of reason. By going about its business, by skillful, reflective, self-critical practice within its own world of discourse, theology will suggest a rather different model of academic life and institutions. It will suggest that the university may be conceived as, and its ideal pursued through, a set of orderly, energetic and curious conversations about differing visions of human life and thought, as a contest between strong claims, including strong claims about the nature of enquiry. In such a context, teachers will play a double role: as partisans, speaking as the intellectual voice of a particular culture, and as those concerned to sponsor high-level articulation of difference, in order that the university may be 'an arena of conflict in which the most fundamental type of moral and theological disagreement [is] accorded recognition'.[26] Such conflicts would not be solved by appeal to universal reason; nor, on the other hand, would they be tolerated by making the university into some sort of perspectival free market of inter-disciplinary discussion in which the only thing that matters is that nothing matters. Both rationalism and indefinite pluralism assume that what is most important about the university is what is neutral among the different versions of reality which are brought to the debate. But may it not be that the academy might flourish if it were to foster sets of practices which would maximize the specific logics of different visions and what animates them; maximize opportunities for encounter and exchange; and minimize factors which inhibit fruitful contests (such as the dominance of only one intellectual procedure)?

What is involved here is the 're-regionalization' of intellectual life, taking seriously 'the death of the notion that there is such a thing as *the* logic of *Wissenschaft*'.[27] An institution in which this kind of conflict is a central pursuit will be less concerned to defend abstract, a-contextual norms, and will be more interested in observing reason as a set of practices with a home in particular traditions which over time have come to formulate and refine standards of intellectual excellence. Filling out this picture of the academy would require us to say much more: about teaching as the engendering of the habits of mind of particular traditions (including their habits of self-critique); about the role to be played by awed reading of classical texts; about the need to deregulate the genres of scholarship.* But what is most important is to state the claim that what is needed is a renewed 'conflict of the faculties', though not one driven by 'the quest for commensuration',[28] but by a confident sense of the importance of non-conformity. And, crucially, what such conflict requires is not just a better epistemology, but a changed anthropology of enquiry and politics of intellectual exchange, so that differences can be seen not as a curse but as the given condition for the university's life.

All this no doubt sounds like a way of smuggling theology (and perhaps other supposedly disreputable disciplines like Marxist aesthetics or feminist studies) in through the back door. But it is more a matter of trying to see what the university looks like in a different projection. And, moreover, it is worth noting that thinking of the academy and of academic theology in this way by no means leaves theology comfortably intact.† Indeed, it requires a quite radical recasting of theology's prevailing self-understanding. Within this recasting, the most important, as well as the most demanding, task is that of re-establishing theology's relation to the culture of Christian faith and practice from which it so often finds itself dissociated. All intellectual acts take place in a particular space or region; that is to say, reflective activity is best understood, not by exquisite analysis of modes of consciousness, but by observing the practices of a cultural world. Christian theology's culture is that of Christian faith – its store of memories, its lexical stock, its ideas, its institutions and roles, its habits of prayer and service and witness, the whole conglomeration of activities through which it offers a 'reading' of reality. That culture precedes and encloses reflective theological enquiry, and it is within, not in isolation from, that sphere that Christian language and concepts acquire their intelligibility. This is why the supposed polarity of enquiry and orthodoxy is specious. For it is only a debased form of orthodoxy which is dominated by the compulsive dynamics of repetition, sameness and closure. Practised well, orthodoxy is not about domination but about what my predecessor, in an essay in honour of another great theologian of this university, has called 'shared attention'.[29] Orthodoxy is participation in a tradition

---

*See especially 'Reading Theology', *Toronto Journal of Theology* 13 (1997): 53–63.
†An ascetical approach to theology follows from this 're-regionalization' precisely because of its eschatological shape. Webster expounds this ascetical bent and its challenge to the sinful status quo in the lectures now published as *CT*. For comparison of his account of intellectual asceticism with that of Sarah Coakley, see Michael Allen, 'Dogmatics as Ascetics', in *The Task of Dogmatics* (ed. Oliver D. Crisp and Fred Sanders; Grand Rapids: Zondervan Academic, 2017), pp. 189–209.

which directs itself to a source of convertedness. It involves a setting of the self – including the knowing self – within patterns of common action and contemplation, of speech and hearing. When they function well, those patterns are sufficiently stable to provide focus, and yet sufficiently aware of their own provisionality to enable self-critical adaptability and to offer a check against stasis. 'Orthodoxy' of this kind enables the theologian to articulate a distinctively theological account of the content, methods and goals of the discipline, and offers much by way of resistance to too ready an acquiescence in the protocols of neighbouring intellectual fields. And it also makes theologians worth talking to, because it means they have something distinctive to say. The vigour of theology and its capacity to contribute in a lively way to the conversations of the academy will in large measure depend upon the confidence, vigour and intelligence with which it inhabits its regions of meaning. Not the least requirement for the theologian in the university is competence in the rules of life of the Christian tradition. Such competence, acquired through observation and application, through habits of prayer and attention and suffering, is a much more serious and fruitful contribution to conversation than the scrupulous bracketing of positive religion which has long been held to be the price of theology's entrance ticket to the world of higher learning.

In the light of considerations such as these, we may see the wisdom of the arrangement whereby this chair straddles the two publics of the academy and the ecclesial community. At first blush, it seems nothing other than a way of making sure that divinity professors know at least the Anglican answer before the evidence is in, once again betraying the interests of free enquiry. After all, was not Kant right that the catchword of the cleric is 'Do not argue, but believe!'?[30] And Kant continued thus in talking of the scholar-priest:

> The use ... which an appointed teacher makes of his reason before his congregation is merely private, because this congregation is only a domestic one ...; with respect to it, as a priest, he is not free, nor can he be free, because he carries out the orders of another. But as a scholar, whose writings speak to his public, the world, the clergyman in the public use of his reason enjoys an unlimited freedom to use his own reason and to speak in his own person.[31]

There is a cluster of assumptions here: about the rational precedence of the world over the congregation; about the inferiority of the merely domestic Christian culture to the free public spaces where reason operates; about the possibility of and necessity for the intellectual to seek out a world without convention and conviction, since freedom and scholarship are antithetical to belonging. But the integration of academy and congregation, of intellect, prayer and attention to Scripture, should serve to highlight the fact that there is no non-local public, no rationality abstract from social practice, no sphere where everything is open for total reflection. The university may not pretend to be such a space, and it may be a particular vocation of theology, when it sticks to its task, to issue that reminder to an institution which has sometimes threatened to convert its customs into axioms.

The university, or, indeed, the faculty of theology where the academic life is envisaged in quite these terms, does not, of course, exist: hence what can be seen as the utopian tone of my remarks. The worldly wise turn away from utopian proposals with a tolerant smile. But the function of utopias is to encourage an ironic distance from prevailing conceptions, and to recount the past and envisage the future from a different point of view, thereby provoking serious self-criticism.* At its best, the university strives to be a place of non-competitive argument from and about interests, in the hope that things could be other than they are. Theological theology has much to contribute to the fostering of that kind of intellectual polity, and the academy has every reason to expect much from its contribution.

Notes

1 An inaugural lecture as Lady Margaret Professor of Divinity, delivered before the University of Oxford on 28 October 1997.
2 The early history of the chair is recounted in J. McConica (ed.), *The History of the University of Oxford III: The Collegiate University* (Oxford: Clarendon Press, 1986), pp. 347–52; and in M. K. Jones and M. G. Underwood, *The King's Mother: Lady Margaret Beaufort, Countess of Richmond and Derby* (Cambridge: Cambridge University Press, 1992), pp. 206–10.
3 N. Wolsterstorff, 'The Travail of Theology in the Modern Academy', in M. Volf et al. (ed.), *The Future of Theology: Essays in Honour of Jurgen Moltmann* (Grand Rapids: Eerdmans, 1996), p. 37.
4 Wolterstorff, 'The Travail of Theology in the Modern Academy', p. 38.
5 G. Grant, 'Research in the Humanities', in *Technology and Justice* (Notre Dame: University of Notre Dame Press, 1986), p. 99.
6 A. MacIntyre, *Three Rival Versions of Moral Enquiry: Encyclopaedia, Genealogy, and Tradition* (Notre Dame: University of Notre Dame Press, 1990), p. 225.
7 Cf. J. Stout, *The Flight from Authority* (Notre Dame: University of Notre Dame Press, 1981), p. 149.
8 I. Kant, 'What Is Enlightenment?', in L. W. Beck (ed.), *Kant on History* (New York: Macmillan, 1963), p. 9.

---

*Eventually Webster would turn not merely to describe the eschatological as a means of prompting of ethical self-criticism but would also supplement this with attention to creation and nature as another means of bringing present tense experience into relief. He affirmed the importance of such primal concerns as early as essays on anthropology in the 1990s, though he only much later began to shade in those lines with textured description of creation in his last decade of writing.

9   E. Charry, *By the Renewing of Your Minds: The Pastoral Function of Christian Doctrine* (Oxford: Oxford University Press, 1997), p. 245.

10   M. J. Buckley, *At the Origins of Modern Atheism* (New Haven: Yale University Press, 1987), p. 67.

11   Buckley, *At the Origins of Modern Atheism*, p. 358.

12   Buckley, *At the Origins of Modern Atheism*, p. 358.

13   R. Thiemann, *Revelation and Theology: The Gospel as Narrated Promise* (Notre Dame: University of Notre Dame Press, 1985), p. 11.

14   See F. Fiorenza, *Foundational Theology: Jesus and the Church* (New York: Crossroad, 1985), pp. 14f.

15   M. Nussbaum, 'Introduction: Form and Content, Philosophy and Literature', in *Love's Knowledge: Essays on Philosophy and Literature* (Oxford: Oxford University Press, 1990), pp. 19f.

16   See, for example, M. Foucault, *The Order of Things: An Archaeology of the Human Sciences* (London: Tavistock, 1970), and *The Archaeology of Knowledge* (London: Tavistock, 1972); J. Guillory, *Cultural Capital: The Problem of Literary Canon Formation* (Chicago: University of Chicago Press, 1993); P. Bourdieu, *Homo Academicus* (Cambridge: Polity Press, 1988); P. A. Bové, *Intellectuals in Power: A Genealogy of Critical Humanism* (Columbia: Columbia University Press, 1986); and *Mastering Discourse: The Politics of Intellectual Culture* (Durham: Duke University Press, 1992).

17   E. Jüngel, 'Die Freiheit der Theologie', in *Entsprechungen. Gott – Wahrheit – Mensch. Theologische Erörterungen* (Munich: Kaiser, 1980), p. 15.

18   C. Gunton, 'The Indispensability of Theological Understanding: Theology in the University', in D. F. Ford and D. L. Stamps (eds), *Essentials of Christian Community: Essays for Daniel W. Hardy* (Edinburgh: T&T Clark, 1996), pp. 276f.

19   For example, C. Gunton, 'The Indispensability of Theological Understanding', p. 275; D. Ford, 'Christian Theology at the Turn of the Millennium', in D. Ford (ed.), *The Modern Theologians: An Introduction to Christian Theology in the Twentieth Century* (Oxford: Blackwell, 2nd edn, 1997), pp. 724f.

20   J. Wollebius, *Compendium theologiae christianae*, Prolegomena 1.III, in J. W. Beardslee (ed.), *Reformed Dogmatics* (Grand Rapids: Baker, 1977), p. 30.

21   G. Schner, *Education for Ministry: Reform and Renewal in Theological Education* (Kansas City: Sheed and Ward, 1993), p. 33.

22   J. Macquarrie, 'Theology and Spirituality', in *Paths in Spirituality* (London: SCM, 1972), p. 70.

23   Macquarrie, 'Theology and Spirituality', p. 64.

24   K. Barth, *Ethics* (Grand Rapids: Eerdmans, 1981), p. 98.

25   J. Milbank, *Theology and Social Theory: Beyond Secular Reason* (Oxford: Blackwell, 1990), p. 381.

26   MacIntyre, *Three Rival Versions of Moral Enquiry*, p. 231.

27   Wolterstorff, 'The Travail of Theology in the Modern Academy', p. 44.

28   R. Rorty, *Philosophy and the Mirror of Nature* (Princeton, NJ: Princeton University Press, 1979), p. 317.

29 R. Williams, 'Does It Make Sense to Speak of pre-Nicene Orthodoxy?', in
    R. Williams (ed.), *The Making of Orthodoxy: Essays in Honour of Henry
    Chadwick* (Cambridge: Cambridge University Press, 1990), p. 18.

30 Kant, 'What Is Enlightenment?', p. 5.

31 Kant, 'What Is Enlightenment?', p. 6.

2

Biblical reasoning

EDITOR'S INTRODUCTION

This essay really does address two themes signalled by the title, drawing together the theme of Holy Scripture with that of human reason. In so doing Webster seeks to probe their interconnection: what does it mean to engage in specifically biblical reasoning? To address that human intellectual question, he backs up and begins by considering the doctrine of God (his inner life and his works or economy). Then he considers the place of Scripture and reason, respectively, within that divine economy. He concludes with observations about the character of theology in both its dogmatic and exegetical modes.

'Biblical reasoning' is neither the first nor the last essay which Webster wrote about the task of theology, and it illustrates two signature moves throughout his writings. First, he locates all moral or intellectual discussions in a deeper assessment of natures (ontology) and ends (teleology) and, second, he looks to the divine economy as the lens by which that ontology and teleology might be grasped. So, for instance, claims about the nature and attributes of Holy Scripture 'ought not to be treated in isolation from the wider redemptive economy'. When considering reason, he describes the way in which it has been alienated from God by sin, and how it now 'is renewed after its self-alienation and treachery against God'. A lengthy excursus differentiates his proposal from that of other theological accounts on offer (i.e. Paul Janz, Oliver Davies), largely worrying that they too glibly relate human reason and the divine mind without registering the metaphysical turbulence provoked by the Creator–creature distinction; similarly, he worries that claims about reason being 'incarnational' frequently glean wrongly that the implication of the incarnation for reason is that it must be material and embodied rather than, primarily, that it is healed and saved in this singular event in redemptive history.

It is fascinating to observe his correction to the regnant anthropology in the intellectual culture of the university. While he alluded to the critiques of critical theory in 'Theological Theology', here he turns to specifically theological challenges to a Kantian or Enlightenment-era epistemology. The project of universal reason is shown to be complicated not so much by contextual and demographic diversity as by the regress of sin, death and devil. In so doing, Webster is not denying the realities of demographic (mal)formation, though he does relativize that standard postmodern criticism of the Enlightenment academy. His attempt at developing a 'theological theology' can be seen in action here as he describes reason's affliction by means of distinctly theological analysis.

A thesis frames his final section: 'Christian theology is biblical reasoning. It is the redeemed intellect's reflective apprehension of God's gospel address through the embassy of Scripture, enabled and corrected by God's presence, and having fellowship with him as its end.' As in other essays, he employs the language of ontological principles and cognitive principles to root theology in the presence and action of God (who alone is its ontological principle and whose Word is its cognitive principle – indeed, Webster highlights that 'the cognitive principle is grounded in the ontological principle'). Theology is first a divine reality, as God knows God, and becomes by grace a creaturely calling and reality, as God shares or reveals his own knowledge.

He describes two modes of biblical reasoning. 'Exegetical reasoning is, most simply, reading the Bible, the intelligent (and therefore spiritual) act of following the words of the text.' The Word is a lively one, and theologians are called to follow it. Thus, commentary provides a primary mode of theological genre, inasmuch as it most directly manifests that 'cursive' practice of listening and following. 'Dogmatic reasoning produces a conceptual representation of what reason has learned from its exegetical following of the scripture text.' Dogmatics does not tidy up matters but gathers 'together what is dispersed through the temporal economy to which the prophets and apostles direct reason's gaze'.

In both modes, Webster argues that theology functions as an ascetical discipline for 'the intellect is drawn away from idols'. He suggests, however, that not all share such a posture, and many might decry the definition of theology as 'biblical reasoning' inasmuch as they look at Scripture apart from the divine economy of God's life-giving involvement and view it merely as a repository of ancient religious texts or a reminder of days past when God did speak.

> One of the deepest fault lines in the church at the present time runs between those who do their theological reasoning on the basis of a conviction that in Scripture the breath of the divine Word quickens reason to knowledge and love of God, and those who fear (or hope?) that neither Scripture nor reason take us any further than human poetics.

In that regard this essay furthers the reform of an anthropology of inquiry (brought up initially in 'Theological Theology') by speaking of the need to avoid having theological subdisciplines (whether dogmatics or exegesis) defined by related disciplines (philosophy and literature, respectively). Webster is offering a prolegomenal essay here (though the previous essay seemed to have chided post-Reformation Protestants for that development), but he works hard to shape the prolegomenal methodology to fit the material content of Christian doctrine by looking first to God and then the full range of the works of God.

Suggested readings

'The Holiness of Theology', in *Holiness* (Grand Rapids, MI: Eerdmans, 2003), pp. 8–30.

'Resurrection and Scripture', in *Christology and Scripture. Interdisciplinary Perspectives* (ed. Andrew Lincoln and Angus Paddison; London: T&T Clark, 2007), pp. 138–55; repr. in DW: 32–49.

'The Domain of the Word', in DW: 3–31.

Darren Sarisky, 'Scripture', in *A Companion to John Webster's Theology* (ed. Michael Allen and R. David Nelson; Grand Rapids, MI: Eerdmans, forthcoming).

Fred Sanders, 'Holy Scripture under the Auspices of the Holy Trinity: On John Webster's Trinitarian Doctrine of Scripture', *International Journal of Systematic Theology* 21, no. 1 (2019): 4–23.

Michael Allen, 'Dogmatics as Ascetics', in *The Task of Dogmatics: Explorations in Theological Methodology* (ed. Oliver D. Crisp and Fred Sanders; Grand Rapids, MI: Zondervan Academic, 2017), pp. 189–209.

Michael Allen, 'Reason', in *A Companion to John Webster's Theology* (ed. Michael Allen and R. David Nelson; Grand Rapids, MI: Eerdmans, forthcoming).

BIBLICAL REASONING

I

Christian theology is biblical reasoning. It is an activity of the created intellect, judged, reconciled, redeemed and sanctified through the works of the Son and the Spirit. More closely, Christian theology is part of reason's answer to the divine Word which addresses creatures through the intelligible service of the prophets and apostles. It has its origin in the Spirit-sustained hearing of the divine Word; it is rational contemplation and articulation of God's communicative presence.

Elucidating this conception of theology requires well-judged theological characterizations of Scripture and reason, their natures and ends. An ontology and a teleology of Scripture and reason are needed; the ontology and teleology should derive from the material content of the Christian confession and, accordingly, should demonstrate a free relation to other considerations of the nature of texts and rationality. We need to ask what Scripture and reason *are* and what they are *for*. Theological answers to those questions are taken from an understanding of the place of Scripture and reason in the divine economy. As I am using it here, the term 'divine economy' bears two closely related senses: it is both the work of the triune God in which he administers the temporal order of creaturely being and activity in accordance with his eternal purpose, and also the sphere of creaturely reality so administered by him: both God's act of *dispensatio* and that which he disposes. This order of reality encloses and forms the nature and activity of creatures; to be and to act as a creature is to be and to act within this ordered realm of being; and, moreover, it is to be in the communicative presence of God. God establishes and maintains fellowship with his creatures by addressing them through his Word, thereby summoning them to address themselves to his address. Fellowship with God includes rational fellowship; and of this rational fellowship, Christian theology is an instance.*

Most of what follows is given over to describing more closely the divine economy in terms of which we can understand Scripture, reason and their relation. This line of approach appears remote from familiar debates about the relation of the Bible and theology, and those debates are commonly predicated on significantly different understandings of texts and their rational reception, or are less direct in invoking

---

*This essay seeks to locate acts of creaturely intellectual life within the economy of the gospel rather than in some neutral space. As he says elsewhere, 'A holy theology has its context and its content in the revelatory presence of the Holy Trinity' (*Holiness*, 12). While it may be obvious that theology treats revelation as its content, Webster wants to push back against modern notions of objectivity in the intellectual life and to push towards an emphasis upon the life of the mind as a spiritual affair (shaped by sin and grace).

theological doctrine. We need, I suggest, to move away from pressing concerns about the proper 'use' of Scripture, the nature of biblical authority or the practice of theological interpretation. Widespread confusion, and impatient and incoherent debate, about these matters should alert us to the need to push back, and to question the adequacy of the terms in which the debates have been conducted and the concepts through which matters have been framed.

With respect to Scripture, for example, lack of clarity about the tasks of biblical interpretation (in which the tug-of-war between 'historical' and 'theological' interpretation is but one episode) is symptomatic of the absence of shared conceptions of the nature of Scripture and of the tasks which it undertakes in the divine economy. The absence of bibliology, and the widespread assumption that a doctrine of Scripture is exegetically and hermeneutically otiose, cannot be compensated for by further refinement of strategies of interpretation. We need to figure out what the text is in order to figure out what to do with it; and we determine what Scripture is by understanding its role in God's self-communication to creatures.

Similarly, discussion of the place of reason in theology is frequently underdetermined by a wider theological conception of God's purposes for creatures. This underdetermination is part of the disorientation of reason.* For Christian theology, an account of rational acts rests on an account of creaturely nature, which in turn rests upon an account of God's purposes for creatures manifest in his works. Neglect of this rule on the part of Christian theology is an aspect of the self-alienation of the Christian religion and its theology from their proper subject matter, which in turn has undermined confidence that the resources of the Christian religion are adequate to describe the nature and context of reason's work. Extracted from its place in the divine economy, reason is exposed to inflammation and distortion. A clear-sighted interpretation of the modern defection of reason, for example, is only possible on the basis of an understanding of reason's proper nature and ends within the economy. It is, indeed, imperative not to frame a theological account of reason simply in reaction to a perceived crisis; corrections made on such a basis are likely to be haphazard and disproportionate.

The argument proceeds in three stages: some initial reflections on the divine economy as the setting in which we can determine the nature of reason and of Scripture; two sections which characterize Scripture and reason, respectively; and a final section which expands the notion of theology as biblical reasoning.

---

*Both hermeneutics and logic can and do frequently replace distinctively Christian reflection on Scripture and reason, respectively, with resources drawn from other disciplines. Webster believes that it is far too easy to assume common sense or shared principles in these areas and that theological theology will return to fundamental matters viewed in a distinctly theological and thus biblical register.

II

Scripture and reason are elements in the economy of God's communication with creatures, aspects of the cognitive fellowship between creatures and their loving creator.

Scripture and reason are not only elements of a religious-cultural economy. The order of reality in which they belong and which shapes their operations is not only that of human exchange; they are not only a field of human communicative agency. Nor are they without residue to be folded into tradition, that is, an assemblage of cultural forms in its passage through time. Certainly Scripture and reason are creaturely realities, participating in the dynamics of cultural production; they are not 'pure', they do not wholly transcend the processes by which human beings express themselves and acquire cognitive purchase on the world. But such descriptions of Scripture and reason, however necessary, are not sufficient. The social and historical dynamic of tradition is penultimate, pointing back to the divine economy, which is the historical form of God's presence to and action upon creatures. Scripture and reason are not only contingent activities of speech and intelligence; they are to be understood in relation to the divine Word and its intelligible and saving address of the creatures of God. In short, Scripture and reason function within the economy of divine revelation.

How may this economy be described more closely? (1) The divine economy is grounded in the immanent perfection of the Holy Trinity. God's dealings with creatures, in which he makes it possible for them to know and love him, are a second, derivative reality. In more directly dogmatic language, the economy is the field of the divine missions: the Father's sending of the Son and the Spirit to gather creatures into fellowship with himself and to uphold them on their way to completion. But this outpouring of love in the divine missions is the external face of the inner divine processions, that is, of the perfect internal relations of the triune persons, the fountain from which the external works of God flow. The *opera Dei externae* are suspended from the *opera Dei ad intra*. The importance of this is not simply that it respects the divine aseity and safeguards the distinction of uncreated and created being. It is also that, by grounding the economy in the inner life of God, it indicates that the creation has *depth*. Creation is not simply contingent temporal surface, arbitrary action. It has a willed shape; it assumes its form under the pressure of the divine intention, and is maintained by unbounded divine benevolence. And so creatures and their acts – including textual and intellectual acts – are referred back to the anterior reality of God, a reference in which alone their substance and continuing operation are secured.

(2) The divine economy unfolds as the history of fellowship in which creatures are summoned to know and love God. God loves creatures. To love is to will

another's good, and God's love of creatures is such that he wills and effects their being, bestowing life upon them. This life is of a particular kind, not simple animal life but life characterized by knowledge and love. Knowledge and love are essential to fellowship, whether with other creatures or, supremely, with the creator himself. Knowledge and love are a transcendent motion, a thirst for that which is other than the creature; they involve *intelligence*, a more than instinctual relation to the world and God. Further, creaturely life is a condition which is also a history; knowledge and love are enacted or exercised, and their enactment is constitutive of the creaturely side of fellowship with God. The divine side, to which the creaturely responds, is God's free communicative self-gift, his 'Word' in which he addresses creatures and his Spirit in which he quickens creatures to love and knowledge. The creator speaks, bestows life and makes himself known and loved above all things.

(3) The divine economy includes the history of redemption. The temporal course of creation is not a steady unfolding of the creature's embrace of the creator's purpose of fellowship, knowledge and love. Rather, fellowship is breached by the wicked and self-destructive refusal of creatures to enact their nature by following their vocation. Creatures repudiate the life-giving Word, defying its summons, choosing instead to instruct themselves in their own good, and so betraying themselves into futility, senselessness and darkness (Rom. 1.21); creatures do not receive the gifts of the Spirit, regarding such gifts as folly, and so make themselves unspiritual (1 Cor. 2.14). Faced with this treachery, God acts to maintain his own glory and his purpose for the creature. Creaturely defiance is overcome, and the creature's fulfilment is secured, in the history of redemption. At the Father's behest, the Son and the Spirit interpose themselves into the history of creation so as to counter the calamity of the fall; through their works, creatures are reconciled to God, sanctified and directed to perfection. Creaturely nature is preserved because remade by the redemptive work of the Word made flesh and the life-giving Spirit.

(4) In all this, the divine economy is revelatory. God is made known in the economy of his creative and redemptive acts. In the history of fellowship, God is present and effects creaturely knowledge of himself. This is the most basic meaning of 'revelation': the eloquence of God's presence and activity, God so acting in relation to creatures that his actions constitute his address of them. In his presence and activity among creatures, God's relation to creatures is not simply one which produces an objective effect; it also communicates to creatures a measure of God's own knowledge of himself. We may speak of the economy as the theatre in which God's Word is heard, in which God is communicatively and intelligibly present. Word, Spirit and intellect are basic to the economy and the way in which creatures participate in it.

The divine economy – founded in God's own life, fellowship-creating, redemptive and revelatory – is fundamental to creaturely being and acts. It is the atmosphere or sustaining context of what creatures are and do. Creaturely communicative activity takes place against this deep metaphysical background, in the situation brought about by the active presence of the triune God and under the impulse of his summons. In this light, what is to be said of Scripture and reason?*

III

God's work in the economy is eloquent, speaking out of itself. Its relation to creatures is not only causal but self-expressive, producing a cognitive relation. The possibility of this cognitive relation resides with God alone. Knowledge of God, *understanding* God's work rather than simply feeling its force, does not lie within creaturely capacity. God intends that the relation between himself and his creatures should not be silent and opaque but a history of intercourse, in which God utters, and creatures live by, his Word, promise, law, ordinances, statutes, precepts and testimonies. Such a history is wholly a matter of the divine initiative, precisely because it is rooted in the inner divine life which turns to creatures in the missions of Son and Spirit.

God is in himself the antecedent, majestic divine Word. In its address of creatures, God's Word is the enunciation of his eternal purpose to make himself an object of creaturely knowledge. God expresses himself. Commenting on the opening phrase of the Fourth Gospel, Calvin says:

> I think he calls the Son of God 'the Word' (*sermo*) simply because, first, he is the eternal wisdom and will of God, and secondly, because he is the express image of his purpose. For just as in men speech is called the expression of the thoughts, so it is not inappropriate to apply this to God and say that he expresses himself to us by his Speech or Word.[1]

Creaturely knowledge of God is made possible by the operation of the *verbum externum*, that is, by the presence and action of the eternal Word. To this external Word there corresponds the *verbum internum*, that is, the presence and action of the Holy Spirit by whom cognitive fellowship between God and creatures is consummated. Like its objective presence, the subjective intelligibility of the divine Word is not achieved by a coordination of divine and created agencies. God is sovereignly at work in the full course of his revelation; he is not one who merely furnishes the occasion or raw material for creaturely work. If creatures hear and know, it is because God the Holy Spirit makes them hear and know. This hearing and knowing are genuine creaturely acts – were they not, there would be no fellowship between God and creatures but simply a divine utterance into a void. But the hearing

---

*The order is significant. God's action in communicating via his Word comes first, followed by his work in creating and then regenerating the human mind which reasons in response to his Word. In both areas, we speak of God's action, but we do move from his action outside us to his action that transforms us, from his speech to his work in drawing out our answer or testimony.

and knowing of creatures are spiritual acts, that is, acts for whose description we must employ language about the Holy Spirit.*

The work of Word and Spirit, through which God gives creatures a share in his knowledge of himself, is mediated through creaturely auxiliaries. Of these, Holy Scripture is the chief; through its ministry of the divine Word in the Spirit's power, God makes himself known and loved. What is to be said of the nature and service of Scripture?

If we are consistent at this point in drawing an understanding of the nature and function of Scripture from theological doctrine about the divine economy, we may find ourselves led to think some unfamiliar thoughts (unfamiliar, that is, in the commonplace narrations of theological progress). But as a consequence we may also discover a measure of freedom from the deism or historical naturalism which in various guises continues to trouble mainstream biblical scholarship.[2] We may be led to say something like this: Scripture is not simply one of a set of immanently conceived communicative practices, a literary-historical entity of which a sufficient description can be given by identifying the natural properties of texts and their agents (whether authorial or interpretative). Nor is Scripture a purely natural entity upon which we superimpose 'religious' evaluations that encourage 'spiritual use' or 'theological interpretation'. Rather, without in any way denying the natural properties of scriptural texts, we may say that Scripture's place in the divine economy of redemption and revelation is determinative of its nature; this nature, in turn, directs its reception.

This might be spelled out further by speaking of Scripture as prophetic and apostolic testimony. 'Prophetic' and 'apostolic' pick out the canon of biblical writings as a unified set of creaturely communicative acts having their origin in God's calling and authorizing certain persons in the communion of the saints. In the assembly which is brought into being by the divine summons and promise there have been those whose words are caused to bear a distinctive relation to the divine Word. Their words are not wholly identical with the divine Word, but they are the subject of a special mission, they are 'sent from God'. This sending is definitive of its subjects: the prophets and apostles *are* those sent by God, and therefore those whose speech is for the sake of the divine Word.† 'Prophetic' and 'apostolic' are ontological, not evaluative, qualifiers, indicating what these persons and their acts most basically are

---

*His doctrine of qualitative divine transcendence enables God to act in such a way that it enables rather than evacuates humans of their own agency. See 'Immensity and Ubiquity of God' for further exposition of this idea.
†He here distinguishes prophetic, scriptural speech from the incarnate Son of God ('the divine Word') rather than the inspired Word of God. He does so to observe that scripture is human attestation sent by God (hence he next uses language of it being 'ambassadorial'). His expansion of this doctrine to speak of 'verbal' and 'plenary' inspiration will only come with a later essay, 'Holy Scripture', in R. Clements and D. Ngien, eds, *Between the Lectern and the Pulpit: Essays in Honour of Victor A. Shepherd* (Vancouver: Regent College Publishing, 2014), 173–81.

(this is shown by the call narratives of the prophets and apostles, which record drastic separation for a task in relation to God's self-utterance).

The particular relation of prophetic and apostolic words to God's own Word is ambassadorial; they are an embassy of God's eloquence. Not by embodiment or continuation but by authorized representation and testimony, the prophets and apostles are instrumental in the communication of the one who commissions them for their task. So commissioned, they bear authority.

They do not do so by virtue of innate capacity; but their commissioning and the providential ordering of their course makes them fitting, drawing them into the movement of God's self-revelation. As God does this, raising up prophets and apostles in the history of the covenant, he makes his people into the community of the Word of God, one in which his Word can be heard in the ministry of his ambassadors.

Holy Scripture is the textual settlement of this embassy. In it, prophetic and apostolic speech is extended into the church's present. Scripture is the availability of prophetic and apostolic ministry beyond its originating occasion. We should note at once that this account of the nature of Scripture does not obliterate its creaturely qualities, but sets them in relation to what Bullinger in a lovely phrase called 'the history of the proceeding of the Word of God'.[3] Scripture is a creaturely reality ordered to divine communication. There is a parallel here with the elements in the Lord's Supper. Bread and wine are signs in the economy of salvation; by them the ascended Christ distributes the benefits of his saving achievement, comforting and nourishing his people by his presence. These functions do not detract from the created materiality of the elements, but indicate, rather, that such created realities are taken up into the divine service. So also Holy Scripture: prophetic and apostolic words are no less creaturely for being servants of the divine Word; indeed, their creaturely nature is therein fulfilled. It is a bad dualist habit which assumes that scriptural texts are most basically products of a religious-cultural world to be investigated as such, and only secondarily describable as prophetic and apostolic testimony. The astonishingly simple and revisionary rule for understanding Scripture (on which the pre-critical exegesis of the church is predicated) is: 'those moved by the Holy Spirit spoke from God' (2 Pet. 1.21).*

Scripture's being and function are in this movement of the Spirit. Scripture is 'inspired' in the sense that its entire course (from pretextual tradition to canonization, including supremely the work of textual production) is superintended by the Spirit. The movement, of which Scripture is part, is a shedding abroad of the knowledge of God. As an element within this divine movement, therefore, Scripture is not a closed reality, a hermetically sealed oracle. It runs its course, and as it does so it commands

---

*For further exposition of this passage, see his 'ὑπὸ πνεύματος ἁγίου φερόμενοι ἐλάλησαν ἀπὸ θεοῦ ἄνθρωποι: On the Inspiration of Holy Scripture', in J. G. McConville and L. K. Pietersen, eds, *Conception, Reception and the Spirit: Essays in Honor of Andrew T. Lincoln* (Eugene, OR: Cascade, 2016), 236–51.

hearing. The necessity for the reception of Scripture ought not to be conceived in such a way that reception becomes the point at which an inert textual deposit acquires vitality by virtue of being used or drawn into an interpretative project: reading is not writing. Yet *abusus non tollit usum*; there is a legitimacy to speaking of the field of the reception of the divine Word in the prophets and apostles. The end of their embassy is that creatures should know and love God, and knowing and loving are creaturely acts. Scripture engenders such acts; it is their occasion and regent. God's Word does not stun creatures into immobility; it moves them, it is a *path* (Ps. 119.35), a divine movement summoning and ruling a corresponding creaturely movement.

This anticipates what will be said shortly about reason in relation to the Word's intelligibility. Here we simply note the bearing of this principle on how the authority of Scripture might be conceived. The authority of Scripture ought not to be treated in isolation from the wider redemptive economy. If it is so isolated, it is easy to fall into the distortions of an abstract conception of authority developed apart from the ends which God has for creatures. The authority of Scripture is its power to command thought, speech and action by virtue of the fact that it brings to bear upon its hearers the purpose of the one who presents himself through its service. Scripture's authority is neither arbitrary nor merely statutory; it heralds the commanding presence of the loving creator. Scripture's authority is *retrospective*, in that it looks back to God as Scripture's primary *auctor*, the one who wills the creature's good and shares with the creature his knowledge of that good. And it is also *prospective*, an authority which engenders or 'authors' creaturely acts. Scripture's authority is a creative, not a sublimating, power. It is *fontalitas*: it creates a situation for the proper exercise of creaturely powers, including the powers of reason. This is not to say that Scripture is merely a stimulus for limitless debate; against such indeterminacy the Reformed scholastics properly insisted that: *sacra scriptura locuta, res decisa est*. But that *locuta* and *decisa* do not eliminate the intelligence, the will or the affections but direct them, putting them to work by freeing them from the pretence that they are at liberty to command themselves.

IV

Reason is 'a grace, and gift of love',[4] and continues to be such despite our descent into depravity, because God has contradicted reason's contradiction of itself and God. The rehabilitation of reason is among the benefits that accrue to creatures from the Word's redeeming work which the Spirit is now realizing in the creaturely realm. By this unified saving action and presence of Word and Spirit, reason's vocation is retrieved from the ruins: its sterile attempt at self-direction is set aside; its dynamism is annexed to God's self-manifesting presence; it regains its function in the ordered friendship between God and creatures.

Explicating such statements about reason requires deft use of the material content of the Christian faith, in order that reason can be seen in its proper setting in creation, redemption and revelation. Within the order of reality established by these works of God, reason undertakes its task; this order of reality is reason's 'law', by which it is formed and brought to life and activity. In this order, constituted by divine acts and rendered intelligible through divinely appointed signs, reason is a primary instrument of fellowship with God. By reason we are brought to apprehend, cleave to and obey God – to 'contemplation' in the sense of intelligent adoration. But this is possible only as reason is first humbled into the realization that it is neither author nor magistrate. The sanctifying Spirit must reorient reason to the divine Word, and only after that reorientation is reason authorized and empowered to judge and direct. Yet, as it is reoriented, reason really is authorized and empowered.* And Christian theology is an instance of this redeemed intellectual judgement.

Though such affirmations are still not common in contemporary theology, of late they have become less rare, and there is greater willingness to consider a concept of reason beyond that which has held sway in, for example, some varieties of philosophy of religion. Promptings in this direction sometimes have come from post-critical, pragmatic epistemology which links knowledge to (for example) the inhabitation of tradition or the cultivation of virtue. From a dogmatic standpoint, these approaches can suffer from a certain immanentism or relativism; and, even when they are associated with a theology of creation, incarnation or church, language about God rather quickly can become secondary to language about creatures and their common lives. More far-reaching revisions of conventional critical-instrumental understandings of reason have been generated by historical work. Genealogies of the fate of reason in the post-mediaeval (and especially post-Enlightenment) period have sought to identify the increasing isolation of reason from its setting in creaturely relations to God, and the inhibition, even sterility, which attends reason's elevation to presidency over a realm of pure nature.[5] For dogmatics, however, the most illuminating historical work is probably not that which traces reason's modern decay but that which explores conceptions of the intellect operative in the earlier Christian tradition, of which Anna Williams' exquisite essay on the intellect in patristic theology is a recent example.[6] By attentive return to the sources, we may recover much that has been lost – above all, the place of the intellect in creaturely redemption – but without recourse to a tragic reading of modernity which can discourage theology from calm deployment of its own resources in making sense of where it is and how it might best proceed.

Reason is created, fallen and redeemed. (a) The creator endows creatures with reason in order that, hearing his intelligible word of promise and command, they

---

*The prophetic process is in play here: deconstruction and then reconstruction of reason. Other relevant terms are those of post-Reformation Reformed soteriology, which speaks to the mortification and vivification of reason or other regenerate realities.

may know him, and so love and obey him. This means, first, that because creatures are *creatures*, they have reason because they have God. To talk of reason, therefore, we have to talk of God (for example, by a doctrine of the divine image). Creaturely reason is contingent. It is not original or self-founding after the manner of the uncreated divine reason. 'Reason', says Turretin, 'cannot and should not draw mysteries from its own treasury. The Word of God alone has this right'.[7] Second, reason gives creatures a capacity to transcend the immediate. Reason is reflective awareness, through which we entertain intentional relations to situations rather than simply registering them.[8] But to act with intention is quite other than to take up a stance of total critique. The movement of critical transcendence is not itself the fulfilment of reason's nature, for that movement drives ahead, to reason's ultimate end, which lies wholly beyond itself in apprehension of God and of all things in God. The fulfilment of created intellect occurs in this movement; reason shares in the dependence, finality, and therefore the goodness, of all created things.

(b) By speaking of reason as a created reality, theology is committed to giving a metaphysical rather than a voluntaristic account: reason acts within an order of being grounded in God himself, and is not simply a tool of the will.[9] But reason's nature is defiled. In the regime of sin, the structure of human desire collapses, because creatures do not give active consent to their creaturely vocation. And in the general collapse, reason also falls into futility and darkness; alienated from the life of God, it is overwhelmed by the callousness and squalor into which we betray ourselves (Eph. 4.17–19). Augustine describes how reason

> does many things through vicious desire, as though in forgetfulness of itself. For it sees some things intrinsically excellent … and whereas it ought to remain steadfast that it may enjoy them, it is turned away from [God] by wishing to appropriate those things to itself, and not to be like to him by his gift, but to be what he is by its own, and it begins to move and slip down gradually into less and less, which it thinks to be more and more; for it is neither sufficient for itself, nor is anything at all sufficient for it, if it withdraw from him who is alone sufficient; and so through want and distress it becomes too intent upon its own actions and upon the unquiet delights which it obtains through them; and thus … it loses its security.[10]

Augustine sees how fallen reason debases itself by spurning its divine vocation; its anxious acquisitiveness, its urgency in rational appropriation of the world, is not only pride but loss, a descent from security into self-securing. Embroiled in the creature's bid for freedom from the creator, reason loses its orientation to its proper end, and so compromises its goodness. It becomes 'pure' reason, reason on its own; and precisely this is its corruption.*

---

*Not surprisingly a secular approach to reason invariably brings with it a more despairing notion of reason devoid of hope (though it may have optimism for a time, it suffers this 'descent from security into self-securing' which can never cease).

Yet reason's corruption is a perversion of its given nature, and so not a ground for repudiating reason *tout court*. Interpretations of the modern history of reason as hubris sometimes stumble at this point. Trapped by the history which they narrate, they can make reason synonymous with the aggressive empirical intellect, and so promote either despair about reason or a kind of voluntaristic view of reason as just the intellectual vanguard of the will. But fallen reason is not the triumphant fulfilment of rational powers; it is their contradiction, substituting a spacious sense of reason's calling with a cramped and anxious desire for certainty without trustful attention to the divine Word and promise. Any talk of reason's depravity and need for renovation must be set under the sign of that Word and promise, that is, under the sign of redemption.

(c) Like all other aspects of created being, weakened and rendered dark and futile by sin, reason is encountered by the assurance and creative power of the forgiveness of sins. Divine judgement renews; it slays in order to make alive. There is not only declension; there is a renewal in the spirit of the mind, a new creaturely nature created after the likeness of God. The gracious, sovereign movement of Word and Spirit outbids the fall.

Reason participates in the dying and rising which are the foundation and pattern of redeemed existence. Reason dies as part of the comprehensive destruction of the wisdom of the world. For Paul in 1 Corinthians, unredeemed reason is one of the 'things that are' which are brought to nothing at the cross (1 Cor. 1.28).[11] But the shaming and bringing to nothing of corrupt reason is the negative condition for the gospel's claim that, in the economy of grace, God remakes creatures precisely by taking from them the evil self-existence which devastates creaturely flourishing. 'God', Paul tells the Corinthian elite, 'is the source of your life in Christ Jesus, whom God made our wisdom' (1 Cor. 1.30). If God in Christ is indeed reason's source of *life*, this restores to reason its orientation to the divine Word and enables it to perform its ministerial role. The depravity of reason means that we may 'err in excess', attributing to it powers which it has forfeited; but the redemption of reason means that we may also 'err in defect' by underrating it.[12] Because of the fall, reason cannot be, as Turretin has it, 'a principle and rule in whose scale the greatest mysteries of reason should be weighed'.[13] But, he goes on, 'a ministerial and organic relation is quite different from a principal and despotic. Reason holds the former relation to theology, not the latter'.[14] If Turretin is instructive here, it is because he stands at the latter end of a long tradition in which the anthropology and teleology of the intellect were derived from its place in the unfolding course of God's creative and saving works.

In short: reason is renewed after its self-alienation and treachery against God, because God *loves* creatures and desires to fulfil their natures, including their rational natures. This is why reason is a grace and a gift of love.

My account of reason in relation to the creative and redeeming work of God differs in significant ways from the striking proposal set out by Oliver Davies in *The Creativity of God*. Like the foregoing account, Davies' presentation suggests that the dominance of Baconian rationality has to be understood in relation to the decline of a Christian theological ontology of creaturely being and activity. On his reading of the matter, what was lost in the early modern period was a premodern participatory cosmology, in which the created intellect is understood as an element within the world, itself viewed as 'the domain of God's creativity',[15] and therefore as a 'theophanic universe':[16] the coinherence of creation and revelation is basic to Davies' proposal.[17] Once reason is isolated from the linguistic and material density of creation, it drifts away from 'what is perhaps the central tenet of the Christian faith: ... God's creativity radically and continuously shapes history, selfhood and world'.[18] Divine creativity, it should be noted, is to be understood not primarily in relation to divine transcendence but in terms of its suffusion and forming of creaturely media.

In accordance with these basic theological principles, the repair of reason can be approached through a semiotics of the participation of creaturely speech in the divine self-communication. This is initially stated through a most provocative account of the nature of Scripture: 'biblical texts make present kinds of human speaking which are interpenetrated by and formed within the creative rhythms of revelatory divine speech'; they are 'inwardly shaped by divine speaking'.[19] The most important element here is that divine and human speech (like creator and creation) are not to be segregated in extrinsicist fashion:

> The presence of God within the creation, as one whose speaking is the origin of the creation, sets the parameters for a distinctively Christian understanding of language, world and sign. This is a model which proposes a double operation of divine language. In the first place divine speech is that which institutes the world. The world, of which we are a part, must therefore be constituted as a domain of signs whereby things created point to the divine creativity as the source of their existence ... That which was spoken by God speaks the Creator, as a text bodies forth its author's voice.[20]

Here the difference from my own proposal surfaces: the underlying theology of creation makes much of the continuity of creator and creatures. Thus the world is 'a divine text: a "text" which is the deposit of the divine speaking and which bodies forth the essence of the communication between the divine Persons that is itself the foundation of the world'.[21] Or again, the world '"bears" or "houses" God's voice ... by extension',[22] for created reality is 'a kind of overflow from the infinitely fecund semiosis that is the inner life of the Trinity'.[23] Revelation gravitates towards a doctrine of creation as effusion, and creation itself is permeable to the being of God.

In this light, what of reason? Reason is integral to a 'creation-centred cosmology',[24] and therefore is to be understood in relation to a Christian semiotics of the participation of creaturely reality in divine self-communication. In this connection, Davies suggests that the eucharist be seen as the 'fundamental paradigm of reality',[25] in that it exemplifies the way in which created reality is transfigured by the divine in which it participates. Reason is thinking 'structured around the basic Christian experience of reality as the body, self-communication, or overwhelming embrace of God'.[26]

This direct appeal to Christian doctrine to reconceive the nature and function of reason is impressive. But too much is allowed to hang on the doctrine of creation, and, indeed, on that doctrine rather narrowly conceived. The pervasive idiom of participation may mute a sense of the sheer difference of the creator and his revelatory operations – the divine Word is almost folded into that which it interpenetrates and which in turn participates in the divine Word as its sign. This is compounded by a curious inattention to the theology of redemption: the economy of which reason is part is that of a participatory cosmology and material signification, not that of the mortification and vivification of creatures in Christ (Christ and his work, indeed, are hardly visible in the proposal).

The eclipse of the theology of redemption by the theology of participation is not uncommon in recent theological accounts of reason. It may also be found in Paul Janz's *God, the Mind's Desire*,[27] a book which shares the fate of others who invest heavily in a certain strand of Bonhoeffer's theology of the penultimate, namely the confusion of incarnation with immanence. Janz's underlying dogmatic principle, which he identifies as 'the heart of the Christian gospel, the heart of orthodoxy', is that 'the Christian God is always God-for-me, God-with-us, in empirical history, the referent in its very *advent*, and not God in his self-existent unconditioned aseity. If the revelation of the transcendent God is truly to be the *revelation* of God to God's creation in any meaningful sense of this term, then it has to be the revelation of the transcendent God-with-us'.[28] This is a pretty drastic rejection of teaching about the freedom of God's life in himself. It affects a theology of reason because reason is an aspect of 'a *creaturely* way of being human' which means 'the attachment to God's creation as a penultimate'.[29] And so theology can embrace 'nature and reason … without fear of jeopardizing the *mystery* of Christ that must remain at the heart of the gospel. For the mystery of Christ is not hidden in secret esoteric depths that require special aptitudes for apprehending it. Empirical reality is not just a "front" for some deeper supra-sensible reality in which the mystery of Christ is "really" hidden as something "subterranean" within immanence. No, the mystery of Christ is hidden in empirical history *as* empirical reality, "in the likeness of sinful flesh".[30] But this surely needs correction by a robust account of the lordly activity of God in Christ as the context in which reason's capacity for intelligence is to be set. To speak of incarnation is not to champion some general theory of the penultimate or the empirical, but to speak of the singular event of the divine Word's assumption of flesh in the context of the fall, human alienation and the reconciling presence of God. What the incarnation tells us is not that reason needs to be embedded in the material but that, in the person and work of the Son, reason is redeemed and its proper finality restored.

V

Christian theology is biblical reasoning. It is the redeemed intellect's reflective apprehension of God's gospel address through the embassy of Scripture, enabled and corrected by God's presence, and having fellowship with him as its end.

Classical Reformed theology spoke of Scripture as the cognitive principle of theology, and of God as its ontological principle.[*] Such talk is no doubt vulnerable to epistemological or metaphysical formalization. But we need not fear that it will always succumb; worries about foundations or ontotheology can be compulsive, and to alleviate them we only need to recall that theology's cognition of its objects is an episode in the unfolding fellowship between God and the creatures to whom he makes himself known. Bearing this in mind, we can say three things. First, Scripture is the cognitive principle of theology in the sense that Scripture is the place to which theology is directed to find its subject matter and the norm by which its representations are evaluated. God himself is this subject matter and norm in his royal address of the creature's intellect. Because of this, second, the ontological principle of theology is God himself – not some proposed entity but the Lord who out of the unfathomable plenitude of his triune being lovingly extends towards creatures in Word and Spirit. Third, therefore, the cognitive principle is grounded in the ontological principle. Holy Scripture is a function of God; its cognitive and revelatory force is not that of a textual deposit but of a loving voice and act of rule.

Christian theological reason is not an indeterminate intellectual activity, reason in search of an object, but reason to which an approach has already been made with unassailable might, to which an object has been given. This object represents itself in textual form. The form does not exhaust its object – how could a mere text fathom the untold depths of God's life? But the form is fitting, and through it theology does encounter the divine summons; and so theology is not a free science, but bound to (and therefore liberated by) the one in whose company it finds itself placed.

Through Scripture God commands creaturely reason, and this command quickens. Even in the economy of redemption reason is not adequate to do the bidding of its creator and redeemer. Turretin speaks of reason as 'sound and healed by grace'.[31] This ought not to be pressed into an anticipation of the eschatological knowledge of the blessed; in its pilgrim state, theological reason remains subject to lingering corruption. Yet reason *is* within the sphere of God's sanctifying and ruling grace, its inadequacies compensated for by a divine promise. The promise is the promise

---

[*]This paired set of principles manifests the fact that Webster clearly thinks of 'God' here as the singular one who reveals himself in Scripture; otherwise, God as ontological principle would never necessitate Scripture as cognitive principle.

of baptism, the effective announcement of regeneration and participation in a new history under the divine rule.

How does reason respond to this rule? There is a temptation to magnify grace by eliminating the work of reason as if reason were by nature an aggressor. But, in the realm of the redeemed creation, reason is neither master nor slave. It is, rather, made ready for lively embrace of the Word, received not in pure passivity but actively, under the Word's direction. Reducing reason to passivity misses the real character of the Word's address and of the reason which it addresses. For, on the one hand, the Word is creative, communicative and intelligible. It does not have its term merely in being uttered, but in being received, in becoming a matter for the intelligence of faith. And, on the other hand, reason is redeemed not for slothful compliance but for a work of knowledge. There is, of course, a disorderly work of reason which considers itself competent to summon the Word into its presence or to take upon itself the Spirit's work of furthering the communicative effectiveness of the Word. But disorder is overcome by order, and in good theological order reason is restored to its proper task of biblical reasoning. For the purposes of exposition, this task can be broken down as exegetical reasoning and dogmatic reasoning.

(a) Exegetical reasoning is, most simply, reading the Bible, the intelligent (and therefore spiritual) act of following the words of the text. Scripture is not an oracular utterance but an instrument through which divine speech evokes the unselfish, loving and obedient tracing of the text's movement which is the work of exegesis. This is the theologically primary act; the principal task of theological reason is figuring out the literal sense, that is, what the text says. This would be an absurdly naïve claim if the literal sense were thought of merely as information to be retrieved from an inert source in which it had been deposited. But the prophets and apostles are *alive*, their texts are their *voices* which herald the *viva vox Dei*. 'Following' these texts is as it were a movement of intellectual repetition, a 'cursive' representation of the text, running alongside it or, perhaps better, running in its wake. To be taken into this movement is the commentator's delight, tempered by the knowledge that we cannot hope to keep pace, because the prophets and apostles always stride ahead of us. This is why following these texts involves the most strenuous application of the powers of the intellect, demanding the utmost concentration to resist habit and to ensure that the text's movement is not arrested in our representation.

One extension of the primacy of exegetical reason is the importance of commentary as a theological genre, more specifically, of commentary as contemplative paraphrase rather than as repository of textual-historical information. Commentarial reason operates naturally in a theological culture in which the text is a determinate, authoritative and, in an important way, *resistant* element, rather than something which is plastic in the hands of the present agents of the culture. Commentary flourishes in a positive rather than a critical theological and spiritual culture, one which regards its essential matter as a given to be received afresh rather than generated.[32] Of course, the very need for commentary indicates that the text upon which the commentary is made is not the end of discourse; the text is a gift which evokes the works of reason. But commentarial reason always points back to the text from which alone it draws its substance; and this reference back is itself both a necessary limitation (even, indeed, mortification) of reason and the occasion of reason's aliveness.[33]

(b) Dogmatic reasoning produces a conceptual representation of what reason has learned from its exegetical following of the scriptural text. In dogmatics, the 'matter' of prophetic and apostolic speech is set out in a different idiom, anatomized. Cursive representation leads to conceptual representation, which abstracts from the textual surface by creating generalized or summary concepts and ordering them topically. This makes easier swift, non-laborious and non-repetitive access to the text's matter. But, in doing this, it does not dispense with Scripture, kicking it away as a temporary scaffold; it simply uses a conceptual and topical form to undertake certain tasks with respect to Scripture. These include: seeing Scripture in its full scope as an unfolding of the one divine economy; seeing its interrelations and canonical unity; seeing its proportions. These larger apprehensions of Scripture then inform exegetical reason as it goes about its work on particular parts of Scripture. Dogmatics is the schematic and analytical presentation of the matter of the gospel. It is 'systematic', not in the sense that it offers a rigidly formalized set of deductions from a master concept, but in the low-level sense of gathering together what is dispersed through the temporal economy to which the prophets and apostles direct reason's gaze. What dogmatic reason may not do is pretend to a firmer grasp of the object of theological reason than can be achieved by following the text. The prophets and apostles are appointed by God, dogmaticians are not; prophetic and apostolic speech is irreducible; the sufficiency of Scripture includes its *rhetorical* sufficiency.[34]

VI

Exegesis and dogmatics are indirectly ascetical disciplines.[*] That is, they are intellectual activities in which the church participates in the mortification of reason which is inescapable if the children of Adam are to become the friends of God. As

---

[*]As John Calvin says, the sum of the Christian life is self-denial (*Institutes*, III.vi.1), including the life of the mind. Exegesis and dogmatics are described here as tools or instruments of that self-denial by God's gracious provision.

theological reason goes about its exegetical and dogmatic tasks, the intellect is drawn away from idols.[35] Mortification, however, is ordered to vivification, which is, indeed, its inner power, and the ground for theological confidence. Christian theology cannot remain content with the contemporary commonplace that reason is not much more than a play of power – a commonplace as lazy as it is hopeless. Oriented by and to the divine Word in the testimonies of the prophets and apostles, reason is a sphere of grace, a sign of the overcoming of the disorder of sin in its forms of ignorance and unbridled invention. May it not be that what afflicts some of the church in its present hermeneutical gridlock is a disorder of the passions, a destructive instability which will not allow itself to be drawn into the self-abandonment (intellectual, moral, political) which is the only way in which redemption will have its way with us? One of the deepest fault lines in the church at the present time runs between those who do their theological reasoning on the basis of a conviction that in Scripture the breath of the divine Word quickens reason to knowledge and love of God, and those who fear (or hope?) that neither Scripture nor reason take us any further than human poetics. The latter choice generates irony and squabbling, and both of these are sicknesses of the soul. The former is more persuasively present than it has been for some long while, and we should seize the day.

Notes

1   J. Calvin, *The Gospel According to St John 1–10* (Edinburgh: St Andrew Press, 1959), p. 7.

2   On deistic views of revelation underlying some kinds of historical biblical scholarship, see E. Stump, 'Revelation and Biblical Exegesis: Augustine, Aquinas, and Swinburne', in A. G. Padgett, ed., *Reason and the Christian Religion. Essays in Honour of Richard Swinburne* (Oxford: Clarendon, 1994), pp. 161–97.

3   H. Bullinger, *The Decades* I & II (Cambridge: Cambridge University Press, 1849), p. 48.

4   D. Turner, *Faith, Reason and the Existence of God* (Cambridge: Cambridge University Press, 2004), p. xiv.

5   For some representative accounts, see: M. Brown, *Restoration of Reason. The Eclipse and Recovery of Truth, Goodness and Beauty* (Grand Rapids: Baker, 2006); I. U. Dalferth, *Becoming Present. An Inquiry into the Christian Sense of the Presence of God* (Leuven: Peeters, 2006), pp. 10–19; I. U. Dalferth, *Die Wirklichkeit des Möglichen. Hermeneutische Religionsphilosophie* (Tübingen: MohrSiebeck, 2003), pp. 209–56; Davies, *The Creativity of God*; L. Dupré, *The Enlightenment and the Intellectual Foundations of Modern Culture* (New Haven, CT: Yale University Press, 2004); P. J. Griffiths and R. Hütter, eds, *Reason and the Reasons of Faith*

(London: T&T Clark, 2005); D. Hardy, 'Reason, Wisdom and the Interpretation of Scripture', in D. Ford and G. Stanton, eds, *Reading Texts, Seeking Wisdom. Scripture and Theology* (London: SCM Press, 2003), pp. 69–88.

6   A. Williams, *The Divine Sense. The Intellect in Patristic Theology* (Cambridge: Cambridge University Press, 2007).

7   F. Turretin, *Institutes of Elenctic Theology* (Phillipsburg: Presbyterian and Reformed, 1992), I.xvi.6 (vol. 1, p. 30).

8   Cf. R. Spaemann, *Persons. The Difference between 'Someone' and 'Something'* (Oxford: Oxford University Press, 2006), p. 63.

9   R. Hütter rightly criticizes the Nietzschean cast of much contemporary writing about reason in 'The Directedness of Reason and the Metaphysics of Creation', in P. J. Griffiths and R. Hütter, eds, *Reason and the Reasons of Faith*, pp. 160–93.

10   Augustine, *On the Trinity* (Peabody, Mass.: Hendrickson, 1994) X.v.7.

11   On the Pauline material, see L. Malcolm, 'The Wisdom of the Cross', in P. J. Griffiths and R. Hütter, eds, *Reason and the Reasons of Faith*, pp. 86–118, and especially J. L. Martyn, 'Epistemology at the Turn of the Ages', in *Theological Issues in the Letters of Paul* (Edinburgh: T&T Clark, 1997), pp. 89–110.

12   Turretin, *Institutes* I.viii.2 (vol. 1, p. 24).

13   Ibid.

14   Turretin, *Institutes* I.viii.6 (vol. 1, p. 25).

15   Davies, *The Creativity of God*, p. 48.

16   Ibid., p. 56.

17   The theme is explored in his earlier book *A Theology of Compassion. Metaphysics of Difference and the Renewal of Tradition* (London: SCM, 2001).

18   Davies, *The Creativity of God*, p. 72.

19   Ibid., p. 75.

20   Ibid., p. 95.

21   Ibid., p. 105.

22   Ibid., p. 108.

23   Ibid., p. 118.

24   Ibid., p. 170.

25   Ibid., p. 179.

26   Ibid., p. 184.

27   Paul Janz, *God, the Mind's Desire. Reference, Reason and Christian Thinking* (Cambridge: Cambridge University Press, 2004).

28   Janz, *God, the Mind's Desire*, pp. 213f.

29   Ibid., p. 219.

30   Ibid., p. 220.

31   Turretin, *Institutes* I.ix.14 (vol. 1, p. 31).

32   See J. B. Henderson, *Scripture, Canon, and Commentary. A Comparison of Confucian and Western Exegesis* (Princeton, NJ: Princeton University Press, 1991); P. J. Griffiths, *Religious Reading. The Place of Reading in the Practice of Religion* (Oxford: Oxford University Press, 1999).

33   Exegetical reason draws upon the services of other forms of rational inquiry, chiefly historical and literary, which enable readers to follow the text that is actually before them in its fullness and integrity. But such inquiries are subordinate, because the task of exegetical reason is to explicate the text, not to generate an account of its historical, religious or cultural conditions of possibility. Scripture is only secondarily an item in the literary history of religion; primarily it is an element in the economy of grace, a letter ordered to the Spirit's presentation of the divine Word and its quickening of reason.

34   T. F. Torrance surely was correct to insist that theological statements are 'genuine statements in so far as they *derive from* [the] Word and *refer back* to it: that is their essential *ana-logic*' ('The Logic and Analogic of Biblical and Theological Statements in the Greek Fathers', in *Divine Meaning*, p. 381). But there is something problematic in his suggestion that 'theological activity … is not concerned merely with biblical exegesis or with the kind of biblical theology that builds up what this or that author in the New Testament taught about the Gospel; it is concerned with the Truth at a deeper level' (p. 385) in so far as it penetrates 'into the interior logic of the apostolic witness, and [allows] the truth that was embedded there to come to view in an orderly and articulate way' (p. 386). The difficulty here is that the work of dogmatic reason appears to generate conceptual improvements on the biblical text (what Torrance calls *paradeigmata*, p. 367), improvements which are more immediately connected to the 'apostolic mind' (p. 388). Torrance is reluctant to order concepts to the letter of the text – a point which comes out in his treatment of Hilary of Poitiers, who, he suggests, 'interprets what is meant rather than just the sense of the words' (p. 395). *Sermo* is certainly subject to *res*; but *paradeigmata* are subservient to *sermo*, and the prophetic and apostolic *sermo* remains the governor of theological discourse, not simply that which we pass through on the way to the *res*.

35   A point made to great effect in M. Levering, *Scripture and Metaphysics. Aquinas and the Renewal of Trinitarian Theology* (Oxford: Blackwell, 2004).

3

The immensity and ubiquity of God

EDITOR'S INTRODUCTION

John Webster devoted significant time not only to commending the centrality of God as both context and content of Christian doctrine but also to confessing something of the singular character of this God who reveals himself through the embassy of the prophets and apostles in Holy Scripture. He addressed matters of triunity, but he also wrote repeatedly on the divine attributes or perfections. 'The immensity and ubiquity of God' was one of two essays on the attributes which appeared in his collection, *Confessing God* (alongside 'The Holiness and Love of God'). Portions of the essay also played a role in the third of his as-yet-unpublished but nonetheless justly famous Kantzer Lecture series on Perfection and Presence.

In this essay he turns to space, presence and omnipresence, but in so doing he turns, as ever, to God. 'The centre of theological concern, we might say, is less the physics of space or the poetics of space than the "economics" of space, its significance in God's ordered administration of created reality.' Again the divine economy provides a matrix within which to consider other concepts, in this case that of space. In this essay he considers the omnipresence of God, and he does so impelled to address both the immensity of God in himself as well as the ubiquity with which God makes himself present in the works of God.

Webster shows a concern to trace the divine attributes 'by offering an analytic depiction of God's identity … [which] is singular and antecedent', thus pushing against tendencies to think God by reflecting on generic deities. Specifically, he differentiates his approach with 'most perfect being' variants that are dominant in the world of the analytic philosophy of religion. Therefore, notice that he labours patiently not merely to identify God's transcendence of space as a negative assertion but also of what it says positively of who God actually is and how God actually makes himself present unto his created beings. He itemizes the most relevant biblical texts for thinking about divine presence (i.e. 1 Kgs 8.27; Jer. 7.4; Ps. 139.7), and in doing so he emphasizes divine presence in temple among Israel and also probes christological issues (e.g. affirming the so-called *extra Calvinisticum*). He engages with classical and contemporary authors (Augustine, Aquinas, Calvin, yes, but also Ingolf Dalferth, Eberhard Jüngel and Thomas Morris) and engages in conceptual glosses of that divine economy and Scriptural elaboration of divine (omni-)presence and, beneath it, in God's transcendence of space in his own perfect life.

Like the previous essay on Christology, this chapter also shows the challenge in thinking about theology and economy and in relating the two themes appropriately. He notes that there's the danger of an abstract account of the attributes on the one hand and the temptation to overreaction by shirking all concern for metaphysical absolutes on the other hand. In this essay he names the danger, then, of secularized thought about space, and he seeks to guide us away from that pathway by reclaiming space as a theological category.

Suggested readings

'Attributes, Divine', in *The Cambridge Dictionary of Christian Theology* (ed. David Fergusson, Karen Kilby, Ian McFarland, and Iain Torrance; Cambridge: Cambridge University Press, 2010).

'God's Aseity', in *Realism and Religion: Philosophical and Theological Perspectives* (ed. Andrew Moore and Michael Scott; Aldershot: Ashgate, 2007), 147–62.

'God's Perfect Life', in *God's Life in Trinity* (ed. Miroslav Volf and Michael Welker; Minneapolis, MN: Fortress, 2006), 143–52.

'The Holiness of God', in *Holiness* (Grand Rapids, MI: Eerdmans, 2003), 31–52.

'The Holiness and Love of God', *Scottish Journal of Theology* 57, no. 3 (2004): 249–68; repr. in *CG*, 109–30.

'Life in and of Himself: Reflections on God's Aseity', in *Engaging the Doctrine of God: Contemporary Protestant Perspectives* (ed. Bruce McCormack; Grand Rapids, MI: Baker, 2008), pp. 107–24; repr. in GWM 1, 13–28.

Christopher, R. J. Holmes, 'Divine Perfections', in *A Companion to John Webster's Theology* (ed. Michael Allen and R. David Nelson; Grand Rapids, MI: Eerdmans, forthcoming).

THE IMMENSITY AND UBIQUITY OF GOD

I

Christian dogmatic language about the divine attributes explicates the nature of the triune God by offering an analytical depiction of God's identity. For the Christian confession, God's identity is singular and antecedent; it is possessed of its own incomparable uniqueness and of a majesty which can only be characterized as it sets itself before us in the free acts of God's aliveness. Because it is responsible rational articulation of the church's confession of that aliveness, Christian dogmatics is a positive science, and so from the beginning it is prohibited from according any orienting or controlling function to abstract considerations of *deitas* in its account of the attributes of God: in dogmatics, questions of the divine nature are wholly resolved into questions of the divine identity, from which alone dogmatics receives its direction. The divine identity is disclosed in the acts of God's being. That is, the singularity of God is learned, not by the adoption, refinement and qualification of a religious, philosophical or ethical conception of deity, but by attention to God's self-enactment in his inner and outer works. God is himself in the plenitude, unity and differentiation of the inner divine life of love and fellowship, in the relations and processions of Father, Son and Spirit. And God is further himself in the unhindered, effortless and wholly loving missions of the triune persons, in willing, reconciling and perfecting creatures as the counterpart to the love and fellowship which God is in himself.* In the inseparability of God's inner and outer works, in their strictly irreversible sequence and no less strict reciprocity, Christian dogmatics has to discern the one who is the object of the church's praise. God's identity becomes a matter for dogmatic explication because it expounds itself in and through the history of God's engagement with humanity, God's creature, sinner and child caught up in the judgement and renewal of all things. That history is the drama of God's self-exposition; in it and through it, the *essentia dei* sets itself forth with majestic force and mercy. The divine *essentia* may not be constructed in advance of or in isolation from that history, nor may that history be considered in advance of or in isolation from the antecedent perfection of God. To offer a dogmatic presentation of the attributes of God is, therefore, to indicate *this one* in the supreme radiance and completeness of

---

*'Effortless' is a statement about God's works that does not qualify them as less effective or significant, but as demanding no cost or diminishment of God in their execution. God is no less even when God makes us more. Webster will elsewhere use the language of fullness and perfection to express this singular character of the divine life and, therefore, also the divine works.

his triune being and act in which he freely turns to his creatures, claiming them and directing them to himself.

In formal terms, this means that if a dogmatics of the divine attributes is to serve the articulation of God's identity, it must achieve a fitting coordination of 'immanent' and 'operative', 'absolute' and 'relative'. In the matter of the divine immensity and ubiquity, this requirement must be obeyed with particular strictness. This is because, like all the so-called 'metaphysical' attributes, immensity and ubiquity have in some measure been bent out of shape by being harnessed to an abstract conception of God as 'perfect being' and to abstract exposition through the 'logic of perfection' or 'supremacy'. Examples are ready to hand in some recent Anglo-American philosophy of religion which explores divine omnipresence by mapping the logic of the concept of a perfect being.[1] Such a being, the argument runs, must of necessity be characterized by freedom from limitation, that is, by infinity, and must therefore be present at once to all things in a manner which is incorporeal, spiritual and lacking in determinate spatial location. In and of themselves, of course, such statements are hardly unexceptionable; what makes them problematic is their attachment to a distinctly formal conception of deity largely uncorrected by the event of God's free self-enactment as Father, Son and Spirit.

Proponents of these styles of philosophical engagement with the attributes of God consider that 'perfect being theology' is continuous in a quite straightforward way with the theology of Augustine, Anselm and Aquinas, and, indeed, often develop their ideas in conversation with classical texts.[2] The similarities are, however, more formal than substantial: there is all the difference in the world between spelling out the logic of *a god* and indicating the particular perfection of the God manifest in Jesus Christ and in the Spirit's presence. The *aliquid quo nihil maius cogitari possit* of pre-modern Christian theology is not so much a proposal about deity as an indicator of a name to be confessed.* It refers back to the divine enactment, and it is concerned with the conceivability of *deitas* only as a consequence of being overtaken by the 'supreme and inaccessible light' before which the eye of the mind is 'dazzled by its splendour, overcome by its fullness, overwhelmed by its immensity, confounded by its capacity'.[3] The antecedent of 'perfect being theology' is thus not the pre-modern theology of the church, but rather the development from the seventeenth century onwards of a systematic natural theology, in which the divine attributes are deduced from a conception of God which is itself established as part of the project of giving a theistic explanation of the world.[4] For the historical forebears of 'perfect being

---

*These first two pages of polemical concern, specifically and lengthily expounding about identifying God and expounding the divine nature only in a way shaped by God's self-manifesting identity revealed in his works, are targeting modern philosophical approaches rather than premodern Christian classics. He will shortly thereafter show that Samuel Clarke's argument has moved a long ways from those of Augustine, Anselm and Aquinas (and note that even Thomas fits the pattern of *fides quarens intellectum* or 'faith seeking understanding' in Webster's assessment).

theology', therefore, we should look not so much to the work of Augustine, Anselm or Aquinas, but – for example – to the Newtonian natural theology of Samuel Clarke, whose *Demonstration of the Being and Attributes of God* (1705) endeavours 'to show to such considering persons as I have already described that the being and attributes of God are not only possible or barely probable in themselves, but also strictly demonstrable to any unprejudiced mind from the most uncontestable principles of right reason'.[5] The setting of such an account of God's perfections is not the prayer of faith – Anselm's 'Your countenance, O Lord, do I seek'[6] – but rather the project of 'demonstration', a project whose norm is only 'the bare force of reasoning', and whose procedure is coherence 'to the rules of strict and demonstrative argumentation'.[7] Thus, like his analytical heirs, Clarke argues from the demonstration of a self-existent being to the proposal that 'the self-existent being must of necessity be infinite and omnipresent', for '[t]o be self-existent … is to exist by an absolute necessity in the nature of the thing itself. Now this necessity being absolute in itself and not depending on any outward cause, it is evident that it must be *everywhere* as well as *always* unalterably the same'. And hence 'the infinity of the self-existent being' must be 'an infinity … of immensity'; this being must exist 'absolutely in every place and be equally present everywhere, and consequently must have a true and absolute infinity both of immensity and wholeness'.[8]

This is surely problematical, not simply because Clarke reaches his affirmation of divine omnipresence by the wrong route, but much more because tucked within the method is substantive teaching about God. Following the method commits him in advance to a theology of omnipresence in which neither the immanent triune life of God nor his loving relations to his creatures play any perceptible role, so reducing omnipresence to a kind of continuous substrate of the coherence of the universe. As a consequence, ubiquity is drastically narrowed by being subsumed under God's (naturally discerned) providential work, thereby eliding its soteriological and pneumatological character. And in this, 'perfect being theology' fares little better, for the same disposition of doctrines (a maximal investment in providence and the cosmological aspects of ubiquity, a correspondingly minimal investment in trinitarian distinctives) is largely retained in exploring the logic of a supreme being. If, by contrast, good dogmatic order is to prevail, what is required is a thoroughgoing theological correction of concepts like 'perfection', 'supremacy' or 'self-existence'. As they have been deployed in natural and philosophical theology, they have been characteristically too abstract, and therefore too susceptible to being laden with the wrong content, in effect answering the question 'What is God?' before the question 'Who is God?'* Something a good deal more descriptively dense and rich is required, something more transparent to the particularity of God's self-enactment. Dogmatics

---

*This statement of order addresses the order of being, not necessarily the order of exposition in a given pedagogical setting.

has no concern with that than which nothing greater can be conceived *in abstracto*; its responsibility is to God's particular perfection. Or, as Barth put it, what matters in an account of God's perfections is '*Gott selber, sein eines, einfaches, eigenes Wesen,* God himself, his one, simple, distinctive being'.[9]

Christian dogmatics attempts to indicate God's enacted singularity.* Yet in pursuing this task, in not allowing itself to be governed by prior conceptions of *deitas* in general, a dogmatics of the divine attributes soon faces another danger, namely, that of countering abstract conceptions of divinity by simply abandoning consideration of the 'metaphysical' or 'absolute' attributes of God and orienting itself exclusively to the economy of God's works *extra se*. But no less than the abstractions of generic notions of deity, this hypertrophy of the *attributa operativa* fails to grasp the perfectly mutual correspondence between God's inner being and his outer works. In the matter of divine omnipresence, as in all the divine attributes, it is of capital importance that, under the tutelage of God's self-enactment, theology does not fall into a bifurcation of the *essentia dei* and God's revealed will and activity. That bifurcation can happen (as in 'perfect being theology') by determining the doctrine of God in advance of God's works. But it can also happen from the other end: by giving a wholly 'economic' account of the attributes of God without roots in God's being *in se*.† Dogmatics can protect itself against this division only by developing an integrated answer to what Chemnitz believed to be the two fundamental questions for a comprehensive dogmatic article *de deo*: 'What is the essence both in the divine unity as well as in the three persons of the Deity?', and 'What is the will of God, revealed in His activity, both in the creation of the universe and the sustaining of all created things, as well as in the creation of special benefits for the sake of His church?'[10]

Consequently, a theology of divine omnipresence needs to offer a fully integrated account of *immensitas dei* and *ubiquitas dei*. There is no *immensitas* which is not known in God's *omnipraesentia operativa*; there is no ubiquity which is not grounded in God's wholly free, transcendent majesty as the measureless one. And if dogmatics affirms this inseparable and equiprimordial character of immensity and ubiquity, it is, once again, not because of some prior conception of what Pannenberg calls the 'true Infinite'[11] – an unhappily detached notion whose persistence throughout his account of the divine attributes is unsettling. Rather, it is because only in this way can

---

*Webster draws on Barth about beginning with divine singularity, but he does not turn to a distinctively Christocentric account. Language here is consistently trinitarian and never reductively Christocentric (as in some readings of Barth and other modern figures). See 'The Place of Christology in Systematic Theology' for further exposition on this front, differentiating Webster's approach to divine singularity from more reductively Christocentric versions of divine singularity.

†Narrative theology cannot solve the problem alone or stand alone; God's self-revelation involves not merely the great works of God (economy) but also its self-exposition which points to roots in the inner life of God too (theology). Narrative cannot be severed from metaphysics, and both must be normed and limited by Holy Scripture as God's self-revelation.

dogmatics hope to indicate the one who as free Lord of all things is without limit and everywhere present in power and mercy.

II

God's immensity is the triune God himself in the boundless plenitude of his being, in which he is unhindered by any spatial constraint, and so is sovereignly free for creative and saving presence to all limited creaturely reality.

God's immensity is commonly identified as a mode of his infinity. Thus Charles Hodge: 'His immensity is the infinitude of his being, viewed as belonging to his nature from eternity.'[12] Accordingly, it is expounded by describing a set of contrasts with limited, spatial reality: possessed of *immensitas*, God is one to whom *ubietas* may not be attributed, for space is a mode of existence pertaining only to creatures, and God is *illocalis*, his being is *sine mensura*. Such a procedure offers formal assistance to dogmatics by some primary conceptual clarifications; but it is an inherently risky enterprise if it is allowed to overwhelm substantive dogmatic considerations. In particular, two weighty qualifications have to be kept in mind. First, the concept of infinity must not be deployed in such a way that it becomes an inverted image of the finite; an *immensitas dei* which is simply the antithesis of the local, which is reached merely by stripping away the attribute of spatiality, will by no means necessarily be adequate to indicate the boundless plenitude of the triune God. Second, therefore, whatever is said by way of negation is only an interim concept, something said on the way to a positive statement of God's immensity, and its function is therefore not so much to deliver a substantive doctrine of what God is not, as to articulate some contrasts which will bring into relief the particular perfection which God is. Infinity is not indefiniteness or indistinctness of being. As the immense one, unconditioned by space and unrestricted by relations of adjacency, God is not unspecific: he is *this one*. Infinity is not lack of identity, but rather the absolute *Istigkeit* of God's being; it is intensive perfection. Immensity, therefore, means that God is – in Bavinck's phrase – 'limitless in the intensive, qualitative, positive sense'.[13] Lack of finitude, transcendence of all circumscriptive measure and limitation, are the backcloth to the particular freedom in and as which God is God; to speak of God's absence of limitation is to indicate the boundless liberty of God to be and act as he determines in relation to space. Immensity concerns the plenitude, richness, sufficiency and effectiveness of God and so of God's disposition of himself in relation to creaturely space.

Immensity is commonly identified as an 'absolute' attribute of God, referring to God *in se*, apart from his relation to creation, and thereby distinguished from the 'relative' attribute of omnipresence, which is his spatial infinity with respect to the creature. The success of any such distinction depends on retaining the integrity and inseparability of 'absolute' and 'relative': only in that way can an account of the divine attributes fittingly refer to the unique and simple identity of the one who in himself and in his acts towards the creation is Father, Son and Spirit. Certainly, the conceptual mapping of God's identity in terms of the distinction between absolute and relative may have a certain formal or heuristic justification (parallel to the distinction between God *in se* and God *pro nobis*, of which it is a corollary). And, more importantly, it may (like, again, a doctrine of the immanent Trinity[14]) preserve the sovereign and gratuitous character of the ways and works of God in the economy. But these distinctions must not be pressed in such a way that the 'absolute' acquires greater weight than the 'economic' in determining the *essentia dei*. In the case of God's immensity, therefore, this means, first, that immensity cannot be expounded without immediate reference to omnipresence, to which it stands in an inseparable and mutually conditioning relation. And it means, second, that, as with all the divine perfections, talk of divine immensity is wholly referred to the enacted identity of God in his sovereign self-presence as Father, Son and Spirit. Accordingly, dogmatics must give precedence to *definition by description* over *definition by analysis*; its account of the being of God and of God's perfections is to be determined at every point by attention to God's given self-identification – and thus by biblical-historical description of the particular freedom which God exercises in his lordly acts – rather than by construction of what is fittingly ascribed to a god.* Certainly we cannot climb out of our concepts, for they are all we have. But neither can we leave them undisturbed, or assume that they are inherently adequate to render God to us. They must be converted, made serviceable by correction, above all through being filled out by descriptive reference to the event and name of the God whom they attempt to indicate.

God's immensity is his transcendence of space. But in theological usage, transcendence, like infinity, is non-comparative: its content cannot be reached either by the magnification of creaturely properties (so that immensity is mere vastness) or by their negation (so that immensity is simply lack of spatial limitation). God's immensity is his qualitative distinction from creaturely reality, and can only be grasped on the basis of its enactment in the ways and works of God. *Immensus*, as MacKenzie notes in a reflection upon the Athanasian Creed, is an aspect of *increatus*, and the latter term 'points to the being of God as utterly qualitatively distinct from the existence of creatures, their attributes and limitations'; immensity is thus not quantitative disparity but a 'differential of quality'.[15] 'In terms of space, size and place are not applicable to him. Neither is he their mere negation. He is qualitatively and utterly other than these, both positively and negatively.'[16] One task, therefore, of the language of immensity is to press theology into a quite different conceptual register, one in which we do not talk about the divine perfections by maximizing a creaturely

---

*This ordering is not a statement of exclusion but of prioritization; description precedes and shapes analysis, not the other way around and not one in place of the other.

conception of immeasurability or infinite extension, but rather by emptying our thinking about God of the connotations of spatiality, positive and negative. But again, this 'emptying' is not an end in itself: if it were, the word 'God' might simply indicate some kind of void. Rather, it is both a preparation for and a consequence of attentiveness to God's wholly unique being and act.* Subject defines predicate; predicate can be resolved in its entirety into subject.

God's immensity is the free, gratuitous, non-necessary character of God's relation to space. As *immensus*, God's being has in itself its own particular depth, its own plenitude and perfection in the relations of Father, Son and Spirit. God stands under no external constraints by virtue of the spatiality of created reality, and his relation to creation does nothing to complete his being. Possessed of immensity, God is self-moved, replete, *ipse sibi et mundus et locus et omnia*.[17] This, once again, differentiates a Christian theology of divine immensity from pantheism or panentheism, which fail because they cannot coherently affirm the difference between God and the world. Not only do they impugn the aseity of God, rendering God and the world mutually constitutive, but they also cannot give a coherent account either of God's action upon the world or of the world's relative independence. Moreover, both assume an abstract conception of divine immensity as pure remoteness, a conception which, if it is to have any cosmological significance, must be secularized by identifying God's immensity with infinite space. It is precisely this abstract conception of immensity which dogmatics must replace with a more richly formed notion of immensity as the surpassing excellence of God which includes within itself the boundless capacity for nearness: immensity is the transcendent fullness of God which is also the energy of his fellowship with his spatial creatures in the works of creation and incarnation.

God is the lordly creator and keeper of the spaces of heaven and earth. His act of creation is a work of effortless supremacy, authority and effectiveness in which he determines that, alongside the utter perfection of his triune life, he will have his being in relation to another reality. This act is *ex nihilo*; that is, it is wholly original, requiring for its fulfilment nothing other than the mighty enactment of God's will. As creator, God brings into being the things that are not, and orders those things by structuring their existence through spatial and temporal relations. Space is not preexistent but a created mode of relation between contingent realities which emerged out of nothing. 'God does not stand in a spatial or temporal relation to the universe but ... spatial and temporal relations are produced through his creation of the universe and maintained through his interaction with what He has made.'[18] God's immensity thus includes his majestic priority over the space which he brings into being; he does not contain space (surrounding it as a vast vessel), nor is he dispersed through it or spatially immanent in it as its life-force, nor is he circumscribed by any of its places. 'Heaven

---

*Jeremiah 1.10 provides a pattern for this epistemological approach; the Word of God deconstructs false impressions and builds up true notions. Theology operates in the full prophetic mode here.

and the highest heaven cannot contain thee' (1 Kgs 8.27). Yet none of this denotes the creator's absence, but rather the free, unconditioned character of his sustaining presence to spatial reality and of his employment of it as one of the media in which he makes himself known. The immensity of the triune creator of heaven and earth is his unqualified transcendence of spatial relation even as the one from whose creative act all spatial relations originate and by whose providential work they are held in being. Immensity is at one and the same time the 'otherness' of God over against created space and the divine capacity to stand in relation to space and to act in space without compromise to the divine freedom.[*]

Something of the same may be suggested of God's interaction with creaturely space in the incarnation. The Word becomes flesh and dwells among creatures; thereby he appropriates to himself creaturely conditions, including spatiality. Yet no less than in the act of creation, the act of incarnation is an act of divine self-movement, a *becoming* or condescension which does not entail the abandonment or restriction of God's immensity. For the Word's entry into space is not to be thought of as local removal; his taking to himself a body does not indicate confinement and thus spell the end of his transcendence over space. The Word becomes flesh, certainly, taking to himself a body of matter and its relations to other bodies. In the passion he enters into the agony of bodily conflict in the constriction and elimination of his space. But he does all this in fulfilment of the divine resolve and in the plenitude of the divine being. He does not need to hide or divest himself of the immensity of deity in order to become flesh. In the form of a slave, obediently taking upon himself the contingencies of space, he is no less in the form of God. Even as one who is embodied, one to whom *ubietas* may be attributed, he fills all things. In his spatiality, he is – to use the Reformed parlance – 'outside' (*extra*), unhindered in his immensity. And again, to speak thus of God's immensity even in the act of incarnation is not to detract from the fullness of his humanity; it is simply to spell out that *vere deus* and *vere homo*, immensity and embodiment, are not competing and mutually contradictory accounts of the identity of the Son of God. Incarnation is not confinement, but the free relation of the Word to his creation – the Word who as creator and incarnate reconciler is *deus immensus*.[†]

In sum: a dogmatic account of God's immensity must follow the rule of all well-ordered thought about the divine perfections, namely, that the integrity and reciprocally determinative character of God's aseity and God's works *ad extra* must not be compromised either by their separation or by the exposition of one

---

[*]Divine immensity is what makes ubiquity possible as one subcategory of a broader principle: divine perfection makes divine presence possible (rather than impossible).

[†]Webster's Reformed bona fides are on full display in this paragraph on the incarnation. He opposes a kenotic reading of the act of assumption, and he affirms the so-called *extra Calvinisticum*. He argues that qualitative divine transcendence undergirds that Reformed approach to the metaphysics of the incarnation and the Chalcedonian formula.

at the expense of the other. On the one hand, an account of God's presence to and in all created things detached from consideration of God's immensity will be incapable of adequate articulation of the sheer liberty and originality of God's omnipresence.[19] On the other hand, an account of God's immensity developed in relative abstraction from consideration of God's creative, saving and perfecting presence will be incapable of adequate articulation of the direction of God's self-movement as *immensus*.[20] Good order will only prevail when the doctrine of the Trinity is allowed to play a determinative role in a theology of the divine attributes.[21] This is not to 'use' the doctrine of the Trinity as a device to achieve a certain result; it is, rather, simply to follow the direction indicated by the church's confession of the coeternity and coequality of Father, Son and Spirit, and to affirm the singular and richly differentiated life and activity of God in which there is enacted the oneness of freedom and fellowship in God's life before, over and with his creatures.

III

The God who is in himself limitlessly majestic is present without restriction in and to his creation. The necessity of this presence is only that of his self-determination to be who he is. But if in this matter theology submits to the instruction of the gospel, it must also say that God's limitless self-determination really includes his determination to be present to the creation, and that this determination is not accidental to his holy being but of its essence. In – not despite – his immensity, God is everywhere present to the whole creation, and is present to order, sustain and perfect it and to direct human creatures to fellowship with himself. To the *immensitas dei* there corresponds in the closest possible way his *omnipraesentia*. This is so because God's immensity is a perfection of his triune life: the full, unhindered majesty of God as Father, Son and Spirit includes his glorious self-presentation as the creator and reconciler who gives to all things their end and brings all things to their fulfilment. His immensity, because it is *his* immensity, is not bare absence of relation, not simply an unchecked will in a void. God is immense as the Father who speaks the limitlessly effective word of creative love, as the Son who is the redeemer and head of the entire creation and as the Spirit who is over all as Lord and giver of life.* In this triune act of self-presentation and relation, God's immensity makes itself operative and known as his omnipresence in the creation.

By way of rough orientation: God's omnipresence is his entire and constant presence in and to all things, the ceaseless and sovereign lordship in which the Most High, who is without measure or limit, inclines to be present to his creation and so holds and renews

---

*The triune life, in and of itself, involves self-communication and, therefore, triune immensity does not involve absence of relation or presence of a bare divine will.

it in life. But how is the omnipresence of the God confessed in Christian faith to be characterized more closely? Once again: the question 'How is the triune God present?' is not the same question as 'How is a god present?' God's triune presence is thus to be characterized, not by thinking of God as 'exemplifying necessarily a maximally perfect set of compossible great-making properties',[22] but rather descriptively, attending to God's particular greatness which is present in the events of his self-naming, to which the prophetic and apostolic witness bears testimony.

In Scripture, God's presence is characteristically to be understood in relation to his exaltation. God is 'God Most High, maker of heaven and earth' (Gen. 14.19, 22; cf. Mt. 11.25), and therefore the one who as transcendent creator possesses and rules the entirety of that which he has brought into being, for he is one to whom 'heaven and the heaven of heavens, the earth and all that is in it' belong (Deut. 10.14; cf. Exod. 19.5). Exalted in this way, he is 'uncontainable' – most particularly in relation to the temple, which cannot in any way 'house' God. 'Will God indeed dwell on the earth? Behold, heaven and the highest heaven cannot contain thee; how much less this house which I have built!' (1 Kgs 8.27; cf. 2 Chron. 2.6, 6.18; the theme is picked up again in Acts 7.4450). In the prophetic tradition, this thought acquires greater polemical force as a protest against locative religion in which God and place can be identified, and sacred space used to guarantee (and so effectively tame or resist) the divine presence. 'Do not trust in these deceptive words: "This is the temple of the Lord, the temple of the Lord, the temple of the Lord"' (Jer. 7.4; cf. 7.14; Isa. 66.1). Yet the correction to this idolatrous conception of local divine presence is to emphasize, not God's remoteness, but rather the entirely gratuitous character of his universal presence as the Most High. There thus takes place, as de Margerie puts it, a simultaneous process of '*délocalisation*' and '*omnilocalisation*' in order to state that '*sans cesser d'être transcendent, Il est proche*'.[23] Precisely as the one who is uncontainable in a particular locale, God is present without restriction; his transcendence as maker and possessor of all space is the unhindered capacity with which he is in all places. His presence is omnipotent and unrestricted, and no creature can block or escape the judgement which it brings. 'Am I a God at hand, says the Lord, and not a God afar off? Can a man hide himself in secret places so that I cannot see him? Do I not fill heaven and earth? says the Lord' (Jer. 23.23f.; cf. 16.16f.; Prov. 15.11; Amos 9.2–4; Obad. 4; Acts 17.27f.; Heb. 4.13). Above all in Psalm 139.7–12, ubiquity concerns God's majestically unconstrained and therefore inescapable presence as the truth which discloses: 'Whither shall I go from thy Spirit? Or whither shall I flee from thy presence?' (Ps. 139.7).

In conceptual terms: God's omnipresence is a free mode of relation. It is free, willed presence, *ubivolpraesentia*, a term used in Lutheran eucharistic theology as a contrast to *omnipraesentia generalis*, but which may fittingly serve to indicate that God's omnipresence is *his* presence, self-moved and wholly original. As *ubivolpraesentia*, omnipresence is not a retraction, setting aside or suspension of divine immensity. It is a movement of the one who is replete in himself. But this does not, however, imply that God's omnipresence is arbitrary, punctiliar or unstable, or that there are occasions or places from which it might be withdrawn. Occasional presence is not omnipresence, for omnipresence is without exception, universal, all places being comprehended in the *ubi* to which God wills to be present. The will of God is simple, and therefore undeviating and dependable. Omnipresence has the unshakeable reality of the divine promise: its certainty and constancy is that of the unqualified divine declaration: 'I am with you always'. But the reliability of a promise is not that of a material or natural condition, and cannot be converted into a state of affairs graspable apart from the will of the giver without falling into idolatry: 'They did not trust that [God] was near them unless they could discern with their eyes a physical symbol of his countenance', Calvin comments on the children of Israel in the wilderness.[24] In its character as *ubivolpraesentia*, therefore, omnipresence repeats the general nature of God's relation to the creation, namely that it is a relation rooted in God's aseity, springing from but in no way completing the limitless sufficiency of God's self-relation as Father, Son and Spirit.[25]

The affirmation of God's omnipresence as willed presence is wholly incompatible with any sort of account of continuity of being between God and the world, whether in Stoicism or in process philosophy.* Where the world is, there is also God? Only in the sense that where the world is, there also God wills to be and act. Otherwise, the fundamental distinction between God and creation is eroded, and no mutuality or fellowship between them is possible, for they are the same substance in the same space. In the relation between God and the world of which omnipresence is part, it is always a matter of the 'sheer inequality' in which God wholly precedes and transcends the creaturely element.[26] Only in precedence and transcendence (but really in them) is God present to all things as Lord. Otherwise, theology simply ends up in the flat contradiction of divine freedom in which 'God is omnipresent of necessity'.[27]

Omnipresence is free *relation*, *ubivolpraesentia*. The direction taken by the freedom of the triune God includes a direction towards relation to the creation in its totality and in each particular. This relation is personal relation. It is not simply a state or condition, which could readily be converted into a natural property of the creation without reference to God. God's omnipresence is not simply the presence of an infinite supersensible reality without physical limitations, but the presence of the Lord God. It is purposive; and it is known not as simple cosmological fact, but in the course of the drama of God's dealings with his creation as its maker and as the agent of its reconciliation and perfection. God's presence is 'the power of his creative

---

*He suggests here that aloofness and self-constitution are two sides of the same metaphysical coin; both Stoicism and process theology treat divine and human presence as qualitatively similar and, therefore, as competitively involved in a zero-sum game. Over against both the aloof God or the God who suffers as we do, Webster argues that God is singularly distinctly, qualitatively transcendent and as such capable of relation in an asymmetrical or unencumbered and truly free mode.

nearness':[28] it is 'that which is absolutely productive and in no sense produced, ceaselessly effective and not effected, utterly self-presenting and never simply there, the absolute event of nearness and never simply a reality which is to hand.'[29] Or in Aquinas' terms, God's omnipresence is the omnipresence of his agency: *Deus est in omnibus rebus, non quidem sicut pars essentiae, vel sicut accidens, sed sicut agens adest ei, in quod agit.*[30] And as the presence of this limitlessly free agent, God's omnipresence is repletive, a presence without bodily or spatial hindrance, filling and acting on all things which have their being in him: God *replet omnia loca, quod dat esse omnibus locatis, quae replent omnia loca.*[31]

Some negations follow: God's presence is not definite, local or circumscriptive, for he is not present in the world after the manner of a finite physical body encompassed by space. The heavy emphasis upon these negative characterizations in the Western theological tradition owes a good deal to Augustine (most of all in Letter 148 and Letter 187, the so-called *de praesentia dei liber*).[32] God is 'a spiritual substance not susceptible of division according to local distance or dimension, or even confined within the limits of bodily members',[33] and so 'is not diffused through space or confined within limits, having one part in one place, another in another, a smaller in less space, a greater in a larger'.[34] This is because the spatial relations of created bodies are definitive, whereas God is defined by no such relations. 'Take away the spatial relations of bodies, they will be nowhere, and because they are nowhere they will not be at all. Take away bodies from the qualities of bodies, there will be no place for them to be, and, as a necessary consequence, they will not exist.'[35] Yet it would be rash to conclude that Augustine is simply repeating neo-Platonic commonplaces. The negations are corollaries of affirmations; Augustine does not stop short at emphasizing the disembodied, non-spatial and non-dimensive character of God's presence, and such denials serve to draw attention to two positive avowals. First, God is simple and therefore, in Augustine's refrain throughout both letters, God is *in se ubique*, or *ubique incorporaliter tota*. Second, this simple, self-moving and wholly present God is present not just as an invisible spiritual substance but *creatively*, sustaining and ruling the world: God is not a *qualitas mundi* but the *substantia creatrix mundi sine labore regens et sine onere continens mundum.*[36] In sum: the triune God is present in all places, in free majesty, undividedly, neither localized nor extended but spiritually, graciously and creatively present to undergird and glorify all things.

God's omnipresence is a confession of faith. Knowledge of it does not derive from inspection of the nature of created reality but from God's self-presentation as the one who is Lord. No less than knowledge of God's mercy, faithfulness or patience, knowledge of his immensity and ubiquity is a matter of a divinely given perception. Yet to emphasize the confessional character of our knowledge of omnipresence is not to restrict the scope of this piece of Christian teaching simply to the soteriological, at cost to its cosmological implications. That kind of restriction has been common enough in modern Christian dogmatics, especially those of an anthropological cast, in which omnipresence quickly becomes a coordinate or perhaps a contrastive background to experiences of being sought and found by God. Thus Macquarrie suggests that the term immensity indicates 'the deeply felt contrast between man's limited, fragile existence and what has in the revelatory moment touched his life – overwhelming Being'.[37] Or Aulén: a Christian theology of omnipresence affirms that 'there is no place closed to the sovereign power of divine love. God can reach us wherever we are, and it is useless for a man to attempt to flee from his power.'[38] In and of themselves, such statements are relatively unexceptionable. But they risk defining omnipresence simply in terms of saving proximity, with the result that, first, the background of ubiquity in God's *in se* immensity is accorded little significance, and, second, its implications for the spatial character of the created order are left unexplored. Some remarks on this last question may be in order.

In brief: for Christian dogmatics, God's relation to the creation as the immense and omnipresent creator and redeemer is fundamental for the determination of the nature of space. Space is not to be considered as a 'fact of nature' whose meaning is self-evident without reference to the divine presence and claim upon creatures. Nor is space simply a field of spatial politics or poetics, ungrounded spatial practices not rooted in the deep structure of being. Space is an objective, given form of created existence and relation, one of the media through which the human creature has its existence in relation to the natural order, to other creatures and to God. Above all, space is defined by God's limitless presence, by the simple confession that God is *in se ubique*. Because creatures have their existence in this form, then space is not a mere *brutum factum*, nor a commodity, nor raw material for manipulation. It is a law of creation in which we are to discern the structure of created being and in which, therefore, we encounter a summons to act fittingly, as the spatial creatures we *are*.

In more detail: the doctrine of *creatio ex nihilo* is to be the 'head and pattern' of theological thinking about space, above all because that doctrine articulates the utter gratuity and contingency of created being: 'It is the doctrine of God so creating all things *ex nihilo* and sustaining them and fulfilling them by that selfsame Word, which is the theological principle guiding and controlling all theology's thoughts about the nature of space and time.'[39] Space is therefore not absolute or unoriginate, some sort of pre-existent medium; nor is it simply a register of acts and attitudes on the part of creatures who make space for themselves by disposing of themselves in the world. In both cases (roughly, that of Newtonian conceptions of space as the *sensorium dei*[40] and that of late modern poetics of space[41]) space has become detached from God's acts of creating and maintaining the creaturely realm and reconciling it to himself. In effect, space is secularized: the measure of space is not God's presence to and action upon creatures but either the immanent bodily relations of things or the project of world-construction. Christian theology resists this secularization by a cluster of trinitarian affirmations: by its doctrine of creation, according to which created reality is not self-originating but contingent on the unoriginate will and activity of God the

Father; by what it has to say of the relations borne to the creation by the Son or Word of God who orders all things as the one 'in whom all things hold together' (Col. 1.17) and who 'upholds all things by his word of power' (Heb. 1.3); and by the confession of the Holy Spirit as the perfecting cause of creation. From the work of the triune God are derived the origin, order and fulfilment of creaturely space. As creator, God is *immensus*, transcending any contingent spatial relations to that which he calls into being; as Lord of creation he is omnipresent, making space into a medium of relations between the creation and its God.

The centre of theological concern, we might say, is less the physics of space or the poetics of space than the 'economics' of space, its significance in God's ordered administration of created reality.[42] This order is, of course, to be conceived dynamically and historically: the economy of creation is not a set of immobile copresences but an unfolding dramatic process of interrelation. Space is brought into being and held in existence by the activity of the omnipresent creator who grants to what he has made its own space in distinction from himself. This spatial distance is precisely the condition for mutuality and togetherness. In thus differentiating the creation from himself, God does not leave the creature in isolation, but stands with and acts upon every creature as the omnipresent Lord from whom nothing is absolutely remote. To this active divine presence there corresponds the creature's active occupancy of the space bestowed by God. In actively occupying its given space, the creature exists with and alongside other creatures, in the mutually determinative relation of distance and proximity.

> Space is closely connected with interpersonal communion. Space acquires and maintains a surer reality when it has reference not only to myself but to other persons as well, of whom I can and must say: from me to such a one the distance is this. Space, like time, is interpersonal relation. It distinguishes and unites us, and indicates the perspective of a still greater nearness.[43]

This mutuality of spatial relation involves the creature's 'making room' for itself in relation to and distinction from other creatures. Space as the 'law' of existence is not simply a static location, some kind of pre-existent slot into which the particular creature is placed. It is, rather, a summons to the creature to fulfil its divine calling by actively entering into its particular nature, for 'God makes room for all creation. He allows everything in the freedom which it has as that which is created to express itself in making its place.'[44]

In this lies the potential for the sinful perversion of spatial relatedness. The relative independence which is the necessary condition for spatial relation can become spatial autonomy; mutual determination of creatures can become agonistics; the gift of space can become possessed territory. At this point, the cosmological and the soteriological converge. The good order of creaturely existence under God's omnipresence (*Allgegenwart*) is restored by God's saving presence (*Heilsgegenwart*) in the Word incarnate and in the Spirit. In Jesus Christ the Word of God takes upon himself the full reality of creatureliness, including its spatiality. The Word does so without abandonment or retraction of his immensity as the Word who upholds all things. But as this one, in free self-disposition, he takes flesh and occupies created space. In his passion he bears the full weight of the creature's hatred of the presence of other creatures and of God. He is 'taken away', 'cut off out of the land of the living'; his presence is destroyed, and his place becomes the no-place of the grave (Isa. 53.8f.). But that is not all: he is risen from the dead, and is seated at the right hand of the Father in the heavenly places, from where he rules all things as their head and fills all places with his presence (Eph. 1.20–23). He has set an end to the wicked project of spatial autonomy. In him all creaturely places are reordered, by being claimed with the full authority of the one who is Lord of heaven and earth, as the spaces in which we are to discover the presence of God. And being so claimed, they are also made into places of adjacency to other creatures. In sum: in Jesus Christ, now present to all places through the Spirit's power, space is made a medium of fellowship. And 'one cannot obtain such a presence of him without, at the same time, possessing life'.[45]

IV

All this is no more than an initial dogmatic sketch, clumsily executed. The most proper language with which to speak of God's omnipresence and ubiquity is that of praise, of which Traherne may offer a fitting example:

> His omnipresence is an ample territory or field of joys, a transparent temple of infinite lustre, a strong tower of defence, a castle of repose, a bulwark of security, a place of delights … a broad and vast extent of fame and glory, a theatre of infinite excellency … Our Bridegroom and our King being everywhere, our Lover and defender watchfully governing all worlds, no danger or enemy can arise to hurt us, but is immediately prevented and suppressed, in all spaces beyond the utmost borders of those unknown habitations which He possesseth. Delights of inestimable value are there preparing, for everything is present by its own existence. The essence of God being therefore all light and knowledge, love and goodness, care and providence, felicity and glory, a pure and simple Act, it is present in its operations, and by those Acts which it eternally exerteth is wholly busied in all parts and places of His dominion, perfecting and completing our bliss and happiness.[46]

Notes

1   E.g., J. Hoffman and G. S. Rosenkrantz, *The Divine Attributes* (Oxford: Blackwell, 2002); K. Rogers, *Perfect Being Theology* (Edinburgh: Edinburgh University Press,

2000); R. Swinburne, *The Coherence of Theism* (Oxford: Oxford University Press, 1993); E. Wierenga, *The Nature of God: An Inquiry into the Divine Attributes* (Ithaca: Cornell University Press, 1989).

2 E.g., S. MacDonald, 'The Divine Nature', in E. Stump and N. Kretzmann (eds), *The Cambridge Companion to Augustine* (Cambridge: Cambridge University Press, 2001), pp. 71–90; E. Wierenga, 'Anselm on Omnipresence', *New Scholasticism* 52 (1998), pp. 30–41; B. Davies, *The Thought of Thomas Aquinas* (Oxford: Oxford University Press, 1992), pp. 98–117.

3 Anselm, *Proslogion* 16, in J. Hopkins and H. Richardson (eds), *Anselm of Canterbury* (London: SCM, 1974), p. 104.

4 See here C. Schwöbel, *God, Action and Revelation* (Kampen: Kok Pharos, 1992), pp. 46–62.

5 S. Clarke, *A Demonstration of the Being and Attributes of God*, ed. E. Vailati (Cambridge: Cambridge University Press, 1998), p. 7.

6 Anselm, *Proslogion* 1, in Hopkins and Richardson (eds), *Anselm of Canterbury*, p. 91.

7 Clarke, *A Demonstration of the Being and Attributes of God*, p. 7.

8 Clarke, *A Demonstration of the Being and Attributes of God*, pp. 32–34.

9 K. Barth, *Die kirchliche Dogmatik* II/1 (Zurich: TVZ, 1946), p. 362; *Church Dogmatics* II/1 (Edinburgh: T&T Clark, 1957), p. 322.

10 M. Chemnitz, *Loci theologici*, vol. 1 (St Louis: Concordia, 1989), p. 55.

11 W. Pannenberg, *Systematic Theology*, vol. 1 (Edinburgh: T&T Clark, 1991), p. 412.

12 C. Hodge, *Systematic Theology*, vol. 1 (New York: Scribner, 1877), p. 383.

13 H. Bavinck, *The Doctrine of God* (Edinburgh: Banner of Truth Trust, 1977), p. 154.

14 See the important recent articulation of the tasks of this doctrine in P. Molnar, *Divine Freedom and the Doctrine of the Immanent Trinity* (London: T&T Clark, 2002).

15 MacKenzie, *The Dynamism of Space: A Theological Study into the Nature of Space* (Norwich: Canterbury Press, 1995), p. 78.

16 MacKenzie, *The Dynamism of Space*, p. 81.

17 Tertullian, *Adv. Prax.* 5.

18 T. F. Torrance, *Space, Time and Incarnation* (Oxford: Oxford University Press, 1969), p. 23.

19 From this point of view, the account offered by H. Berkhof, *Christian Faith* (Grand Rapids: Eerdmans, 1986) is unsatisfactory. Berkhof takes 'God's condescendence' as his starting point (p. 121), and so reinterprets those attributes which appear to suggest God's supernatural exaltation, seeking to relate them more effectively to revelational encounter with God. Accordingly, the conception of divine omnipresence 'rests on the belief that God, who often seems far away, has the unlimited ability to be present with his judgement and grace, his help and guidance, even when man does not in the least expect it. One who begins to see that dares to believe that such a God will never and nowhere lose sight of his creation, and may *therefore* be said to be present everywhere' (p. 122, my italics). 'Therefore' gives it away: omnipresence is experientially deduced, and the result is that, precisely because it lacks roots in God's *immensitas in se*, the 'unlimited ability' of God is not allowed any depth of its own, but is of only ancillary significance,

as the 'whence' of a human 'belief'. In effect, the divine *perfections* become little more than divine *benefits*. Inattention to *immensitas dei* is often motivated by an (entirely justifiable) resistance to the incursion of metaphysics into the doctrine of God; the resistance emerges as a desire to give priority to (salvific or existential) 'presence' over ubiquity (see, for example, O. Weber, *Foundations of Dogmatics*, vol. 1 (Grand Rapids: Eerdmans, 1981), pp. 449f.). At other times it is motivated by a concentration on biblical-historical-economic concerns without due consideration of God *in se* (for a good example, see Y. Congar, *Le Mystère du temple ou l'Economie de la présence de Dieu à sa créature de la Genèse à l'Apocalypse* (Paris: Editions du Cerf, 1958)). More effective integration of aseity and economic presence can be found in, for example, H. Thielicke, *The Evangelical Faith*, vol. 2 (Edinburgh: T&T Clark, 1978), pp. 122f., or C. Schwöbel, *God, Action and Revelation*, pp. 57–61.

20   Immensity is thus not simply (to use Kathryn Rogers' term) 'aspatiality' (*Perfect Being Theology*, p. 59): the term lacks a proper sense that God's immensity is the energy of his personal movement in the economy. Much the same can be said of Schleiermacher's scruples about talk of the presence of God as 'repletive', which he believes takes us too close to 'the analogy with expansive forms' (F. D. E. Schleiermacher, *The Christian Faith* (Edinburgh: T&T Clark, 1928), p. 209), and his resistance even to the notion of immensity which he again reads as a material idea of 'infinity regarded as substance' (p. 210). On the basis of these scruples, Schleiermacher prefers the stripped-down notions that 'God is in Himself' (p. 209), or 'the absolutely spaceless causality of God' (p. 206). Although Schleiermacher concedes that 'the effects of [God's] causal being-in-Himself are everywhere' (p. 209), his account as a whole is vitiated by a division of immanent and economic, and therefore of immensity and presence.

21   On this, see C. Gunton, *Act and Being: Towards a Theology of the Divine Attributes* (London: SCM, 2002).

22   T. V. Morris, 'Jesus and the Attributes of Deity', in *The Logic of God Incarnate* (Ithaca: Cornell University Press, 1986), p. 76.

23   B. de Margerie, *Les perfections du Dieu de Jésus-Christ* (Paris: Editions du Cerf, 1981), pp. 196f.

24   J. Calvin, *Institutes of the Christian Religion* I.xi.8 (London: SCM, 1960), p. 108.

25   This point is sometimes stated by a dialectical pairing of concepts (such as remoteness/proximity or presence/absence). These expressions are a little unhappy, in that they may suggest that immensity and omnipresence are in some way in tension with one another. The language of *ubivolpraesentia* offers a way of talking of omnipresence as the self-movement of the limitless God which is both more concrete and more effective in integrating transcendence and presence.

26   Barth, *Church Dogmatics* II/1, p. 312.

27   H. Martensen, *Christian Dogmatics* (Edinburgh: T&T Clark, 1898), p. 94.

28   I. U. Dalferth, *Gott. Philosophisch-theologische Denkversuche* (Tübingen: Mohr, 1992), p. 9.

29   Dalferth, *Gott*, p. 8.

30   Aquinas, *Summa Theologiae* I.8.i.

31 Aquinas, *Summa Theologiae* I.8.ii.

32 The best account remains S. J. Grabowski, *The All-Present God: A Study in St Augustine* (St Louis: Herder, 1954).

33 Augustine, *Ep. cxlviii*, I.ii (Corpus scriptorum ecclesiasticorum latinorum 44, p. 333).

34 Augustine, *Ep. cxlviii*, I.iii (p. 333); see also *Ep. clxxxvii*, XI (Corpus scriptorum ecclesiasticorum latinorum 57, p. 90) and XIV (p. 92): God 'is not distributed through space by size so that half of him should be in half of the world and half of him in the other half of it'.

35 Augustine, *Ep. clxxxvii*, XVIII (p. 96).

36 Augustine, *Ep. clxxxvii*, XVIII (p. 96).

37 J. Macquarrie, *Principles of Christian Theology* (London: SCM, 1966), p. 188.

38 G. Aulén, *The Faith of the Christian Church* (London: SCM, 1961), pp. 150f.

39 MacKenzie, *The Dynamism of Space*, p. 21.

40 The classic account is A. Koyré, *From the Closed World to the Infinite Universe* (Baltimore: Johns Hopkins University Press, 1996). For the longer perspective, see E. Grant, *Much Ado about Nothing: Theories of Space and Vacuum from the Middle Ages to the Scientific Revolution* (Cambridge: Cambridge University Press, 1981); and A. A. Davenport, *Measure of a Different Greatness: The Intensive Infinite, 1250–1650* (Leiden: Brill, 1999).

41 See G. Bachelard, *The Poetics of Space* (Boston: Beacon Press, 1969); H. Lefebvre, *The Production of Space* (Oxford: Blackwell, 1991); D. Harvey, *The Condition of Postmodernity* (Oxford: Blackwell, 1990).

42 Cf. MacKenzie, *The Dynamism of Space*, p. 136: 'Through his Word [God] orders all things. He administers οἰκονομία, the ordering of the household of creation … He is Place, for he is the bestower of place for every constituent part of what he has brought into being, and on his Place all things depend.'

43 D. Staniloae, *The Experience of God: Orthodox Dogmatic Theology*, vol. 1 (Brookline: Holy Cross Orthodox Press, 1994), p. 173.

44 MacKenzie, *The Dynamism of Space*, p. 138.

45 Calvin, *Institutes* II.x.8 (p. 435).

46 T. Traherne, 'The Fifth Century', 9f. in *Centuries* (London: Faith Press, 1960), pp. 227f.

4

The place of Christology in systematic theology

EDITOR'S INTRODUCTION

John Webster addressed the subject of Christology on several occasions. In these essays he repeatedly turned to consider how the doctrine of Christ fit within the wider architecture of Christian theology. In fact, he regularly used that language of architecture to get at the systematic character of doctrine, that it exhibits not merely interrelations but also order and prioritization. He had an eye for not merely the errant but especially the disproportionate (that which is inflated or unhealthily reduced). His concern for matters of scope and sequence explain why this essay traffics in more conceptual, less overtly exegetical arguments regarding the architectural schematics of Christian doctrine. He is inquiring less about the décor of a given room than a plotting of the home's floorplan.

This essay – originally published under the simple title 'The Place of Christology in Systematic Theology' – examines the nature of systematic theology (its 'object, sources, ends, settings and practitioners') before turning to consider how Christology relates to its two great themes: God and the works of God (otherwise put, 'all things relative to God'). Webster examined the way in which Christology demanded development in terms of the inner life of God as well as the economy of God's works relative to his creatures. As he came to put it, 'Christology considers both the eternal Word, intrinsic to God's inner being, and the Word's temporal mission in creation, providence and supremely in the person and work of Jesus Christ. Because of this, Christology is a distributed doctrine, not restricted to one or other domain.'

Webster sketches his own mapping of the terrain, moving from theology to economy and seeking to maintain their distinction, connection and sequence/order. He notes, however, that modern Protestant divinity has not tended towards his approach, and he seeks to patiently examine six principles that have marked major trajectories in modern theology. To give more specific exposition, he looks at the place of Christology in the work of Isaak Dorner, Albrecht Ritschl and Karl Barth. They represent a trajectory that could be extended more widely towards Christocentric theological method (in diverse manifestations). 'Some modern systematic theologies have found it difficult to maintain this relation between the two domains, and the corollary placement of Christology.' While Webster would have sounded a similar note in his earlier works (including essays in *Word and Church*), he soon developed a sense that modern Christocentrism has not helpfully attuned readers to catch the full span of biblical teaching nor even, ironically enough, to appreciate the spectrum of specifically Christological material.

His as-yet-unpublished Kantzer Lectures from fall 2007 provide a mapping of this broader approach to Christological thinking. They began with the doctrine of God in and of himself before turning to consider the missions of God and the electing turn of God towards creatures in the covenant of redemption. Having prefaced the economy with theology, they do not even then jump to speak of incarnation before they consider the way in which God makes himself present to creatures in the works of nature and of providence. Finally the metaphysical and moral turbulence of the coming of the Son of God can be registered when, after these reference points are in place, he turns to consider the teaching of John 1.14. While Webster insists that Christology cannot be the 'starting point or centre of Christian teaching', he nonetheless affirms it as 'one indispensable element of a complex whole'.

While Webster had spoken elsewhere of two distributed doctrines (trinity and creation), he here speaks of Christology also as a distributed doctrine. That terminology is pushed to its breaking point when one considers those three items. Trinity and Christology can appear across the topical span, inasmuch as they both pertain to matters in God's own life, first, and then to the works of God, secondly. Creation does not apply to the inner life of God in the same way, even if we appreciated God's creative will prior to his external work of making. In employing the terminology of distribution, Webster is not speaking technically but drawing out the intellectual reality that certain doctrines demand attention at various points (and some more than others). In so doing he is giving some concrete specificity to his earlier calls for theology to be systematic in a low-level way that helps keep one close not only to the material but also to the rhetoric of Scripture; in this case, viewing Christology in terms of God's own life and then of God's works helps keep one abreast of various ways in which diverse canonical texts speak of this Son (i.e. the Word, the Bridegroom, Lady Wisdom, the Christ).

Might it be accurate to say that here Webster is beckoning towards a 'theological Christology'? Such a project would involve talking of God first and fundamentally in speaking of incarnation, rather than presuming to work in a historical idiom predominantly. Earthly history comes, of course, but it can only be appreciated in light of eternity and heaven. A systematic Christology will seek to attend to that history as a work of grace, that is, a free divine act that follows upon the prior kindness of God's work of nature in creation and even upon God's antecedent life in himself.

'Well-conducted, it will draw upon resources (intellectual and moral-spiritual) to check the malign bent to total knowledge – most of all, awareness of the ineffability of its object and of the fact that the renovation of human knowledge of God remains unfinished.' Perhaps nowhere is this epistemological temptation more challenging than in Christology, where premature closure can allure and historical availability can entice. Even here – perhaps especially here – Webster longed for the presence of the incarnate God to be understood as the presence of the perfect, triune God and, thus, as a mysterious glory in our midst.

Suggested readings

'Alyssa Lyra Pitstick, *Light in Darkness: Hans Urs von Balthasar and the Catholic Doctrine of Christ's Descent into Hell*', *Scottish Journal of Theology* 62 (2009), 202–10.

'Eternal Generation', in GWM 1, 29–41.

'Jesus in Modernity: Reflections on Jüngel's Christology', *Calvin Theological Journal* 32, no. 1 (1997): 43–71; repr. in *WC*, 151–90.

'One Who Is Son: Theological Reflections on the Exordium to the Epistle to the Hebrews', in *The Epistle to the Hebrews and Christian Theology* (ed. Richard J. Bauckham et al.; Grand Rapids, MI: Eerdmans, 2009), pp. 69–94; repr. in GWM 1, 59–80.

Katherine Sonderegger, 'Christ', in *A Companion to John Webster's Theology* (ed. Michael Allen and R. David Nelson; Grand Rapids, MI: Eerdmans, forthcoming).

Kenneth Oakes, 'Theology, Economy and Christology in John Webster's *God Without Measure* and Some Earlier Works', *International Journal of Systematic Theology* 19, no. 4 (2018): 491–504.

THE PLACE OF CHRISTOLOGY IN SYSTEMATIC THEOLOGY

I

To say that each element of Christian teaching bears some relation to Christology is to state an analytical judgement, to reiterate the inherent and permanent referent of the term 'Christian'. Further reflection, however, prompts two questions: What kind of relation? and What kind of Christology?

What kind of relation obtains between Christological teaching and other doctrinal topics? It may be considered a relation of derivation, such that Christology is the source – cognitive and ontological – from which are drawn all other Christian teachings, whose Christian identity and authenticity are to be ascertained by demonstrable origination from and determination by Christological doctrine.* 'Within theological thinking generally unconditional priority must be given to thinking which is attentive to the existence of the living person of Jesus Christ . . . so that *per definitionem* Christological thinking forms the unconditional basis for all other theological thinking . . . The only decisions which have any place are those which follow after, which are consistent with thinking which follows him, which arise in the course of Christological thinking and the related investigations, definitions and conclusions' – so Barth.[1]

Another, less straightforwardly deductive conception of the relation between Christology and other doctrines – one which on occasions Barth also maintained – considers Christology, not as in and of itself the basis, centre or starting-point of everything else, but rather as a principal part of Christian teaching having wide dispersal across the doctrinal corpus by virtue of the fact that it is an integral element of the doctrine of the Trinity. The formative status and specifying function of Christology in relation to other topics of Christian teaching, that is, arise from the governance of the entire body of Christian divinity by teaching about the triune God. On this account of the matter, it is not Christology *per se* but a doctrine of God's triune being and his inner and outer works (including the godhead of the Son and his works in time) which occupies the pre-eminent and commanding place in Christian teaching.

---

*Webster first addressed what he called the 'principle of derivation' in the second of his six Kantzer Lectures on divine perfection and presence (that version of which remains still unpublished). He frequently spoke of theology being about everything though not everything about that everything, which one might understand as speaking of global interest paired with a resolutely distinct focus or looking at all things always in one particular way (as related to God).

Further: what kind of Christology? A complete Christology comprises two integral parts: teaching about the eternal Son or Word, his deity and the relations which he bears to the Father and the Spirit; and teaching about the Son's temporal mission, especially in the assumption of flesh to redeem lost rational creatures. Where Christology is located in a comprehensive treatment of Christian doctrine, its size, and the relations which it bears to other doctrines, will be determined in part by decisions about the content of each of the two parts, their relative proportions and the priority of one part over the other, as well as by expectations or demands placed on each part.

Any systematic presentation of Christian doctrine adopts a stance on the function and scope of Christology, implicitly or explicitly. The stance is visible both in the way in which the subject matter of Christian doctrine as a whole is conceived, and in the expository arrangement of its various components. In much modern (and notably, but not exclusively, Protestant) systematic theology these matters have acquired a special prominence, because discrete teaching about the person and work of Christ has often annexed the fundamental role which earlier theologies more naturally recognized in teaching about the Trinity, and so has come to serve as the hallmark of the genuineness, purity and distinctiveness of Christian doctrine.

To anatomize the matter, we look first at the nature and subject matter of systematic theology, and then consider the place of Christology in relation to God's inner life ('theology') and God's work towards creatures ('economy').

II

Though the term 'systematic theology' is sometimes used to designate any constructive (rather than simply exegetical or historical) treatment of Christian doctrine, it is best reserved for accounts of Christian teaching which aim at comprehensiveness and coherence, setting forth the content of Christian belief in its entirety with attention to the congruity of its parts.* Theological systematization attracts a range of criticisms: dominance by a governing principle abstracted from the range of Christian teaching; reduction of the internal variety of Christian beliefs; over-reliance on deduction in the construction of doctrine; aspirations to finality which accord ill with the incompleteness and liability to revision of temporal knowledge of God. However, systematicity in theology properly derives not from pretentions to perfect understanding but from contemplation of the scope and internal relations of its object. A theological system is not so much a projection as an acknowledgement and reiteration of the order which obtains between the various elements of Christian belief. Well-conducted, it will draw upon resources (intellectual and moral-spiritual)

---

*For discussion of these two approaches to systematic theology, see especially A. N. Williams, *The Architecture of Theology* (Oxford: Oxford University Press, 2011).

to check the malign bent to total knowledge – most of all, awareness of the ineffability of its object and of the fact that the renovation of human knowledge of God remains unfinished.*

The character of a systematic theology is a function of a number of factors. (1) A determination of the object or matter (*res*) of Christian teaching, both as a whole and in its various divisions. This will include judgements about which are the principal parts of Christian teaching, about which parts are derivative and how they may be derived, and about which parts may most properly be expected to set the distinctive nature of the system. (2) A judgement about the cognitive principles or sources of Christian teaching and their relative values, and about the ways in which systematic theology gives expression to the matter which these sources communicate. Such sources may be internal (such as Scripture or dogma), or external and ancillary (such as philosophy, history or aspects of human culture held to be normative). (3) A conception of the end or purpose of systematic theology. This will include answers to such questions as: Is systematic theology a 'positive' science with a given, antecedently established matter of which it is an exposition, or is it critical, reconstructive enquiry? How should contemplative, speculative, didactic, apostolic and apologetic purposes be ranked in the construction of a system of Christian doctrine? (4) A set of judgements about the ecclesial and extra-ecclesial settings of systematic theology, including judgements of circumstance, that is, determinations about which parts of Christian teaching should receive especial attention in a given set of conditions. (5) A conception of the virtues required of the systematic theologian. Such virtues may be intellectual (exegetical, historical and conceptual) skills and (if theology is considered to be itself an exercise of religion) moral-spiritual powers.

Decisions about the object, sources, ends, settings and practitioners of systematic theology exercise a formative influence on the rhetoric of a system of Christian doctrine, in particular upon the ways in which its genre and voice may echo the primary modes of expression of Christian faith while at the same time striving for conceptual regularity and argumentative clarity. Further, the overall character of a systematic theology will be inscribed in its organization. A system is composed of an orderly arrangement of parts according to a scheme. The design of a systematic theology requires attention to matters of overall sequence: Where are the different elements to be placed? Is the sequence or order of exposition to be a direct transcription of the material order or the order of knowing? Do the various elements simply relate to each other serially, or is there a more complex set of interrelations? Do certain topics require more ample consideration and others more cursory treatment?

---

*The two primary reasons for avoiding claims of totalizing knowledge are God's ineffability and human sinfulness; demographic limitations based on race, class, gender and so on are not unimportant, though they are not primary theological categories and are better treated subordinate to the terms of the divine economy.

These formal questions about location, proportion and relative influence are of considerable weight in deciding the proper place of Christology in a system of Christian doctrine. They are, however, consequent upon material determination of the object of Christian faith and theology, which is God and the creatures of God. What is the place – location, role and rank – of Christology in systematic theological exposition of that object?

III

Systematic theology has a single but not simple object: God and all things relative to God. '[A]ll things are dealt with in holy teaching in terms of God, either because they are God himself or because they are relative to him as their origin and end'.[2] This one complex matter may therefore be divided into (1) God absolutely considered, that is, considered in himself in his inner life as Father, Son and Spirit (theology), and (2) God relatively considered, that is, considered in his outer works and in relation to his creatures (economy). Systematic theology is enquiry into God and into created realities under the formality of God.

There is a material order in this one complex object according to which theology has preponderance over economy. This is because though it is entirely possible (indeed, necessary) to conceive of the triune God without creatures, it is not possible to conceive of creatures without God. God is from himself and in himself; he is self-subsistent and self-sufficient, and does not receive his being from any other, for he is the first principle and cause of all that is not himself. All other beings, however, are not from themselves; they receive being from him and are sustained by him as they enact the being which they have received. The material priority in systematic theology of God in himself is an acknowledgement of the unqualified priority of the creator over the creature; God is first in being, and so theology precedes economy.

Yet three qualifications must be made. First, to speak of the primacy of theology over economy is to make a distinction, not a separation. The pre-eminence of theology does not mean that economy is an accidental or inessential element of systematic theology. Quite the contrary: consideration of the economy is indispensable because there is not only God in himself but God who of his will and goodness reaches beyond his own being and gives life. A system of theology which failed to treat the economy would not correspond to its object's full range. The material primacy of theology does not eliminate or depreciate all else relative to God; it indicates that theology treats the uncaused cause of all other things, and economy treats those things which are caused.

Second, to say that primacy belongs to God's inner works, not to his economic acts, does not entail that the latter offer no instruction about God's inner being. The outer works of God are *his* works, not some remote operation which is not proper to him, and this continuity of acting subject means that God's economic acts elucidate his inner being, even though they do not exhaust it. God's triune life is not closed in upon itself; it is also communicative or externally relative, and so manifest in acts towards creatures.

Third, the material primacy of theology is not necessarily mirrored in the order of knowing or in the order of exposition adopted in a theological system.* The thought that God is the origin of all things – of created being, and of the world's redemption – may arise in our minds as we are moved to reflect on our contingency or on the sheer gratuity of the Christian life. In the order of knowing, we may begin from contemplation of God's outer works which prompt us to trace them to the worker of these works. In systematic theology, what matters is not that the cognitive order reduplicate the material order but that the cognitive order not be allowed to overwhelm the proper material order: first the worker, then the work. Similarly, the order of exposition is a matter of relative indifference. Provided that the material order remains undisturbed, expository arrangements may be invented or adapted according to the requirements of didactic circumstances.

The matter treated in Christology straddles the two subject-domains of systematic theology. Christology considers both the eternal Word, intrinsic to God's inner being, and the Word's temporal mission in creation, providence and supremely in the person and work of Jesus Christ. Because of this, Christology is a distributed doctrine, not restricted to one or other domain; and it is so because it treats one of the triune persons, each of whom is to be considered both immanently and relatively.

If it is properly to reflect the scope and distribution of Christology in a system of Christian teaching, treatment of any particular Christological topic must keep in mind this double matter. No treatment of the doctrine of the incarnation, for example, may so concentrate upon the historical density of the Word made flesh that it neglects the way in which that history refers back to its antecedent ground in the eternal inner-triune persons and relations.† The Word which became flesh is the Word which was 'in the beginning' (John 1.14, 1); the Son who was for a little while made lower than the angels and partook of flesh and blood does so as one eternally begotten of the Father, bearing the very stamp of God's nature (Heb. 2.9, 14; 1.5, 3). To understand the Word made flesh, theological intelligence must consider its *terminus a quo*; systematic Christology connects teaching about incarnation to the doctrine of the immanent Trinity. Equally, theological investigation of the eternal Word will be incomplete if it neglects the way in which this same Word, possessed of

---

*Webster himself does consistently match the order of exposition with the order of being, because he deems the contemporary climate to privilege the historical. His beginning with God's inner life served as a polemical and pedagogical reorientation of that drift towards a focus upon the immanent in contemporary dogmatics. He also consistently notes, as here, that other pedagogical orders could be faithful to the material order, and other times and circumstances may call for such variety of presentation.

†This criticism applies to 'early high Christology' in modern historical analysis as well as to more revisionary accounts.

the infinite beatitude and completeness of God's simple being, also has a *terminus ad quem* in his external, relative acts as maker, sustainer and reconciler of created life. Systematic Christology also considers the work of the Word in time.

The adequacy of a systematic Christology is partly a matter of how these two *termini* are defined and set in relation. In treating the *terminus a quo*, systematic theology is not proposing some abstract, speculative reality unconnected to the history of the incarnation. It is simply following the rule of Christian faith that the invisible God is infinitely more real than any visible thing, the one by virtue of whom any visible thing has being and effect. The visible reality of the Word in time emerges from his participation in the entire sufficiency and repose of God. In himself the Word lacks nothing, and in his relation to creatures he receives no augmentation, for he is antecedently perfect. To this perfect fulfilment of the processions within the godhead, in which the Son is eternally begotten of the Father and one from whom the Spirit eternally proceeds, there corresponds the Son's movement towards that which is not God. God's infinite beatitude includes infinite love extended outwards; it is an inner bliss which is causal, limitlessly generous, that by virtue of which created history comes to be.

Again, in treating Christology's *terminus ad quem*, the outward movement of the Word has to be understood as arising from his anterior completeness. It is not the accumulation of properties which extend the Word's identity. In the course of his movement from immanent origin to economic goal, the Word acquires nothing, remains immutable and simple, entirely resolved and composed. Whatever relations the Word bears to creatures are on his side non-real (that is, non-constitutive). Yet, once more, God's perfect goodness is confirmed in creative causality. God is the 'absolutely supreme good' in as much as he is 'the first source of every perfection things desire'.[3]

By way of initial summary: (1) Christology is a division of the doctrine of the Trinity; (2) as a division of the doctrine of the Trinity, Christology is concerned with both theology and economy, theology first, economy by derivation; (3) Christology is not restricted to one particular locus of a system of Christian teaching, but is widely spread; (4) Christology is not in and of itself the starting-point or centre of Christian teaching, but one indispensable element of a complex whole.

A brief exemplification of this arrangement may be found in Aquinas's incomplete *Compendium of Theology*, a summary exposition of Christian teaching structured as a treatment of faith, hope and love. 'The whole knowledge of faith involves. . . two things', Aquinas states at the beginning, 'namely the divinity of the Trinity and the humanity of Christ'.[4] Aquinas treats these two topics according to what he takes to be their proper material sequence: the doctrine of the Trinity, followed by the doctrine of the incarnation. In investigating the divinity, attention to three topics is necessary: 'first, the unity of essence; second, the Trinity of persons; and third, the effects of divinity'.[5] Once again, the succession of the topics is significant. Only after giving a substantial amount of space to the oneness and the triunity of God

(I.3–67) does Aquinas turn to consider the 'effects' or outer works of God in creation, providence and redemption. Moreover, the treatment of faith in the humanity of Christ and of the restoration of creatures through the incarnation does not begin until I.185, when Aquinas surveys the nature of sin, the nature of the incarnation, Christ's conception and birth, the paschal mystery and his exaltation and future work of judgement. The delay in introducing Christological material is, however, merely apparent, and does not indicate that Aquinas considers the incarnate Christ and his work of reparation a negligible matter: a treatment of faith which did not proceed beyond the divine essence and triunity to the effects of God would be Christianly unthinkable. But these effects, including the incarnation of the Word, are just that: *effects*, only intelligible when their cause is grasped. Christ's humanity and his enactment of his office as saviour cannot be understood *per se*, but only as it is 'related to his divinity as an instrument'.[6] The language of instrumentality, perhaps initially alarming, does not diminish the full reality of the Word's becoming flesh.[*] It simply indicates that this 'becoming' and all that follows from it is 'assumption', that assumption does not compromise the integrity of the two natures, and that the assumed nature is to be understood not from its historical phenomenality, but from the divine person and act of the one who assumes it. 'We . . . judge the disposition and quality of instruments by their purpose, though also by the dignity of the one using them. Therefore, it is appropriate to esteem the quality of the human nature assumed by the Word of God in accordance with these norms'.[7] Once this is in place, exposition of Christ's person and work follows naturally and completes the sequential treatment of the objects of faith.

We turn to further elaboration of the place of Christology in the two domains of theology and economy.

IV

The first domain of Christology is theology. After any formal or prolegomenal matters about the nature, tasks and cognitive principles of theology have been dealt with (not, of course, without reference to the substance of Christian teaching, including Christology), a system of Christian doctrine opens its material exposition with consideration of the Christian doctrine of God, and it is at this point that Christology receives its first extended treatment: in the course of the explanation of the doctrine of the Trinity, the eternal Son of God enters as an object of reflection.

---

*Webster here clarifies that language of the 'instrumental' character of the human nature of the incarnate Son does not diminish its historical or existential reality but locates those properties metaphysically relative to the divine person of the Son. Only a foolhardy attempt to treat divine and human predicates as parallel would view the term as somehow diminishing the humanity of the Son. Because divine and human being function in a quantitatively different way, the one may be instrumental to the other without either being diminished.

Three tracts of material are treated in this Christological domain. First, consideration is given to the Son's eternal deity: his consubstantiality with the Father and the Spirit as one who participates in the undivided divine essence, and the properties which are his according to that divine essence. Here systematic theology turns its contemplative gaze and analytical intelligence to the Son's self-subsistent perfection, his infinity, simplicity, immutability and impassibility as one beyond composition or disintegration, in other words, his entire beatitude. At the same time, systematic theology directs its attention to the Son's omnipotence and omniscience, and his unlimited goodness, wisdom and justice. This is followed in a second stretch of argument by consideration of the Son's place in the processions which are God's infinite aliveness, that is, the Son's relation to the Father and the Spirit by origin, order and operation. Here systematic theology gives an account of the eternal generation of the Son – the reality that he is 'begotten of the Father before all worlds, God from God, light from light, true God from true God, begotten not made', and so that the relation of the Son and the Father is wholly natural, consubstantial and non-sequential rather than external, causal or temporal. In similar fashion, attention is given to the Son as one from whom with the Father the Spirit proceeds. Treatment of these matters is then concluded, third, by an explanation of the personal property which is his as Son, namely 'filiation', the property of being one begotten by the Father before all worlds.*

If it is to occupy its given place in the system of Christian teaching, a presentation of this threefold material needs to keep two thoughts in mind at every point. First: the Son is complete without creatures – not because he does not will to create creatures out of love, but precisely because he creates out of fullness of love rather than out of some indigence by which he is afflicted. Second, therefore, the interior, wholly resolved life of the eternal Son is also fraught with movement beyond itself, willing to direct itself outwards, and in so doing neither completes itself nor is at variance with itself, because the divine Son is supremely good and therefore creative.

In systematic consideration of Christology in the domain of theology, therefore, an account of the missions or external acts of the Son of God will be preceded by an account of the divine procession which is their vital principle. The procession of the Son from the Father is an 'immanent' act, having no external basis or object, but as such it is the uncaused cause of the history of the incarnation. This is why such a systematic treatment risks distortion if it goes directly to the history of Jesus Christ. His identity as the divine-human agent of that history, as well as the nature, purpose, power and effect of his acts, cannot be understood in isolation from his eternal relation of origin. The ground of his history, presupposed in each of its episodes and manifest, declared or confessed in some, is: 'I have come'.[8] Formally

---

*These aspects are most fully worked out in his essay 'Eternal Generation' (GWM 1.29–42).

expressed: a divine mission includes within itself and refers to an eternal procession by which the identity of its agent is constituted. Thus the coming of the Son and his reception by creatures has its source and character in the fact that the Son is of one substance with the Father, by whom he is sent and from whom he comes into the world. This coming repeats in outward activity the relation of origin and the oneness of substance proper to Father and Son as eternal divine persons. The Son's entry into audible, visible, tangible presence is the manifestation of 'that which was from the beginning' (1 John 1.1).*

From this, a number of observations about the place of Christology in a system of theology may be drawn. (1) Christology is intrinsic to the doctrine of God, and receives its first treatment in the course of exposition of the doctrine of the Trinity. What is said subsequently about the Son of God relatively considered rests wholly upon what is first said about his eternal deity absolutely considered. One of the finest English divines from the mid- to late-seventeenth century, John Owen, phrases it thus: 'The person of Christ is the next [nearest] foundation of all acceptable religion and worship'; but 'the divine being itself is the first formal reason, foundation and object of all religion'.[9] Again: 'Were he not the *essential* image of the Father in his *own divine person*, he could not be the *representative* image unto us as incarnate'[10] – and this, because 'God himself is the first and only essential truth'.[11] (2) The first material on the Son's divine essence carries within itself reference to his economic activity. Commenting on Prov. 8.22f. ('The Lord created me at the beginning of his work . . .'), Owen writes: 'The eternal personal existence of the Son of God is supposed [presupposed] in these expressions. . . Without it, none of these things could be affirmed of him. But there is a regard in them, both unto his future incarnation, and the accomplishment of the counsels of God thereby'.[12] (3) A systematic theology will be adequate to its object if it constructs its exposition in a way that makes visible this mutual reference of absolute and relative, procession and mission, inner and outer work. This may be achieved by argumentative devices of anticipation and recapitulation, to ensure both that the full extent of Christology is kept in mind as completely and consistently as possible, and that the *loci* are not isolated from one another. (4) Christological knowledge is *knowledge by causes*: the visible reality of Jesus Christ becomes an object of understanding only when its underlying invisible principle is kept in mind as that by virtue of which it has phenomenal form. This is because in all its human density that visible form is an effect, that *from* which theological intelligence moves backwards to trace its foundation and source in God's being and will itself, and that *towards* which theological intelligence moves when it considers God's being and will. Christology is therefore only derivatively

---

*Webster draws the language of divine processions and missions not only from Thomas Aquinas but specifically from his reading of Gilles Emery, *The Trinitarian Theology of St. Thomas Aquinas* (Oxford: Oxford University Press, 2007).

(yet also necessarily) an historical science.* As we shall see shortly, one effect upon Christology of the decline of knowledge by causes or first principles and the prestige of immanent historical explanation has been atrophy of the first domain of Christology and expansion of the second domain, such that the proportions and location of Christological material have undergone extensive alteration.†

V

The second domain of Christology is economy. Arising from and extending the 'absolute' consideration of the Son of God which is its formative principle, there is a 'relative' consideration of his mission in time and its telos in the renewal of creaturely existence. This second tract of Christological material is no less indispensable than the first; in its absence, systematic Christology would be a fragment.

The necessity of theological study of the Son's acts in time properly does not arise from suspicion that theology remains abstract or merely noumenal until its historical force is registered. Nor is it properly any supposed restriction of human knowledge and experience to the phenomenal realm which necessitates attention to the economy, as if that realm were more immediately accessible and could be more readily turned to account. Rather, the second Christological domain is a matter for attention because theological intelligence traces the outer movement of God's communicative goodness – that is, God's determination that at the Father's behest the eternal Son should be the giver of life. 'He was in the beginning with God; all things were made through him' (John 1.2f.); 'as the Father has life in himself, so he has granted the Son also to have life in himself' (John 5.26); and so, 'the Son gives life to whom he will' (John 5.21).

Stated in a slightly different register, the hinge between the inner works of God and his economic activity is the divine will. To ground the economy in the divine will is to say that God's external works are not mere indifferent or accidental happenings, but purposive, the fruit of something akin to a decision (though without the deliberative, discursive sequence of a human decision). This divine purpose is eternal, antecedent, wholly spontaneous and unconditioned by any consequent, 'before the foundation of the world' (Eph. 1.5), arising solely from God and not a response to some reality

---

*Here is an epistemological or methodological corollary of the earlier 'principle of derivation'; in this case, historical study of Jesus follows theological study by way of derivation. Webster's concerns about overinflated or disordered approaches to historical Jesus study go all the way back to his intimate engagement with the corpus of Jüngel in the 1980s and early 1990s.

†This atrophy and malformed proportionality of the elements of Christology serves as another example of what 'Theological Theology' identifies as a failure of nerve to consider doctrinal material in its Christian areas of concern; in this case, study of Christology under the banner of historical study of Jesus alone allows external categories (drawn from the study of antique history) to dominate the discussion and unhelpfully limit its range.

alongside God (*creatio ex nihilo* is fundamental to the being and history of that which is blessed by the divine purpose). Further, the divine purpose is not the imposition of an alien will, but that by virtue of which creatures come to have life and to flourish. This is because God's will is inseparable from his goodness and wisdom, and so is the gift of life.

God's outer works may be divided into two spheres: that of his work of nature, and that of his work of grace. The first sphere comprises creation and providence, the second the redemption and perfection of creatures. The agent of these works is the undivided Trinity, whose external acts are indivisible, though particular works may be especially appropriated to particular persons. This last point is of some consequence in retaining the correct proportions of Christology in a treatment of the economy. To say that the Son is the agent of redemption is not to concentrate the entirety of God's outer work upon this one person. This is because the Son acts *ad extra* as one who shares in the one divine essence, and so is not a discrete agent. Moreover, attribution of some work to him is *eminent* but not *exclusive* attribution, for in each divine work in time the Father is its fount, the Son its medium and the Spirit its terminus.

With these preliminaries in mind, what material is treated in the second Christological domain? The Son's work is spread across the two spheres of nature and grace. He is the agent of creation ('in him all things were created', Col. 1.16) and of the providential maintenance and ordering of what has been made ('in him all things hold together', Col. 1.17). This being so, Christological material will have a considerable presence in a systematic account of the bringing into being and preservation of creatures; Christology is not exhausted by the history of redemption.

In the sphere of grace, Christology presents an analysis of the full scope of the Son's divine-human mission. This begins with an account of the act of incarnation (the conception of Christ; the Word's assumption of human nature and the union of the divine and human natures in Christ's person); his earthly ministry as the herald and agent of the Kingdom of God; his passion and death in their saving effect; his exaltation in his resurrection, ascension and heavenly session; his continued operation through the Spirit in calling, sanctifying and governing the church and in ruling the course of the world; his future coming as judge and deliverer. Once again, Christology is widely extended, because its matter comprehends the person of the mediator and soteriology in its objective and subjective aspects, as well as ecclesiology and the Christian life. This complex of material may be arranged in various ways: as a relatively straightforward narrative sequence, or through conceptual structures such as the names and titles of the incarnate one (Jesus, Messiah, Christ, Lord, servant, and so forth), his offices (prophet, priest and king) or his states (humiliation and exaltation). In practice, most systematic treatments offer some sort of combination of all or most of these various schemes.

In a well-ordered systematic theology, the extensive material on the second domain of Christian teaching will arise naturally from and make appropriate backward reference to the material on the first domain; economy is most fully seen when illuminated by theology, which it in turn illuminates. Some modern systematic theologies have found it difficult to maintain this relation between the two domains, and the corollary placement of Christology. The difficulty arises because well-established principles of modern theological reason, both formal and material, tend to favour a rather different set of arrangements. These principles may be set out schematically as follows (not all modern systematic theologies exhibit any or all of these features, or exhibit them in unmixed form). (1) The differentiating characteristic of the Christian religion is the reference of all its various elements to Jesus Christ. As Schleiermacher puts it, in Christianity 'everything is related to the redemption accomplished by Jesus of Nazareth'.[13] (2) The Christology to which all other elements refer is one in which the personal history of Jesus is irreducible, possessing a certain absoluteness which prohibits its resolution into a cause of which it is an external instrument. (3) In a doctrine of the incarnation, preservation of the integrity of Jesus Christ as unified personal agent takes priority over scrupulous distinction of and ordering of his divine and human natures. (4) In a Christian doctrine of God, God's being is act, and God's act principally understood as external (or externally manifest) operation, in terms of its *terminus ad quem*. (5) In systematic theology, priority is therefore to be assigned to the outer works of God; theology is an extrapolation from economy. (6) The specification of the Christian doctrine of God – its protection from abstraction and from being laden with unbecoming attributes – is to be effected by Christological doctrine rather than by teaching about the immanent Trinity.

Formation of Christology by some or all of these principles may result from various factors, theological and non-theological. Chief among the theological factors is a commitment to a view of divine revelation as embodied divine self-manifestation: in effect, revelation *is* incarnation.* One consequence of this strong identity between the divine Word and the historical form which it assumes is to close the space between God absolutely considered and God relatively considered. By virtue of the incarnational union of deity and humanity, there is consubstantiality between God's immanent self and God's revealed self, so that 'inner' and 'outer' are not simply coherent but identical. Theology cannot 'get behind the back of Jesus to the eternal Son of God'.[14] The non-theological factors are more diverse and less easy to specify. They include such matters as: consent to the metaphysical restrictions imposed by Kant's placing of the noumenal beyond the reach of the human intellect; the effects of historical naturalism on interpretation of New Testament Christology; a valorization

---

*The tendency stems from (though does not remain limited to) Lutheran Christology. Webster offers a Reformed rebuttal; for a parallel account that celebrates Reformed breadth over Lutheran atomization in its Christology, see Rowan Williams, *Christ the Heart of Creation* (London: Bloomsbury, 2018), 142–55 (a work which is notably dedicated to Webster by his predecessor as Lady Margaret Professor at Oxford and by the man who would speak at his memorial service in 2016).

of history as first reality; a concomitant loss of confidence in the explanation of temporal events, acts and agents by reduction to their causes.

In their widely varied forms, such principles have made a deep impression on some major systematic Christologies in the last two centuries, though others have been resistant to them. Where they do exercise sway, the result is commonly an expansion of the domain of economy, a corresponding contraction of the domain of theology, and an intensification of expectations surrounding the person and acts of Jesus Christ considered as historical quantities. As the one who constitutes all proper Christian knowledge, he is that reality around which may be ordered an entire account of Christian teaching, of which he is the centre (the metaphor is widely-used and informative).

To illustrate the variety of responses to these factors, we may turn briefly to three examples from the history of Protestant systematic theology.*

1. We look first at a theologian largely (though not entirely) unaffected by these trends, Izaak Dorner, in his *System of Christian Doctrine* (1879–81), a work whose wealth of historical observation, analytical finesse and spiritual cogency is without equal in the school of 'mediating theology' with which he is usually associated. In treating Christology, Dorner sought to eschew any antithesis of theology and economy. He accomplished this partly by emphasis upon Christ's pre-existence, which he regarded as 'the doctrine of the living, real possibility and necessity of the incarnation', or 'the living potentiality, the productive ground of the possibility of the incarnation . . . eternally in God'.[15] This directed Dorner's mind to the immanent Trinity, to which teaching about the person of Christ must always be 'conjoined'.[16] Yet what the doctrine of the immanent Trinity secures is not so much God's perfection apart from the incarnation but rather the fact that there is in God 'an eternal self-disposition for incarnation';[17] the Word is principally one who is 'to be incarnate'. Dorner made this move in part because it was for him a rule that 'evangelical piety starts with the world of revelation, and therefore with the revealed Trinity, with historical redemption and justification . . . and does not start with the doctrine of the immanent Trinity'.[18] There is more than a hint here that the order of knowing (from economy to theology) is coming to be regarded also as the material order. Yet for all this, Dorner remained clear that systematic reflection 'cannot halt' at this point of departure, and must advance to consider the fact 'that there corresponds to the peculiar and permanent being of God in Christ an eternal determination of the divine essence',[19] a 'ground in God'[20] for the incarnation

---

*The absence of Jüngel here is notable, though unexplained. See *WC*, 151–90 for a parallel reflection on the first object of Webster's historical analysis.

such that God's self-communication in Christ is without divine self-detriment or self-realization. This ground is 'the will of perfect self-communication'.[21]

2.   With Dorner's slightly younger contemporary, Albrecht Ritschl, matters took on a very different air. In the Christology set out in the third volume of his deeply impressive *Christian Doctrine of Justification and Reconciliation* (1874), Ritschl transposed Kant's separation of noumenal and phenomenal into a severance of theology from economy. The Christological effect of this proved drastic: Christology restricts itself to the effects of Christ in their reception by and formation of the moral existence of community of faith; nothing is gained from speculation about the eternal Son as the cause of those effects and their reception and power to shape. It is the significance of Christ – not his being in himself or his origin in God – which constitutes the proper object of Christological reflection, and that significance is only intelligible to (almost, indeed, constituted by) 'the consciousness of those who believe in him'.[22] Here Ritschl explicitly differentiated himself from classical theology, which starts from an idea of original divine perfection and so fails to envisage 'every part of the system from the standpoint of the redeemed community of Christ'.[23] Ritschl's work is an exemplary instance of how, when detached from its trinitarian source, Christology may quite quickly collapse into soteriology, and soteriology into analysis of religious fellowship in its experiential and ethical dimensions. Within such a system, the doctrine of God's inner perfection can have very little Christological import: knowledge of God is exhausted in knowledge of his will to enact his love. In a remarkably voluntarist judgement, Ritschl maintained that 'when God is conceived as love, through the relation of his will to his Son and the community of the Kingdom of God, he is not conceived as being anything apart from or prior to his self-determination as love. He is either conceived as love, or simply not at all'.[24] In terms of Christology, the consequence is that Christ's deity is not his immanent essence but purely economically operative: 'the godhead of Christ is not exhausted by maintaining the existence in Christ of the divine nature; the chief point is that in his exertions as man his godhead is manifest and savingly effective'.[25] In short: Christ's origin 'transcends all inquiry'.[26]

3.   A final example is that of Barth, generally judged the most consistently Christocentric modern theologian. The unequalled intellectual grandeur of Barth's achievement in the *Church Dogmatics*, along with its rhetorical, imaginative and spiritual force and its descriptive prowess, have combined to convey an impression of originality about his concentration on Christology, an impression which Barth himself did not discourage. However, his indebtedness to the great dogmaticians of the nineteenth century ought not to be understated (Barth himself did not understate it). What was original to Barth was not his Christological concentration so much as his combination of it with classical

conciliar incarnational dogma and Reformed teaching about the hypostatic union, and his refusal to concur with the moralization of Christology into the soteriological background to religious-ethical society.

Barth's concentration on Christology is more complex than admirers and critics often allow, and than some of his own programmatic statements about the place and function of Christology suggest (understanding the *Church Dogmatics* requires attention both to Barth's uncompromising enunciations of principles and his often much more nuanced and fine-grained exposition of detail).* There are certainly many occasions when he announces the Christological determination of all dogmatic *loci*: revelation, the being of God in his freedom and his love, the election of humankind, human nature, sin, the Spirit, and more besides. Often the vigour of Barth's statements derives from his resistance to what he considered the corrosive effects of natural theology. Moreover, the fourth volume of the *Dogmatics*, which treats the doctrine of reconciliation by an innovative interlaced account of the person and work of Christ, his natures, offices and states and their saving efficacy, is without doubt the point at which Barth's powers are at full stretch. In the details of his exposition, however, Barth rarely reduces all other doctrines to derivatives or implicates of Christology. In part this is because he fears systematic master principles, even dogmatic ones, and seeks to preserve the freedom of the Word of God in dogmatic construction. In part, too, it is because he has a well-developed sense of the range of dogmatics, and an especially strong conviction that, in a dogmatics in which the covenant between God and humanity is of primary import, Christology in the economy must not overwhelm either the freedom of the eternal divine decision or the integrity of the human creature. In addition, Barth remains convinced that Christology and Trinity are inseparable and mutually implicating, and that teaching about the immanent Trinity is of great Christological import (this may be lost from view if Barth's doctrine of reconciliation is detached from his doctrine of the Trinity in *Church Dogmatics* I). Jesus Christ is the name, form and act of God; yet where those in Ritschl's school (including the theological existentialists with whom Barth engaged in skirmishes in the 1950s whilst writing *Church Dogmatics* IV) took this as permission to set theology proper to one side in favour of an exclusively economic orientation, Barth continued to think that teaching about the eternal Son is essential to identifying the acting subject of revelation and reconciliation. In the overall sweep of his exposition of Christian doctrine, Barth does not allow theology to atrophy, though he is consistently and powerfully attentive to the economy as the sphere of the Son's presence and action.

---

*One common observation in Webster's Barth scholarship is that Barth's pronouncements of principle may oftentimes express a polemical or hyperbolic claim that his actual exposition (of Scripture especially but also historical–textual engagement) does not sustain. Thus, to read Barth well demands not merely reading theses or introductory statements but following his argument all the way through (both through any given section or sub-section and through to the last fragments of what he prepared for Volume Four).

VI

No element in a system of theology is unrelated to Christology: to contemplate any of its parts is to have one's mind drawn irresistibly to the name and figure of Jesus Christ. Why is this so? Barth judged that it was so because Christian theology 'does not know and proclaim anything side by side with or apart from Jesus Christ, because it knows and proclaims all things only as his things . . . For it, there is no something other side by side with or apart from him. For it, there is nothing worthy of mention that is not as such his. Everything that it knows and proclaims as worthy of mention, it does so as his'.[27] This is, perhaps, stated in an unqualified way; yet there is here something incontestably correct and wholesome, namely, that Jesus Christ is not merely the exponent or symbol of some reality available apart from him, for he is (the term is Hans Frei's) 'unsubstitutable'.[28] Yet if this conviction – so ample and loving in its dedication to the Word incarnate – is not to occasion over-intensification of one indispensable element of Christology and attenuation of the way in which that element directs attention to God's inner life, systematic theology must specify with some scruple the sense in which God is the formal object of each Christian doctrine, Christology included. In assembling all its various matters into a scheme, systematic theology acknowledges that faith gives assent to many things; but it does so because by those many things faith is conducted to God as first truth. Theology takes things other than God into account as 'the workings of God'.[29] The breadth and spread of Christology derive from the fact that in it theology considers both God himself as first truth and God's effects. Study of the incarnate Word may not pass too quickly over his phenomenal form; but nor may it terminate there, for it must allow this human history to direct us to the triune God.[30] Yet, again, instruction about this formal object may be had by observation of its extensions or external working: we demonstrate 'something about a cause through its effect'.[31] And so when systematic reflection is directed to God as first truth, the incarnation is not left behind, because to apprehend this first truth is also to apprehend that the eternal Word participates in God's infinite communicative and creative goodness and is the exemplary cause of God's works in time. When these material – trinitarian – principles govern the content and proportions of a systematic presentation of Christian teaching, the place, extent and formative role of Christology will be properly delimited and secured.

Notes

1 K. Barth, *Church Dogmatics* IV/3 (Edinburgh: T&T Clark, 1961), p. 175.

2 Aquinas, *Summa theologiae* Ia.1.7 resp.

3 Aquinas, *Summa theologiae* Ia.6.2 resp.
4 Aquinas, *Compendium of Theology* (Oxford: Oxford University Press, 2009), I.2.
5 Aquinas, *Compendium of Theology* I.2.
6 Aquinas, *Compendium of Theology* I.213.
7 Aquinas, *Compendium of Theology* I.213 (translation altered).
8 On this, see S. J. Gathercole, *The Pre-existent Son. Recovering the Christologies of Matthew, Mark and Luke* (Grand Rapids, MI: Eerdmans, 2006).
9 J. Owen, *Christologia, or A Declaration of the Glorious Mystery of the Person of Christ* [1679], in *The Works of John Owen*, vol. 1 (Edinburgh: Banner of Truth Trust, 1965), p. 44.
10 Owen, *Christologia*, p. 78.
11 Owen, *Christologia*, p. 79.
12 Owen, *Christologia*, p. 54.
13 F. D. E. Schleiermacher, *The Christian Faith*, p. 52.
14 T. F. Torrance, 'The Place of Christology in Biblical and Dogmatic Theology', in *Theology in Reconstruction* (London: SCM Press, 1965), p. 130.
15 I. A. Dorner, *A System of Christian Doctrine*, vol. 3, p. 284.
16 Dorner, *A System of Christian Doctrine*, vol. 3, p. 284.
17 Dorner, *A System of Christian Doctrine*, vol. 3, p. 285.
18 Dorner, *A System of Christian Doctrine*, vol. 3, p. 286.
19 Dorner, *A System of Christian Doctrine*, vol. 3, p. 286.
20 Dorner, *A System of Christian Doctrine*, vol. 3, p. 297.
21 Dorner, *A System of Christian Doctrine*, vol. 3, p. 293.
22 A. Ritschl, *The Christian Doctrine of Justification and Reconciliation III: The Positive Development of the Doctrine* (Edinburgh: T&T Clark, 1902), p. 1.
23 Ritschl, *The Christian Doctrine of Justification and Reconciliation III*, p. 5.
24 Ritschl, *The Christian Doctrine of Justification and Reconciliation III*, p. 282.
25 Ritschl, *The Christian Doctrine of Justification and Reconciliation III*, p. 393.
26 Ritschl, *The Christian Doctrine of Justification and Reconciliation III*, p. 451.
27 Barth, K. *Church Dogmatics* IV/1 (Edinburgh: T&T Clark, 1956), p. 21.
28 H. Frei, *The Identity of Jesus Christ. The Hermeneutical Bases of Dogmatic Theology* (Philadelphia: Fortress Press, 1975), p. 49.
29 Aquinas, *Summa theologiae* IIaIIae 1.1 resp.
30 See Aquinas, *Summa theologiae* IIaIIae 1.1 ad 1.
31 Aquinas, *Summa theologiae* Ia.1.7 ad 1.

5

Non ex aequo: God's relation to creatures

EDITOR'S INTRODUCTION

Repeatedly throughout his writings, Webster turned to consider and respond to the increasing dominance of language about creaturely participation in God. He observed that participation had played a signal role in *la nouvelle théologie* within Roman Catholicism prior to and especially after the Second Vatican Council, and he worried about the inroads made – oftentimes without any sign of critical self-awareness – within the Protestant world.

'The Christian doctrines of the Trinity and of creation alike entail that the relation of God and creatures is a "mixed" relation, "real" on the side of the creature but a "relation of reason" on the side of God.' Webster takes this asymmetry in language and non-reciprocal relation from Thomas Aquinas (*De potentia*, III.3, resp; *ST* 1a.54.3, *ad* 1). Noting that this language of the 'mixed relation' has garnered contempt, Webster offers a defence of the claim. To do so, he begins three steps back by considering relations within the Godhead before considering what it might mean for God to relate to a being that is not God. He analyses Trinitarian theology, the place of creation in theology more broadly, and the scope of a viable doctrine of creation. Then he turns to examining how these moves shape our understanding of God's relating to human creatures.

Like many post-Reformation Reformed dogmatics (though unlike so many modern theologians, even many within his own Reformed tradition), Webster pairs a Thomistically infused account of creational metaphysics with an emphasis on the language of covenant fellowship. This essay serves as the most specific and nuanced statement of his reflection on what is going on when God relates to creatures. He does not here describe moral expectations or theological provisions; he lingers patiently over the metaphysical language necessary to depict such communication and union. He wagers that 'teaching about God the creator and his work exercises considerable sway in articulating the work of grace, whose intelligibility depends in some measure upon principles about the coming-to-be and the nature of created things in relation to God which are laid down in a theology of creation'. Thus, Webster would speak regularly in his latter years of creation serving alongside Trinity as a distributed doctrine that inflects all other topics regarding the economy of God's works. Attending to creation as such a distributed doctrine helps avoid inflation of the gospel economy, inasmuch as it sustains an operative sense of the gratuity and goodness of creation, existence and nature within which the dramas of sin and redemption will occur.

While many argue that a non-reciprocal relation is plainly not a legitimate relation, Webster (picking up this thread from Thomas Aquinas) disagrees. 'In God, absence of reciprocity is not absence of relation but the ground of limitless relation. God does not stand in relation to the creature as some commensurable particular agent in the same order of being, but more intimately and comprehensively as the principle of all being.' Indeed the conclusion of the essay circles back round to the promise of hope offered here: 'Only because the God who is for us is in himself God, entire without us, is his being for us more than a projection of our corrupt longing.' While he suggests that there will be 'ascetical' implications for us to adopt if this is true, he also claims that herein lies genuine hope from beyond. Because this relation is odd (owing to its asymmetry), it has the potential to be truly life-giving. Were it not strange in such a manner, it would be yet another relation of blasé reciprocity.

Suggested readings

'The Dignity of Creatures', in GWM 2, 29–48.
'Perfection and Participation', in *The Analogy of Being: Invention of the Antichrist or Wisdom from God?* (ed. Thomas Joseph White; Grand Rapids, MI: Eerdmans, 2010), 379–94.
'Trinity and Creation', *International Journal of Systematic Theology* 12 (2010): 4–19; repr. in GWM 1, 83–98.
Michael Allen, 'Survey of Covenant in Recent Modern Theology', in *Covenant Theology: Biblical, Theological, and Historical Perspectives* (ed. Guy Waters et al.; Wheaton: Crossway, forthcoming), where Webster's covenant theology is analysed and compared to other recent accounts.
Ian McFarland, 'The Gift of the *Non Aliud*: Creation from Nothing as a Metaphysics of Abundance', *International Journal of Systematic Theology* 21, no. 1 (2019): 44–58.
Tyler Wittman, 'Metaphysics', in *A Companion to John Webster's Theology* (ed. Michael Allen and R. David Nelson; Grand Rapids, MI: Eerdmans, forthcoming).

NON EX AEQUO: GOD'S RELATION TO CREATURES

I

'[T]he creature by its very name is referred to the creator and depends on the creator who does not depend on it. Wherefore the relation whereby the creature is referred to the creator must be a real relation, while in God it is only a logical relation.'[1] The Christian doctrines of the Trinity and of creation alike entail that the relation of God and creatures is a 'mixed' relation, 'real' on the side of the creature but a 'relation of reason' on the side of God.[*] This teaching – refined in mediaeval theology but having its early authority in a passage of Augustine's *De trinitate* on *ex tempore* predication[2] – commonly draws the reproach that it takes for granted a doctrine of God whose lines are drawn in advance of consideration of the economy of revelation and grace, a doctrine in which God's commerce with creatures is accorded no constitutive role. Its real import, however, is not to deny God's relation to creatures but to invest that relation with a specific character. It accomplishes this specification by indicating that God's simple perfection is such that he is not one term in a dyad, relatively or contrastively defined, and, by consequence, that God's creative will and action are unrestrictedly benevolent and beneficent, giving life simply for the creature's good. Precisely because God's relation to created things has no effect on the divine integrity, it is the outward enactment of his goodness.

Displaying the intellectual and religious cogency of this teaching requires (1) articulation of a spacious theology of creation which treats the simple being of the triune creator in his inner and outer works, before moving to consider his act of creation and the natures of created things; (2) attention to the proper proportions and sequence of these various elements of the doctrine of creation, and to their place and function in a system of Christian theology; (3) observation of some formal principles of theological inquiry which follow from the material doctrine of creation; (4) the presence of a range of moral and spiritual dispositions on the part of inquirers which put them in the frame to regard this teaching with complacency. Further, understanding this part (and some other parts) of Christian teaching necessitates struggle to attain freedom from some constraints of metaphysical and religious custom. Most of all it requires the ordering of theological intelligence and spiritual appetite away from a conception of the Christian faith in which the phenomenon of

---

*The claim that the relation is 'not real' on God's side seems farcical at first glance to modern readers. For clarification of its conceptual background and argument for its importance, see section 4.

God's engagement with creatures in time is considered *id quo maius cogitari nequit* – a conception so widely shared by dogmaticians and exegetes as to be largely invisible, yet one whose possession of some of the chief elements of divine instruction is insecure.[*]

II

Theological consideration of the asymmetrical relation of God and creatures requires recall of the principal elements of the Christian doctrine of creation of which it is an extension. Present circumstances, however, demand that this rehearsal be prefaced by consideration of the place and function of teaching about creation in Christian dogmatics, because misunderstanding of or antipathy to the concept of mixed relations are often symptomatic of a misplaced, atrophied or insufficiently operative doctrine of creation.

Modern Christian dogmatics (if the portmanteau term be allowed) manifests a certain disorder or misalignment generated by excessive attention to the divine economy, which may be identified in the following way.

The matter of Christian divinity is God and all things in relation to God. A systematic account of Christian teaching, which presents this matter by topical anatomy and sequential arrangement, has two chief divisions. It begins by considering God's being in himself in his inner works as Father, Son and Spirit, and then, without relinquishing its first theme but enlarging it and following its scope and direction, turns to consider God's *opera ad extra*, the first body of material (the divine processions) constituting the founding principles of the second (the divine missions). The second body of material on God's outer works may then itself be divided into consideration of the work of nature (creation and providence) and the work of grace (election, reconciliation and the consummation of all things).

In such an arrangement of Christian teaching, two related features of the doctrine of creation may be observed. First, it is the bridge by which consideration of God *in se* passes over to consideration of God *ad extra*; it is the ground of the fact that Christian doctrine is responsible to attend not to a single but a double theme (God and all things). The categorical difference between these two themes, and the absolute subordination of the latter to the former, does not compromise the necessity of attention to created as well as to uncreated being. Christian dogmatics cannot be adequate to the range of its matter if it does not treat with full seriousness the fact that to the confession *credo in Deum* there corresponds *creator caeli et terrae*.

---

[*]The call to a theological theology again involves a reorientation, here from a fixation on God's works with and among us to a prioritization of God in and of himself. Eternity crowns time, a point which can only be grasped if we see its primacy and privilege relative to time.

Second, the doctrine of creation is one of two distributed doctrines in the corpus of Christian dogmatics.* The first (both in sequence and in material primacy) distributed doctrine is the doctrine of the Trinity, of which all other articles of Christian teaching are an amplification or application, and which therefore permeates theological affirmations about every matter; theology talks about everything by talking about God. The doctrine of creation is the second distributed doctrine, although, because its scope is restricted to the *opera Dei ad extra*, its distribution is less comprehensive than that of the doctrine of the Trinity. Within this limit, the doctrine of creation is ubiquitous. It is not restricted to one particular point in the sequence of Christian doctrine, but provides orientation and a measure of governance to all that theology has to say about all things in relation to God.

The pervasiveness of teaching about creation – the way in which it brackets and qualifies everything that is said about the nature and course of all that is not God – is such, however, that it is often implicit, built into a wide range of doctrinal material on, for example, providence, anthropology, soteriology or the theology of the sacraments, but not necessarily breaking the surface and becoming visible. The general inconspicuousness of the doctrine after its initial explicit treatment as the first external work of God belies its systematic range and bearing. 'God's first effect in things is existence itself, which all other effects presuppose, and on which they are founded.'[3]

Teaching about creation 'opens the logical and theological space for other Christian beliefs and mysteries',[4] because contemplation of that teaching enables discernment of essential properties of the relation between God and created things which will be further displayed when considering the history of their interaction as it unfolds in the economy. This does not entail that all other doctrines are to be derived from the doctrine of creation, or that those other doctrines do not also in their turn illuminate teaching about creation. Consideration of the *opus gratiae* enriches and extends what is said about the *opus naturae*, most of all by enabling closer identification of the archetype and agent of creation ('in him all things were created') and of its telos ('all things were created through him and for him', Col. 1.16). At the same time, teaching about God the creator and his work exercises considerable sway in articulating the work of grace, whose intelligibility depends in some measure upon principles about the coming-to-be and the nature of created things in relation to God which are laid down in a theology of creation.

---

*A 'distributed doctrine' is a doctrine that must be unfolded at various points in the course of Christian dogmatics. Most broadly, Webster says the trinity of God is globally distributed, relevant at all points; creation is next most distributed in that it bears upon every aspect of the economy (though not the topic of God in himself). Admittedly, the systematicity of all doctrine means that all doctrines are distributed in some sense, but Webster means to highlight a certain conceptual range that extends further in some cases (not least when, as with creation, it is so present as to be overlooked).

In much modern exegetical and dogmatic theology, the doctrine of creation does not have this place and function. This may be attributed in part to the way in which in all conceptions of the matter of Christian teaching some doctrines achieve prominence and others contract. Concentration on the outer works of God, for example, may be such that the first body of dogmatic material on God's infinite perfection *in se* receives only slight attention. By consequence, the existence and history of created things may be assumed as a given, quasi-necessary, reality, rather than a wholly surprising effect of divine goodness, astonishment at which pervades all Christian teaching. Moreover, treatment of the *opera Dei externae* may be so structured that the *opus gratiae* has precedence over the *opus naturae*, of which it is the 'inner ground'. Exposition of the history of grace as the final cause of creation takes priority over contemplation of God the creator and God's act of creation as the first cause of created being and history, including the history of redemption. The resultant conceptions of Christian doctrine are customarily 'historical' or 'dramatic' in idiom, presenting the relation of God and creatures as one between divine and human persons and agents who, for all their differences, are strangely commensurable, engaging one another in the same space, deciding, acting and interacting in the world as a commonly-inhabited field of reality. This may be especially the case when, in the absence of other considerations, the person and career of Jesus are deemed irreducible, since he is the one as whom God is and acts as God. The setting of the work of grace in the work of nature (as well as in the divine processions) thereby recedes from view because of the sheer prominence and human intensity of the central subject and episode of redemption history.[*]

Such an arrangement of Christian doctrine raises an expectation that what needs to be said about the natures of God and the creatures of God, and therefore of their relation, may be determined almost exhaustively by attending to the economy of salvation – the history of election and reconciliation in the external missions of the Son and the Holy Spirit. Accordingly, if God and creature are chiefly conceived as *dramatis personae* in an enacted sequence of lost and regained fellowship, talk of the non-reciprocity of their relation seems theologically and religiously unbecoming.

It is, however, possible to exhibit Christian doctrine in a different arrangement, with differences of proportion and placement as well as of material content. Such a reordering entails no diminishment of the importance of the work of grace, though it does not allow it constitutive significance as the *principium* of all talk of God and creatures. Moreover, it presents a conception of Christian teaching in which the *non ex aequo* character of the relation of God and creatures can be seen as fitting to the natures of both and to the unrestricted intimacy of God's presence in the world.

---

[*]So-called 'biblical theology' or 'the history of redemption' can narrow one's focus to the economy if it is not also bounded by attention to theological metaphysics (as addressed by the doctrines of God and of creation).

III

The Christian doctrine of creation treats four topics: the Holy Trinity as creator, the act of creation, the nature of created things, and the relation of God and creatures. The topical division corresponds to the scope of Christian teaching, which studies both God *in se* and God as *principium rerum*,[5] and also follows its material sequence: 'after treating of the procession of the divine persons, we must consider the procession of creatures from God.'[6] Theological thought about creation begins with contemplation of God's immanent being and only then moves to reflect upon God's transitive acts. '[I]n the teaching of faith, which considers creatures only in their relation to God, the consideration of God comes first, that of creatures afterwards.'[7] Moreover, the way in which each subsequent topic is handled is determined by the first topic's treatment of the triune being of God, this opening material being 'first' not simply in sequence but in rank, because the divine processions are the *causa et ratio* of the making of creatures.[8]

1. Christian teaching about creation is ordered by confession and acclamation of God's matchless self-sufficiency. In his inner works as Father, Son and Spirit, God is plenitude of life and incomparable excellence. The creator is 'the blessed and only sovereign, the king of kings and lord of lords, who alone has immortality and dwells in unapproachable light, whom no one has ever seen or can see' (1 Tim. 6.15f.; cf. Deut. 10.17; Dan. 2.47; Rev. 17.14, 19.16). God's kingship and lordship have no common measure with any other reality; he is not merely contingently superior to other powers, but incomparable, unaffected and undisturbed in relation to them, falling outside the set of kings and lords. In the perfection of his immanent triune life, God 'only' is God, and God is 'alone'.

    This confession, made in the wake of divine instruction, may be explicated through a range of concepts, which also serve to characterize in an initial way the relation of God and created things. God is unoriginate and self-subsistent, having his being not through or in relation to some other, but *per se*. God is fully actual, possessing no potency whose realization would extend or complete his being. God is immutable – already infinitely sufficient and complete and therefore beyond alteration or acquisition – and impassible – inexhaustibly alive, stable and entire in himself and so beyond the reach of any agent or act of contestation or depredation.

    Concepts such as these direct the mind to two elements of the Christian doctrine of God which prove especially important in forming an understanding of the relation of God to creatures: God's radically non-composite or simple nature, and God's absolute otherness from the world.

Simplicity is a broad term for the fact that God is not formed from elements, whether internal or external; God has no career, no process of coming-to-be. Simplicity indicates the intrinsic absence or need for derivation in God and, further, betokens that God is not ordered to anything else, even as the most excellent or supreme being. The world, therefore, is not a concomitant to God. '[I]t is absolutely necessary that God should be differently related to his effects than any other possible cause to its effects and that he should possess his nature in a different way from any other possible being. The concept of "incompositeness" enables us to secure the assertion of these things.'[9]

Because God is simple, he is absolutely and not merely contingently other than the world. God's not being part of the world is not such that he is some reality alongside and contrasted with the world, as if God and the world formed a pair with their respective natures determined in part by their divergence and differentiation from each other. The otherness of God as creator is not an instance of correlativity or complementarity. God is *non aliud*,* beyond relations of similarity or contrast. 'Creatures are not related to God as to a thing of a different genus, but as to something outside of and prior to all genera.'[10]

2.   The act of creation is determined by the nature of its agent: God has his being *per se* and so creates *ex nihilo*. To say *ex nihilo* is simply to say 'God alone'. For the coming-to-be of creatures, nothing is required but God. The act of creation effects 'the issuing of the whole of being from the universal cause,'[11] and is undertaken in relation to nothing.

This may be drawn out by a series of negations. The act of creation does not presuppose something other than God, and is not an act which forms antecedent matter, for it has no material cause, there being no patient entity to receive the divine work. Nor is the act of creation an act *against* anything, the assertion of mastery over contending forces. It is not a 'dramatic enactment … the absolute power of God realizing itself in achievement and relationship,'[12] because 'absolute' excludes self-realization, achievement and constitutive relationship. Again, the act of creation is not an instance of efficient causality: it is without labour (not the exercise of force in relation to some opposing reality but the effortless introduction of being) and without temporal extension (not discursive achievement but instantaneous production), and it effects no change (the movement from non-existence to existence is not the modification of a common subject of 'before' and 'after').

The negatives serve both to distinguish the act of creation from any contingent work of making and also to characterize the agent of creation. As

---

*Literally: 'not other'. God's transcendence cannot be characterized as merely 'other' like any other alien or foreigner. God is transcendent even in his difference, exceeding the bounds of distinction qualitatively, not merely quantitatively.

the one who creates *ex nihilo*, God is not simply an agent of formation, effecting an alteration, but 'the universal cause of being'[13] or 'the universal principle of being'.[14] Further, as *causa universalis totius esse*[15] God is entirely beyond the totality of all things. There is in God no *esse-ad*, no constitutive relation to that which is not himself. The act of creation acquires a measure of intelligibility only as we respect its sheer incomparability, stripping those properties which we normally ascribe to particular acts and agents from our conception of the divine making, and so repeating in thought the confession that God the creator is ὁ μακάριος καὶ μόνος δυνάστης (1 Tim. 6.15).

3.   More briefly: what of the nature of created things? First, a creature *is* a 'thing made' (Isa. 29.16; Ps. 100.3, Jn. 1.3,10), a work of God's hands. Creatures have their being in such a way that both in coming-to-be and in continuance they are marked by entire ontological deficiency apart from the person and act of the creator in his infinite charity. The being of the creator is *per se*, that of the creature 'an existing which is a relation to a source'.[16] This is not to deny that the creature possesses being, but to indicate whence and how it does so. The creature emerges from the non-condition of absolute privation; its 'background' is the non-being of the creaturely subject, to which nothing, no potentiality or expectation of being, may be ascribed. 'A creature is nothing but the relation of dependence upon the proper cause of its being: *tantum esse ad Deum*.'[17]

Second, created being is entirely gratuitous, that which might not have been.* Created being is therefore not that in terms of which other things are explained, but that which stands in need of explanation by reference to an external principle. Created things are *principiata*, their phenomenal reality directing understanding beyond themselves to their source, in relation to which they have and enact their being, and apart from which they possess neither amplitude nor duration.

IV

What is said of the first three topics of the doctrine of creation prepares us for consideration of its fourth division, the relation of God and creatures. '[I]n God [the relationship to the creature] is not a real relation, but only conceptual. The relation of the creature to God, however, is real'.[18]

In this matter theological reflection makes its way with more than usual difficulty, because, as Aquinas observes, 'our mind struggles [*nititur*] to describe God as a most

---

*Contingency and grace are bound up together. That creatures need not have existed means that their existence is in fact a free and gracious reality. A metaphysical term (contingency) and a moral-relational term (grace) are bound up conceptually with one another here.

perfect being'.[19] The struggle arises because thought about God operates under a double constraint, made all the more acute by its subjection to divine instruction in Holy Scripture. On the one hand, the created intellects of the prophetic and apostolic writers represent the relation of God and creatures as a reciprocal history of encounter or communion, drawing on conceptions of the kind of mutual relations which obtain between human persons: 'all our knowledge takes its rise from sensation. Congenially, then, holy Scripture delivers spiritual things to us beneath metaphors taken from bodily things.'[20] On the other hand, everything said of the relation of God and creatures must recognize that God is *perfectissimus* and so an entirely unconventional matter for creaturely thought and speech. Excessive or exclusive submission to either constraint unframes theology. To say that 'it is not in keeping with this teaching to convey divine things under the symbolic representation of bodily things'[21] is to incapacitate divine revelation, to fail to trust its ability to resist being extinguished by the imagery of temporal interaction.[22] Yet theology may be so absorbed by Scripture's dramatic-historical presentation of God's relation to creatures that the distinction between God and the world comes to be pictured in comparative or relatively contrastive terms as a distinction within the world, one between commensurable historical agents.

Both strategies evade the conversion or recasting of the sense of terms *in divinis* which accompanies all theological talk of creation and finds especial application in the term 'relation'.* Divine instruction engenders intellectual and semantic mobility: 'the minds of those given the revelation are not allowed to remain arrested with the images but are lifted up to their meaning.'[23] This mobility alerts us to the originality and unlikeness of the use of the term 'relation', as well as to the fittingness of its retention. Such conceptual adaptability readies theology for overcoming the obstacles placed in its way by a univocal concept of relation learned from dealings with created things. Its exegetical and dogmatic fruitfulness depends upon theology's readiness to be unseated from habits of mind, and also upon persuasion that teaching about God's self-subsistent and wholly realized being has primacy in ordering thought about creation and creatures, that such teaching enables us to read Scripture well, and that it envisages no restriction to God's loving and active presence among the works of his hands.

First, then, relation to the creator is real on the side of the creature. Without this relation the creature would not be, because the creature is ordered to God and constituted by that ordering. '[T]hings that are ordered to something [*res habentes ordinem ad aliquid*] must be really related to it, and this relation must be some real thing in them. Now all creatures are ordered to God both as to their beginning and as to their end . . . Therefore creatures are really related to God, and this relation is

---

*Relations, like all other notions and terms, require ascetic transformation in the theologian's mind, for they do not apply to God as to any other object of study.

something real in the creature.'[24] This *ad aliquid* relation, however, does not come into being in the history of fellowship between God and the patriarchs, kings, prophets and all the people of Israel and the church; it is, rather, the *principium* of that history, that by virtue of which there is a creation and therefore an unfolding covenant – namely, the original gift of being by the creator, along with its providential maintenance, in relation to which the creature lives and moves and has its being.

Second, the relation of God to the creature is a relation of reason. This requires some amplification . . .

Two kinds of relation may be predicated of God: relations *ad intra* and relations *ad extra*. The relations *ad intra* – the divine processions – are eternal real relations, intrinsic to God's perfection. To speak of paternity, filiation and spiration as real relations, however, requires a special sense of relatedness, of being *ad aliud*, in which relation is irreducible (this is a principal task for trinitarian theology). For at first glance it might seem that relations in God would be capable of resolution into the antecedent undivided divine essence. 'Seeing that God is the first beginning and last end of things, anything that is reducible to something previous cannot be in God, but only those things to which others are reduced . . . Now everything that denotes " 'to-another' " [*ad aliud*] being is reducible to absolute or " 'to-itself' " [*ad se*] being. Therefore in God nothing is relative to another but all is absolute.'[25] However, the relations between the divine persons are not accidental to God's being; they simply *are* God's being. The relations of Father, Son and Spirit are not some extended process in the course of which God acquires supplementary properties, behind which lies the unchanging divine essence. Thus, although 'the movable and the accidental are reducible to something previous as the imperfect to the perfect', nevertheless 'relation sometimes follows from the perfection of a thing'. Accordingly, 'the divine perfection does not hinder us from ascribing relations to God, as it forbids us to ascribe movement and accident to him.'[26]

God's relations *ad extra* are relations of reason and do not 'follow from his perfection'. Understanding why this is so requires alertness to the natural tendency of our minds to represent God and creatures as symmetrically related: on the basis of the fact that creatures are really related to God, we conceive of God's relation to creatures in a similar way. '[T]he mind sometimes considers something in relation to another inasmuch as it is the term of the relationship of another thing to it, and yet itself is not related to the other: as when it considers something knowable as terminating the relationship of knowledge to it; and thus it imputes to the thing knowable a certain relation to knowledge, and such a relation is purely logical. In like manner, our mind attributes to God certain relative terms, inasmuch as it considers God as the term of the creature's relation to him: wherefore such relations are purely logical.'[27] That is, the mind may treat relations in which there is only one accident (on the side of the creature) as if we were dealing with a pair of mutual *relata*, a relative and a co-relative: this, because we are 'unable to conceive one thing related to another, without on the other hand conceiving that relation to be reciprocal.'[28] The distinction between real relations and relations of reason is partly intended to inhibit this tendency, and so to give proper regard to the way in which God's perfection *in se* unsettles conventions about relations.*

However, though the concept of logical relations encourages vigilance against the way in which the mind's operations may entice us into metaphysical error, it is primarily a corollary of the dogmatics of God the creator, and follows from a double assertion: that God the creator is not ordered to another, and that God is wholly outside the genus of that which is ordered to him.

Consider Aquinas's extended denial in *De potentia* VII of 'reciprocity in the relations of God and the creature'.[29] A real relation 'consists in the ordering of one thing to another',[30] and is mutually real when in both terms of the relation 'there is the same reason for mutual order'[31] – that is, 'mutual real relations require foundations of the same type'.[32] This may be seen in instances of causality. Agents 'sometimes have an order to their respective patients',[33] as in those agents who produce their like in species. But this is not invariably the case: 'there are some things to which others are ordered, but not vice-versa, because they are wholly foreign to the genus of actions or power from which that order arises [*omnino extrinseca ab illo genere actionum vel virtutum quas consequitur talis ordo*]'.[34] Aquinas offers a number of examples: the way in which the thing known is not touched by the act of knowing; the relative location of a person and a pillar; the relation of money and price; the relation of depicted object to its artistic representation. So in the case of God's relation to creatures: God's 'action is his substance and is wholly outside the genus of created being whereby the creature is related to him.'[35]

Aquinas's analysis applies the dogmatic principle that, unlike God's wisdom or will, God's relations to creatures are not expressive of his essence.[36] Simple and entirely realized, God 'is not made happy by making things, but through being all-sufficient to himself and needing not the things he made.'[37] The non-interdependence of God and creatures is reinforced by contemplation both of God's rest on the seventh day of creation, which indicates that God 'is happy in himself and needs not creatures',[38] and of the way in which the 'newness' of the world demonstrates its non-necessity for God's eternal bliss.[39] The existence of creation adds nothing to God, and in its absence God would be undiminished.

Many recoil from this. In *The Divine Relativity* – a work which evokes admiration and exasperation in equal measure – Hartshorne argued not without passion that 'if . . . God is wholly absolute, a term but never a subject of relations, it follows that God does not know or love or will us, his creatures.'[40] *Sed contra*: it is precisely

---

*The terminology of 'real relations' and 'logical relations/relations of reason' serves to slow us down and remind us that they are not simply of the same sort. Relations of nature within the Godhead are essential and eternal, whereas relations with creations by grace are willed and experienced with the inception and gift of time.

because God's relation to creatures is not 'real' that his love is of infinite scope and benevolence.*

In God, absence of reciprocity is not absence of relation but the ground of limitless relation. God does not stand in relation to the creature as some commensurable particular agent in the same order of being, but more intimately and comprehensively as the principle of all being. '[A]lthough God is not in the same genus as the creature as a thing contained in a genus, he is nevertheless in every genus as the principle of the genus; and for this reason there can be a relation between the creature and God as between effect (*principiata*) and principle.'[41] As *principium* God is the universal cause rather than a particular circumscribed agent, and so there are no bounds to his relation: he is 'in every genus', though contained within none. Further, God's simplicity excludes any relation to creatures in which God receives an augmentation of his being from that to which he relates. But divine simplicity also means the absence of composition in God. God is not an aggregate of particular actions and interactions, and therefore his relation to all that he has made has limitless breadth. '[I]t is not incompatible with a thing's simplicity to have many relations towards other things; indeed, the more simple a thing is the greater the number of its concomitant relations, since its power is so much the less limited and consequently its causality so much the more extended . . . Accordingly, from God's supreme simplicity there results an infinite number of respects or relations between creatures and him.'[42]

Because God's infinitely extended relations to created things neither add to nor subtract from his being, his work of bringing into being and maintaining creatures is wholly benevolent and beneficent. God is in himself infinitely happy, in need of nothing from the creature: how could the perfect be perfected? His work of creation is pure generosity: he makes things for their own sake, not for his. This, in turn, is the ground of the integrity of the creature and of its proper efficacy. Because God can be opposed by nothing – because, again, he is not a particular being acting upon others and acted upon by them – he is beyond envy of the creature, and there is in him no reluctance to bestow upon the creature its own intrinsic substance and powers.

V

Consideration of Christian teaching about creation requires ascetical as well as intellectual virtues. Most of all, it obliges those who consider it to recover the posture

---

*Much of Webster's concern here can be traced back to the spiritual urgency that the notion of a suffering or vulnerable god ultimately does not constitute good news (contra Jürgen Moltmann and others writing in his wake). Only an impassible, transcendent God who assumes our plight without in any way demeaning or diminishing himself can be truly good news for the suffering.

of creatures, the dependence and gratitude of derivation and the repudiation of self-subsistence.* This is acutely hard for the children of Adam, for we contend against our creaturely nature and calling, from stupidity or pride or fear that unless we snatch at our being and make ourselves authors of its perpetuation and dignity, it will slip away from us. And so we propose to ourselves, sometimes a little guiltily, sometimes with frank confidence, that we constitute a given reality around which all else is arranged. Even God may be so placed, as God 'for us', a protagonist whose identity, not wholly unlike our own, is bound to us, and whose presence confirms the limitless importance of the human drama. All this must be set aside, and, by the loving missions of the Word and the Spirit, it is already being set aside as the mortification and renewal of our spiritual, intellectual and moral nature proceeds. As it is left behind, we may begin to understand how it is that God is indeed for us. Only because the God who is for us is in himself God, entire without us, is his being for us more than a projection of our corrupt longing for a satisfying divine counterpart. The burden of the Christian doctrines of the Trinity, creation and incarnation is that, because God is from and in himself, he is God for us in ways we can scarcely imagine.

Notes

1   Aquinas, *De potentia* III.3 resp.; see also *Summa theologiae* Ia.45.3 ad 1. My reading of Aquinas in what follows is indebted to a range of commentators: R. Acar, *Talking About God and Talking About Creation. Avicenna's and Thomas Aquinas' Positions* (Leiden: Brill, 2005); Braine, *The Reality of Time and the Existence of God*; F. C. Bauerschmidt, *Thomas Aquinas. Faith, Reason, and Following Christ* (Oxford: Oxford University Press, 2013), pp. 107–17; D. Burrell, *Knowing the Unknowable God*; idem and B. McGinn, ed., *God and Creation*; idem, *Freedom and Creation in Three Traditions*; idem, 'Creation, Metaphysics and Ethics'; idem, 'Aquinas' Appropriation of *Liber de causis* to Articulate the Creator as Cause-of-Being', in F. Kerr, ed., *Contemplating Aquinas*, pp. 75–83; idem, *Faith and Freedom. An Interfaith Perspective* (Oxford: Blackwell, 2004); idem, et al., ed., *Creation and the God of Abraham* (Cambridge: Cambridge University Press, 2010); M. J. Dodds, 'Ultimacy and Intimacy: Aquinas on the Relation between God and the World', in C-J. P. de Oliviera, ed., *Ordo Sapientiae et Amoris* (Freiburg: Editions Universitaires, 1993), pp. 211–27; G. Emery, 'Trinity and Creation', in R. van Nieuwenhove, J. Wawrykow, ed., *The Theology of Thomas Aquinas* (Notre Dame: University of Notre Dame Press, 2005), pp. 58–76; M. G. Henninger, 'Aquinas on the Ontological Status of Relations', *Journal of the History of Philosophy* 25 (1987), 491–515; idem, *Relations. Mediaeval Theories, 1250–1325* (Oxford: Oxford University Press, 1989);

---

*The ethical conclusion is not unrelated to the metaphysical principles. Creaturely dependence will not be perceived or embraced apart from dependently receiving God's reorientation of our self-perception.

M. R. McWhorter, 'Aquinas on God's Relation to the World', *New Blackfriars* 94 (2013), pp. 3–18; A. Krempel, *La doctrine de la relation chez saint Thomas* (Paris: Vrin: 1952); E. Muller, 'Real Relations and the Divine: Issues in Thomas's Understanding of God's Relation to the World', *Theological Studies* 56 (1995), pp. 673–95; P. Masterson, *The Sense of Creation. Experience and the God Beyond* (Aldershot: Ashgate, 2008); Schmitz, *The Gift: Creation*; idem, *The Texture of Being*; R. Sokolowski, *The God of Faith and Reason*; idem, *Eucharistic Presence*.

2 Augustine, *De trinitate* V.16f.

3 Aquinas, *Compendium of Theology* I.68.

4 R. Sokolowski, 'Creation and Christian Understanding', in Burrell and McGinn, ed., *God and Creation*, p. 179.

5 Aquinas, *Summa theologiae* Ia.2 prologue.

6 Aquinas, *Summa theologiae* Ia.44 prologue (translation from Fathers of the English Dominican Province [London: Burns, Oates and Washbourne, 1921]).

7 Aquinas, *Summa Contra Gentiles* II.4.5.

8 Aquinas, *Scriptum super Sententiis* bk. I, d. 14, q. 1, a. 1.

9 Braine, *The Reality of Time and the Existence of God*, p. 353.

10 Aquinas, *Summa theologiae* Ia.4.3 ad 2; cf. *De potentia* VIII.8 ad 2.

11 Aquinas, *Summa theologiae* Ia.45.1 resp.

12 J. Levenson, *Creation and the Persistence of Evil. The Jewish Drama of Divine Omnipotence* (Princeton: Princeton University Press, 1994), p. xvi.

13 Aquinas, *Summa Contra Gentiles* II.16.3.

14 Aquinas, *Summa Contra Gentiles* II.16.5.

15 Aquinas, *Summa theologiae* Ia.45.2 resp.

16 D. Burrell, 'Act of Creation with its Theological Consequences', in T. G. Weinandy, et al., *Aquinas on Doctrine*, p. 39.

17 K. L. Schmitz, *The Texture of Being*, pp. 122f.

18 quinas, *Summa theologiae* Ia.45.3 ad 1.

19 *De potentia* I.1 resp, translation altered.

20 Aquinas, *Summa theologiae* Ia.1.9 resp.

21 Aquinas, *Summa theologiae* Ia.1.9 obj. 2.

22 Aquinas, *Summa theologiae* Ia.1.9 ad 2.

23 Aquinas, *Summa theologiae* Ia.1.9 ad 2.

24 Aquinas, *De potentia* VII.9 resp.

25 Aquinas, *De potentia* VIII.1 obj. 9.

26 Aquinas, *De potentia* VIII.1 ad 9.

27 Aquinas, *De potentia* VII.11 resp.; cf. *De veritate* IV.5 resp.

28 Aquinas, *De potentia* I.1 ad 10; cf. *Summa Contra Gentiles* II.13.4; *De veritate* IV.5 resp.

29 *De potentia* VII.10 s.c.

30 *De potentia* VII.10 resp.

31 *De potentia* VII.10 resp.

32 Henninger, 'Aquinas on the Ontological Status of Relations', p. 512.

33 *De potentia* VII.10 resp.

34 *De potentia* VII.10 resp.

35 *De potentia* VII.10 resp.; cf. *Summa theologiae* Ia.13.7 resp.

36 *Summa Contra Gentiles* II.13.5.

37 *De potentia* IV.2 ad 5.

38 *De potentia* IV.2 ad 5; cf. *Summa theologiae* Ia.73.2.

39 *De potentia* IV.2 ad 5.

40 C. Hartshorne, *The Divine Relativity* (New Haven: Yale University Press, 1948), p. 17.

41 Aquinas, *De potentia* VII.8 ad 2.

42 Aquinas, *De potentia* VII.8 resp.

6

'It was the will of the Lord to bruise him': Soteriology and the doctrine of God

EDITOR'S INTRODUCTION

John Webster sought to address soteriology in light of biblical teaching, which meant with an appropriate sense of its breadth, particular emphases and connections to other doctrines. For him, 'biblical reasoning' takes the form not simply of cherry-picking your doctrine from spots in Scripture but in attending to the whole counsel of God. Here also he identifies some fundamental missteps plaguing much modern theology, wherein soteriology became central or fundamental and in so doing constricted or narrowed the scope of Christian teaching. Just as Trinitarian theology in modernity has often slanted sharply towards an exclusive focus on the economy of God's works, so soteriology has frequently played a leading role in that fixation on the economy. Such an approach offers purportedly powerful benefits to pastoral theology. 'Only the suffering God can help' has become a watchword in much recent theology.

This essay, contrariwise, lays out Webster's account of the gospel: 'The matter of the Christian gospel is, first, the eternal God who has life in himself, and then temporal creatures who have life in him … So conceived, soteriology pervades the entire corpus of Christian teaching, and its exposition necessarily entails sustained attention to Trinitarian and incarnational dogma as well as to the theology of creatures and their ends.' Webster begins by enumerating four principles for thinking about the gospel in a mode of what he repeatedly calls 'biblical reasoning':

- 'order its presentation of the material with a firm eye on the dramatic sequence of the biblical economy of salvation, both in the larger plot of covenantal history and in the concentrated episode of the work of the Word incarnate;'

- 'acknowledge the priority of biblical concepts and titles;'
- 'allow itself only such conceptual inventiveness and argumentative reordering of this material as serves to direct us to the biblical *positum*;'
- 'be cautious about ordering its material around some theme ... or as a response to a perceived problem.'

These four principles apply his broader programmatic method to the question of soteriology specifically. This essay, however, focuses upon a specific question regarding how we honour the First Commandment as what Barth called an 'axiom' for theology or what Wolfhart Pannenberg said exercises a 'claim' upon all theology. How do we avoid idolatry *here* in speaking of salvation? To that end, the essay reflects on the place of soteriology in systematic theology, on the relationship of the doctrine of the Trinity to salvation (particularly as developed around the concepts of divine processions and divine missions) and, finally, with a brief conclusion regarding the 'human history of the Saviour'. Along the way Webster draws at length upon Jonathan Edwards and Thomas Aquinas, not infrequently turning to Calvin as well. In this published version he compressed material from an earlier oral version of this essay that turned also to address as a parallel concept the covenant of redemption as developed in the federal dogmatics of the post-Reformation Reformed orthodox. He plainly does not shirk the covenant concept, for he still cites Edwards on the subject, but it does not play the larger, parallel role to the (more overtly Thomistic) material on divine processions and missions.

A range of soteriological issues go unexplored in Webster's writings: double predestination (towards which he offered a brief affirmation in a 2009 Q & A at Covenant College), sacrifice, the order of salvation's application to particular persons and so on. Much exegetical work no doubt remained unexpressed, if not underdeveloped. This essay gives a representative and brilliant taste of what he did write on the matter: concerned regarding its order and principles, attentive to its call to be biblical reasoning, a sense of calm about trends and problems in light of the great matter which Scripture itself portrays and the terms it provides and ultimately a concern here also to root what happens in the variegated history of redemption not merely in the doctrine of creation but, first and foremost, in the doctrine of the triune God's own life. Whether he was writing on Holy Scripture or salvation, then, Webster was reminding his readers always to be thinking first of what this or that matter says of God, how it flows from God's singular life, what connections can be traced from the triune perfection to a particular work of that triune God of the gospel.

Modern theologians have tended to relate the doctrine of God and soteriology in a rather direct manner. God comes near, enters into our plight and suffers; in its most vivid forms, God is the 'Crucified God' (Moltmann). Webster offers a counterproposal that does not shirk from speaking first and foremost of the character of God but does so in a wholly different light, namely, in light of God's perfection and fullness in and of himself. To honour the first commandment as a theological axiom, then, takes the form of thinking from the inner life and glory of God towards its expression in the varied works of God, not least in the mercy shown to sinners in the sending of the incarnate Son.

Suggested readings

'Gospel', in K. J. Vanhoozer, ed., *Dictionary for Theological Interpretation of the Bible* (London: SPCK; Grand Rapids, MI: Baker, 2005), pp. 263–4.

'*Rector et iudex super omnia genera doctrinarum*? The place of the doctrine of justification', in M. Weinrich, J. P. Burgess (ed.), *What Is Justification about? Reformed Contributions to an Ecumenical Theme* (Grand Rapids, MI: Eerdmans, 2009), pp. 35–56; repr. in GWM 1: 159–76.

'What is the Gospel?' in T. Bradshaw (ed.), *Grace and Truth in the Secular Age* (Grand Rapids, MI: Eerdmans, 1998), pp. 109–18.

'What's Evangelical about Evangelical Soteriology?', in J. G. Stackhouse (ed.), *What Does It Mean to Be Saved? Expanding Evangelical Horizons of Salvation* (Grand Rapids, MI: Baker, 2002), pp. 179–84.

Ivor Davidson, 'Salvation', in Michael Allen and R. David Nelson (eds), *A Companion to the Theology of John Webster* (Grand Rapids, MI: Eerdmans, forthcoming).

'IT WAS THE WILL OF THE LORD TO BRUISE HIM': SOTERIOLOGY AND THE DOCTRINE OF GOD

I

The chief task of Christian soteriology is to show how the bruising of the man Jesus, the servant of God, saves lost creatures and reconciles them to their creator. In the matter of salvation, Christian theology tries to show that this servant – marred, Isaiah tells us, beyond human semblance, without form or comeliness or beauty – is the one in and as whom God's purpose for creatures triumphs over their wickedness. His oppression and affliction, his being put out of the land of the living, is in truth not his defeat at the hands of superior forces, but his own divine act in which he takes upon himself, and so takes away from us, the iniquity of us all. How can this be? How can his chastisement make us whole? How can others be healed by his stripes? Because, Isaiah tells us, it was the will of the Lord to bruise him; because God has put him to grief; because it is God who makes the servant's soul an offering for sin. And just because this is so – just because he is smitten by God and afflicted – then the will of the Lord shall prosper in his hand, and the servant himself shall prosper and be exalted. And not only this: the servant shall also see the fruit of the travail of his soul and be satisfied; he shall see his offspring.

As it tries to explicate how God is savingly at work in the affliction of his servant, Christian soteriology stretches both backwards and forwards from this central event.[*] It traces the work of salvation back into the will of God, and forward into the life of the many who by it are made righteous. Soteriology thus participates in the double theme of all Christian theology, namely God and all things in God. The matter of the Christian gospel is, first, the eternal God who has life in himself, and then temporal creatures who have life in him. The gospel, that is, concerns the history of fellowship – covenant – between God and creatures; Christian soteriology follows this double theme as it is unfolded in time. In following its theme, soteriology undertakes the task of displaying the identities of those who participate in this history and the material order of their relations. The Lord who puts his servant to grief is this one, dogmatics tells us; this is his servant, these the transgressors who will be accounted righteous.

---

[*]Reference has been made several times already to the need to move backwards and forwards from the incarnational narratives to the pre-existence and post-existence, respectively, of the divine Son, so as to avoid any distortions that come in by way of narrowing or reducing the Christological material. The temptation is great, especially because the incarnational narrative can seem so much more accessible via historical inquiry.

So conceived, soteriology pervades the entire corpus of Christian teaching, and its exposition necessarily entails sustained attention to trinitarian and incarnational dogma, as well as to the theology of creatures and their ends. Indeed, no part of Christian teaching is unrelated to soteriology, whether immediately or indirectly. This does not mean that all other Christian teaching can be resolved into soteriology, or that other teaching is to be arranged around soteriology as its centre. Quite the contrary: making some variant of soteriology (such as the theology of the cross, or justification) into the *rector et iudex super omnia genera doctrinarum* distorts the order and proportions of Christian dogmatics. Soteriology is a derivative doctrine, and no derivative doctrine may occupy the material place which is properly reserved for the Christian doctrine of God, from which alone all other doctrines derive. The question from which soteriology takes its rise, and which accompanies each particular soteriological statement is: *Quis sit deus?*

The answer which dogmatic soteriology gives to that question takes the form of an exercise in biblical reasoning. Biblical reasoning is the analytical and schematic presentation of the Christian gospel as it is announced in Holy Scripture. Dogmatics is a work of reason which is set in motion by, and at every point answerable to, the self-communicative presence and action of God the Lord; it operates in the sphere of God's rule, in particular, that rule exercised in the work of revelation. Dogmatic soteriology can, therefore, only be undertaken as attentiveness to the instruction of God in the gospel, the 'word of reconciliation' (2 Cor. 5.19). Further, attending to this reconciling instruction requires that reason itself be reconciled to God, for in the aftermath of the fall reason has lost its way, becoming estranged from and hostile towards God (Col. 1.21). If it is to discharge its office, therefore, reason must acquire renewed pliability and consent to God, teachableness. In practical terms, this means that as an exercise of theological reason soteriology is at every point directed to the prophetic and apostolic testimonies of Scripture, since they are the sanctified creaturely auxiliaries of God's revealing and reconciling presence.[*] Through their ministry, God addresses and quickens. This is why soteriology is *repetitio Sacrae Scripturae*.[1]

How does this conception of the task of soteriology govern the way in which it goes about its work? First, it presses soteriology to order its presentation of the material with a firm eye on the dramatic sequence of the biblical economy of salvation, both in the larger plot of covenantal history and in the concentrated episode of the work of the Word incarnate.[2] Second, soteriology will acknowledge the priority of biblical concepts and titles, drawing upon them as the normative prophetic and apostolic stock of language and ideas which constitute the governing material content of dogmatic reflection. Third, soteriology will allow itself only such conceptual inventiveness and argumentative reordering of this material as serves to direct us

---

[*]This paragraph compresses much of the argument of the earlier chapter, 'Biblical Reasoning'.

to the biblical *positum* – by, for example, drawing attention to features of biblical economy through conceptual summary, or by setting forth the identities of the agents in that economy. Fourth, accordingly, soteriology will be cautious about ordering its material around some theme (such as 'facing'[3] or 'hospitality'[4]), or as a response to a perceived problem (such as violence[5]). Thematic or problem-oriented presentations are commonly nominalist and moralistic, since their centre of gravity lies, not in the irreducible person and work of God but rather in some human experience or action of which theological talk of salvation is symbolic. Soteriology must fall under the rule which governs all dogmatic work, namely 'the claim of the First Commandment'.[6] To speak of dogmatic soteriology as biblical reasoning is to press home the noetic application of that claim.

But what of the material extension of the first commandment – that the doctrine of God precedes and governs all other Christian teaching? What follows is given over to reflecting on this matter, the argument proceeding in three stages. (1) A sketch of the setting of soteriology in the corpus of Christian doctrine is offered; this is followed by (2) an analysis of the subordination of soteriology to the doctrine of the Trinity, and especially to teaching about the processions and missions of God's eternal and living fullness, and about the eternal purpose of God; (3) a brief concluding note on the human history of the Saviour. The argument in its entirety is to be regarded as no more than an extended gloss on a statement of Aquinas: 'knowledge of the divine persons was necessary for us . . . so that we may have the right view of the salvation of humankind, accomplished by the incarnate Son and by the gift of the Holy Spirit.'[7] Only on this basis, I suggest, can we understand why it is good and wholesome to confess that 'it was the will of the Lord to bruise him' (Is. 53.10).

II

The bedrock of soteriology is the doctrine of the Trinity. The perfect life of the Holy Trinity is the all-encompassing and first reality from whose completeness all else derives. God's perfection is the fullness and inexhaustibility in which the triune God is and acts as the one he is. His perfection is not mere absence of derivation or restriction; it is his positive plenitude. God's perfection is his identity as *this one*, an identity which is unqualified and wholly realized: 'I am who I am' – what the scholastic divines called the *perfectio integralis* in which God's life is complete in itself. That completeness is fullness of *life*, the effortless activity in which God confirms his excellence as Father, Son and Spirit. God *lives* from himself, he is perfect movement, the eternally fresh act of self-iteration. This act is the 'processions' or personal relations which constitute God's absolute vitality: the Father who begets the Son and breathes the Spirit, the Son who is eternally begotten, the Spirit who proceeds – all this is the positive wholeness and richness of God's life in himself.

God's boundless immanent life is the ground of his communication of life. God lives in himself and gives life. He is not locked up in his aseity; his blessedness is not self-absorbed, for alongside the immanent personal works of God's self-relation there are God's external works in which of his own will he brings into being life other than his own, the life of creatures. He does so graciously, without compromise of his own freedom; he is not constituted or completed by the works of his hands, since as their creator he transcends them absolutely. And he does so lovingly, bestowing genuine life upon all that he makes and ennobling the human creature by appointing it for fellowship with himself.

In his free and loving act of creation, God gives to creatures their several natures and ends. To be a creature is to have a nature, to be a determinate reality having its being as *this*. And to have a nature is to be appointed to a history in which that nature is perfected. In the case of human creatures, the enactment of nature through time involves consent, that is, conscious, willing and active affirmation of nature. Human creatureliness involves (though it is not exhausted in) spontaneity. Beasts give no consent to their nature and end; human creatures do so, and their consent is necessary for the completion on the creaturely side of the fellowship with God for which their nature determines them.

These summary references to the doctrines of God and creation form the deep background to the economy of God's saving works, helping us to identify the agents in that economy. This, according to dogmatics, is what goes on in created time: the high and eternal God who is life in himself gives life to creatures. Against this background, what is to be said of the divine work of salvation?

Creatureliness is basic to being human. The nature and end granted by God the creator, and the consent in which they are enacted, are what it is to be human. Human being is being in fellowship, human history is the enactment of that being towards perfection. It is, however, inexplicably the case that creatures resist and repudiate their given nature and end, and refuse to participate in fellowship with God. Sin is trespass against creatureliness, but beneath that lies an even deeper wickedness, contempt for the creator in all its forms – pride, resentment, disordered desire, anxiety, self-hatred, a catastrophic regime of evil which the creature unleashes by creating a nature for itself and assuming responsibility for its own course. By sin the creature is brought to ruin, for as fellowship with God is breached, the creature is estranged from the source of its life and condemned to exist in death's shadow. Sin humiliates the creature, robbing the creature of the dignity which it can have only as it fulfils its destiny for fellowship with God.

What stands between the creature and death? What secures the fulfilment of creaturely being against self-destruction? This is the subject matter of soteriology. Creaturely defiance and self-alienation from God cannot overtake the creator's purpose; God will confirm his own glory by glorifying the creature. The form in which God realizes this determination is a special creaturely history, a particular history which represents and gathers into itself all others. This is the history of divine election and of the covenant to which it gives rise – the history of God's determination of creatures for fellowship on the sole basis of his mercy. In it, God undertakes to bring human nature to perfection in accordance with his purpose. Its human subjects are the patriarchs, Israel and the church, that is, all who stand beneath God's promise and summons. At its centre lies the time of the Word made flesh. He enacts the covenant fidelity of God; as this one, God stands by his creature, and puts an end to its distress. And he does so, moreover, in the face of the creature's contradiction of his fidelity. Faced by its Lord and reconciler, the creature consummates its hatred of God and of itself in an act of staggering wickedness: 'You killed the Author of life' (Acts 3.15). The slaying of God's Son and servant is an undisguised attack on the one by whom he is sent, namely the life-giver himself – made even more base by the fact that 'you asked for a murderer to be granted to you' (Acts 3.14). If the wickedness is staggering, so is the absurdity: how can the creature who has no life in itself extinguish the one who is life's ἀρχηγός? The Son's death is comprehended within the life-giving purpose of the Father, and by it the wicked creature is turned back to God and blessed (Acts 3.26). In the Son's death there takes place the death of death. The Author of life having demonstrated himself to be the one he is – life's *Author*, majestically and limitlessly alive – God's special history with creatures lies open at its further side, expanding and annexing to itself creaturely history. Through the Holy Spirit, creaturely history is directed to fulfilment; the covenant determination: 'I will be your God' is now fulfilled as the Spirit generates its creaturely correspondent: 'You shall be my people'.

Such, in brief compass, is one possible construal of the overall shape of Christian soteriology. It is structured as three moments or loci: the eternal purpose of the perfect God; the establishment of that purpose in the history which culminates in the ministry of the incarnate Son; and the consummation of that purpose in the Spirit. A soteriology will only attain the necessary scope if it attends to all three moments in their integrity and due order. In modern Protestant divinity, the first and third moments were routinely eclipsed, the first often replaced by an abstract theology of divine love, the third by moral or hermeneutical theory. Recent work has done much to correct this latter deficiency, notably in linking soteriology to pneumatology, thereby easing a constrictive focus simply on the passion. But we still await a soteriology in which the first article plays more than a negligible role.[*] Reasons for the neglect lie ready to hand: the dominance of the 'economic' in much contemporary trinitarian dogmatics; hesitancy about the metaphysics of God *in se*;

---

[*]This need for a beginning with the first article – with God in and of himself, in his eternal triune life – stands against tendencies to simply begin with economy or history. It involves a demand for contemplation, not merely narration; for knowing God, not merely his divine works; for looking beneath the surface, not merely attending to the manifestations of divine presence.

functionalist readings of the biblical materials; the high profile enjoyed by Lutheran rather than Reformed incarnational teaching. Left unchecked, these tendencies can promote a soteriology in which the foundations of salvation in the will of the Lord remain inadequately articulated. What may be suggested by way of a remedy?

III

The salvation of creatures is a great affair, but not the greatest, which is God's majesty and its promulgation. 'He saved them for his name's sake,' the psalmist tells us, 'that he might make known his mighty power' (Ps. 106.8). Salvation occurs as part of the divine self-exposition; its final end is the reiteration of God's majesty and the glorification of God by all creatures. Soteriology therefore has its place within the theology of the *mysterium trinitatis*, that is, God's inherent and communicated richness of life as Father, Son and Holy Spirit.

That soteriology has a trinitarian shape is relatively uncontroversial, at least in the more recent literature.[8] So, for example, Christoph Schwöbel argues that 'the doctrine of the Trinity makes explicit the identity of the God of the Christian faith';[9] it is the 'conceptual explication of the *understanding of God* contained within the *relation* to God of Christian faith'.[10] In soteriological terms, this means, first, that the doctrine of the Trinity furnishes an identity-description of the agent of salvation, upon which a definition of salvation depends: 'The character of that which is believed, experienced and expected as "salvation" can only be determined precisely by referring to the identity of the God who is believed in and worshipped as the subject of the activity which brings about salvation.'[11] And, second, trinitarian teaching holds together creation, salvation and eschatological perfection by grounding them in 'the unity of the trinitarian being of God'.[12] The doctrine of the Trinity thus blocks soteriological nominalism and the isolation of teaching about salvation from the other loci of dogmatics.

Yet more is required for an adequate theology of salvation. Working towards the doctrine of the Trinity by retrospection from the divine economy of salvation is certainly possible; but it may leave obscure the antecedent conditions of that economy in the life of God *in se*. If we only look at the saving economy as it were from the angle of its temporal occurrence, we may mischaracterize the kind of temporal occurrence which it is. The economy of salvation is the long history of the works of God, ingredient within the mystery of the Trinity. 'Mystery' (Eph. 1.9f.) is God's self-disclosing act in which he sets forth his will; it emerges from and is fully charged with his unfathomable prevenient purpose. 'Mystery' is revelation in time, a 'making known'; but its energy is from 'before the foundation of the world'; and it takes temporal form under pressure from 'the counsel of his will'. Salvation-history is thus special history, reaching back into the immanent life of the triune God.

Aquinas again: 'Without faith in the Trinity it is not possible to believe explicitly in the mystery of Christ's incarnation; the mystery of the incarnation of Christ includes that the Son of God took flesh, that he redeemed the world through the grace of the Holy Spirit, and that he was conceived of the Holy Spirit.'[13] The renewal of the world by Christ and the Spirit – the fact that, as Aquinas puts it, we now live *post tempus gratiae divulgatae*, after the revelation of grace – means that 'all are bound to believe the mystery of the Trinity explicitly'.[14] And for Aquinas that means confessing not only the trinitarian contours of God's action in the economy, but also the antecedent personal relations within the Godhead which bear up the visible missions of Son and Spirit.[*]

If this is so, then soteriology – figuring out what happens when the servant is put to grief by the Lord – requires a theological metaphysics of God *in se*; only within the setting of God's own life in its glorious self-sufficiency can the history of salvation be seen as divulging divine grace to us. Few theologians in the tradition saw this with greater penetration than Jonathan Edwards. A celebrated sermon from 1730, 'God Glorified in Man's Dependence' expounds 'what God aims at in the disposition of things in the affair of redemption, viz., that man should not glory in himself, but alone in God'.[15] 'There is an absolute and universal dependence of the redeemed on God.'[16] Which God? The Father, the Son and the Holy Spirit: 'that [God] be the cause and original whence all our good comes, thereon it is *of* him; that he be the medium by which is obtained and conveyed, therein they have it *through* him; and that he be that good itself that is given and conveyed, therein it is *in* him.'[17] In this, of course, Edwards echoes ancient tradition:[18] 'There is an absolute dependence of the creature on every one [of the triune persons] for all: all is *of* the Father, all *through* the Son, and all *in* the Holy Ghost. Thus God appears in the work of redemption, as all in all'.[19] And, crucially, that God does so appear is rooted in what Edwards elsewhere calls the 'eternal and necessary subsistence of the persons of the Trinity.'[20] The ground of salvation is the internal works of God.

Yet we should not let this train of thought pass without pausing to note a worry which it might evoke. Does not this talk of God *in se*, of the antecedent purpose of God, of God's eternal and necessary subsistence, quickly regress into metaphysics uncorrected by the gospel drama? Does it not fold the economy of God's works – above all, the agony of the cross – back into pretemporality, in such a way that the economy lacks any *constitutive* significance, as if we were saved by a divine plan rather than by its enactment? Do not Jesus and his death threaten to disappear? The objection has been raised on a number of occasions by Robert Jenson, who argues

---

[*]This paragraph parses two rather different ways of being 'trinitarian': one, a serious focus upon the triune economy as being understood in its breadth only by tending to all three persons and their unified action; the other, pursuing that concern only as it has also probed the depths of that economy by first tending to God's own perfection in himself and in his triune happiness (against which only may the economy be prized as truly free and gracious).

(with characteristic boldness) that formulations of atonement theory commonly assume that the saving power of Jesus's death somehow lies behind the event itself with which it is not wholly identical. Jenson, by contrast, denies any such antecedents: 'The Gospels tell a powerful and biblically integrated story of the Crucifixion; this story *is* just so the story of God's act to bring us back to himself at his own cost, and of our being brought back. There is no story behind or beyond it that is the real story of what God does to reconcile us, no story of mythic battles or of a deal between God and his Son or of our being moved to live reconciled lives. The Gospel's passion narrative is the authentic and entire account of God's reconciling action and our reconciliation, as events in his life and ours. Therefore what is first and principally required as the Crucifixion's right interpretation is for us to tell this story to one another and to God as a story about him and about ourselves.'[21] This is why he can elsewhere speak of 'reconciliation in God':[22] God's life *is* the evangelical drama, and the economy of reconciliation is, we might say, groundless.

By way of response: To say that God's eternity undergirds the history of God's servant is to specify that history's origin, character and end; it is not to reduce it to a mere illustration of metaphysical objects, or to neglect its covenantal or relational structure,[23] or to translate moral drama into ontology.[24] The history of salvation is divinely willed history; it is preceded and enclosed by the great statement of God's eternal fullness: 'In the beginning . . .'; it is necessary history, history of which we can only say: 'it must be so' (δεῖ). Atonement, Barth wrote, is not a contingent event which might have turned out differently, but 'a necessary happening'[25] because its central agent, Jesus Christ, is 'very God and very man, born and living and acting and suffering and conquering in time', and 'as such the one eternal Word of God at the beginning of all things.'[26] To read the canonical Gospels is to read a history which is accidental only at its surface; the tensions of the whole, and of each incident in the whole, are pushed along by 'the divine "must"'.[27] If this is the case, then no small part of any soteriology will be the exhibition of the divine necessity by which the economy is ordered. Calvin was correct to indicate that the task of the theology of salvation is to ask about 'the purpose for which Christ was sent by the Father, and what he conferred upon us':[28] soteriology concerns a history and its effects. Dogmatics answers those questions about the purpose and blessings of God's saving work in time precisely by exploring that work's 'divine connection'.[29]

This does not entail that, in its actual presentation of its subject, soteriology must start from the dogmatics of the immanent Trinity. It would be quite possible to begin at some other point – with the fall and sin, or the cross, or the risen and exalted Christ. What matters is not starting-point but scope, scale and distribution of weight.* In any given set of circumstances a theologian might judge it more prudent to start from

---

*A common observation is made again here: the order of teaching or instruction may vary (based on circumstance), but the order of being or material order needs to be honoured in all such circumstances.

(for example) grace as benefit rather than from the divine counsel. Provided that the full range of material is covered, without disproportion or distortion, and provided also that the *material* order is recognized even when the order of exposition may run in a different direction, method is arbitrary. Further, soteriology must always remind itself that the conceptual idiom and order of dogmatics is subservient to the idiom and order of Holy Scripture. The primary task of theology is commentary on the prophetic and apostolic texts, and its dogmatic-metaphysical explorations have little purpose if they do not serve this undertaking.

In a theological culture such as our own, which instinctively conflates being and time, the proportions of gospel soteriology are best displayed by drawing attention to God *in se*. This is necessary; but it is not sufficient, and soteriology requires for its completion a spacious exposition of the history of the covenant – a joyful and demanding task which cannot be attempted here. Instead, I restrict myself to exhibiting how, correctly made, the distinction and ordered relation of created and uncreated being is soteriologically fundamental. '[I]n the teaching of faith,' Aquinas tells us, 'the consideration of God comes first, that of creatures afterwards. And thus the doctrine of faith is more perfect . . .'[30]

IV

The principle of God's saving acts in the missions of the Son and the Spirit is the eternal divine processions. 'Processions' and 'missions' are formal terms to characterize God's being as being in relation. Taken together, they signify that the relations between Father, Son and Spirit which constitute God's eternal life in himself are the spring of his relations with the creatures whom he elects as his companions in the covenant of grace, and whom he saves and perfects through Christ and the Spirit.

The divine processions are the eternal relations of origin in which God's perfect life consists; in them he confirms his self-existent self-sufficiency. The Father begets the Son, God from God; God *is* this perfectly enacted paternity and filiation. And, further, God is perfect as the Father and Son who together breathe the Spirit, and so as the Spirit who proceeds from them. Paternity, filiation and spiration are the life-filled abundance of God's being, his pure act in which he is who he is. To speak of these as relations of *origin* is not, of course, to refer to events in the past, for they are eternal relations and not completed acts of self-constitution. The Son is the Son, not because he *has been* originated by the Father's paternal act, but because God *is* eternally the relation of paternity and filiation. Nor does the language of origin indicate any subordination within the triune life. Between the persons of the Trinity there is 'priority of subsistence':[31] the Father is the fount of the life of the Godhead, the one from whom Son and Spirit proceed, but who is himself *a nemine*, from no one. But there is no ontological disparity here; there is 'dependence without inferiority of deity',[32] and so no 'natural subjection'.[33] God's unified, singular and wholly realized life is these relations; they are not as it were the process by which God becomes God; neither God's unity nor his personal differentiation precedes them. These relations are what God is; the processions are the infinitely mobile, wholly achieved life of God; they constitute what Edwards calls 'the economy of the persons of the Trinity',[34] the inner order in which God lives and to which the external economy of God's works is anchored.

The divine missions are the further movement of God's being in which he relates to what he freely creates to be other than himself. In the context of soteriology, missions refer to the Father's sending of the Son, the Son's fulfilment of his office as reconciler, and the Spirit's being sent to sanctify and perfect creatures. These missions repeat *ad extra* the relations *ad intra* (hence they can be called 'temporal processions'). In speaking of the divine missions, we are, crucially, still in the sphere of God's perfect life, his uncreated movement; but we look at it as it were from a vantage point in which our eye is trained on that divine movement as it draws near to creatures. The mission of each person is constituted, first, by the eternal procession of the person (the person's orientation to the sender or origin), and, second, by the person's orientation to the one to whom that person is sent (the mission's destination). Again, 'sending' implies no inequality of status between 'sender' and 'sent'; it simply indicates the mode in which each person enjoys full deity in its outward movement. The divine missions are thus the pure divine energy of God's self-giving, the fact that his self-communicative and saving presence to creatures has its ground in God's very self.

Hence the rule: the divine missions follow the divine processions. This means, first, that the works of God repeat the immanent being of God and are 'agreeable to the order of their subsisting'.[35] It means, second, that the engagement of each person in its mission is not a 'becoming' on the part of the one sent, in the sense of an expansion of identity: the Son, for example, is not more Son by virtue of his obedience to the Father's appointment of him to the office of redeemer.[36] The divine missions are already anticipated, included within the life of relations which is God's being. The realm of the divine missions is not contingent or mutable, for they rest on God's unchangeable completeness. But, third, the processions cannot be segregated from the missions. The 'origin' of each person is not a mere *whence*, but a whence which includes a *whither*. Filiation and sending, spiration and outpouring, are inseparable. Because God is *this one*, we are not required to choose between a-historical essentialism (which isolates the processions) and the constitution of God's being as a temporal project (which isolates the missions).[37] Origin is not divine self-absorption; mission is not divine self-completion.

The technicalities are soteriologically charged. Using concepts to apprehend the mystery of the Trinity which the drama of salvation sets before us, they attempt to describe the history of saving fellowship by exhibiting its divine depth, the conditions of its occurrence which lie in the infinite recess of God's very self. The conceptual apparatus is not a speculative replacement for that history, as if the latter were a mere shadow cast by a high metaphysical object: how could incarnation and passion be grasped without reference to their peculiar creaturely-historical intensity? Rather, the theological metaphysics functions a bit like the Johannine Prologue: this is where saving history is *from*, it says, it is from this that saving history is suspended, this is its divine agent, this its inexhaustible inner saving power.

Why is this imperative in the theology of salvation? Because what happens in the Son's work of redemption and the Spirit's gift of life is – in a lovely phrase of Gilles Emery's – 'an embassy of the eternal, bringing a part of its home country into our history'.[38] What we encounter with concentrated historical force in Son and Spirit is the reality in time of a divine movement of sending which is itself the repetition of God's self. Saving history emerges from and points us back towards God's entire adequacy. Here, at least, the adage *quae supra nos nihil ad nos* is untrue. The hidden life of God – precisely in its inaccessibility and completeness – is the ground of creaturely well-being. It is because of the divine processions and the missions which rest upon them that there is a creature, and a servant of God to come to that creature's aid, and a Spirit to bestow life.

The trinitarian setting of a doctrine of salvation thus has much to do with the matter of assurance. Salvation is secure because the works of the redeemer and the sanctifier can be traced to the inner life of God, behind which there lies nothing.[*] And so for Calvin, trinitarian doctrine locates the source of salvation in God, thereby eradicating fear. Commenting on the phrase 'God sent his Son' in 1 John 4.10, he writes: 'it was from God's mere goodness, as from a fountain, that Christ flowed to us with all his blessings. And just as it is necessary to know that we have salvation in Christ because our heavenly Father has loved us of his own accord, so when we are seeking a solid and complete certainty of the divine love, we have to look to none other than to Christ'.[39] The waste and deprivation of sin is countered by God's own self which overflows in abundance. 'The secret love in which our heavenly Father embraced us to himself is, since it flows from his eternal good pleasure, precedent to all other causes'.[40] This is why the servant has prospered; this is why he is authorized and able to bear our griefs and carry our sorrows.

V

So far my concern has been to trace the *backward* reference of soteriology, its indication of the infinite divine milieu which encompasses salvation's temporal occurrence. But, however necessary this indication, it does not exhaust the task of a theology of salvation. Having set forth its all-important first principles, soteriology

---

[*]Because the economy is not arbitrary but a fitting expression of the inner processions in the outer divine missions, the saving acts of the economy can be trusted in all circumstances. Trinitarian contemplation serves to give substance to Christian assurance.

moves to presentation of the economy of salvation as it unfurls itself through time: because there are the processions and missions, then a creaturely history unfolds. This history is *of God*; and what is of God really is *this history*, the human history of the Saviour. By way of conclusion, we may consider briefly this second element.

One of the functions of trinitarian teaching in soteriology is to instruct us in how to read rightly the evangelical narratives of the Saviour, by specifying the identity of their active subject. Trinitarian doctrine shows who indeed it is that bears our griefs, whose chastisement it is that makes us whole. To say that external saving history is just that – 'external', a sequence of acts and sufferings referring back to the infinite, groundless life of God in his inner relations – is not to reduce saving history to a mirage, but simply to indicate what takes place in that history. To contemplate the principles of the history of salvation in the divine processions and missions is to attempt conceptual penetration of the Saviour's evangelical ministry and self-announcement: 'I am the living bread which came down from heaven; if any one eats of this bread, he will live for ever; and the bread which I shall give for the life of the world is my flesh' (John 6.51).

Teaching about the Trinity thus clarifies what *kind* of human history is 'of God': 'flesh', certainly and inescapably, because this is what the eternal Word unreservedly *became*. Yet 'becoming' indicates a relation of Word to flesh which is not simple identity, and this particular mode of relation (in which the Word is not exhausted in his act of self-identification in the historical activity of Jesus of Nazareth) is fundamental to the Saviour's temporal identity. Jesus's human history is the taking place of a 'descent from heaven', a giving of living bread, the enactment and manifestation of the divine ἐγώ εἰμι. Certainly a full soteriology would be impossibly idealist without a presentation of the human history of the Saviour. But such a presentation could not proceed as if Jesus's human history were in some straightforward way comparable with our own and narratable as such; it would need, rather, to exhibit the special character of that history, the mystery of its occurrence at the intersection of created time and divine eternity. Jesus's history is incomparably and irreducibly strange,[*] and the strangeness (as Donald MacKinnon put it in a searching essay) 'may be judged rooted in, and expressive of, the way in which he lived uniquely on the frontier of the familiar and the transcendent, the relative and the absolute'.[41]

The human history of Jesus *is* the divulgence in time of divine grace. Yet if the force of 'is' there is properly to be seized, considerable restraint is needed: the human history of Jesus may not be allowed to become *in and of itself* soteriologically primitive or constitutive.[42] Certainly, the humanity of the Saviour – his living of this

---

[*]Whereas narrative expression may tempt because it seems transparent and comparable to our own human social and psychological experience, this language about metaphysics of the incarnation is meant to remind us that the incarnational events are, in point of fact, 'strange' and thus anything but transparent. There is revelation here, but it is overwhelming, singular and, as such, remains incomprehensible.

human life – is soteriologically indispensable, for only in that way, as Calvin puts it, can we be reassured that Christ is 'comrade and partner in the same nature with us',[43] that there is indeed *naturae societas*, fellowship of nature, between him and us. 'Ungrudgingly he took our nature upon himself to impart to us what was his, and to become both Son of God and Son of man in common with us'.[44] Yet already Calvin's reference there to *Dei filius* shows that Jesus's human history is not a quantity in itself. There is no human history of Jesus *in se*, in abstraction from its enhypostatic[*] relation to the divine Word; the only history of Jesus which there is is the history of the God-man. Jesus's history *is* the Son's mission in the world; the Son's sending is not some additional element, superimposed upon the history of Jesus or concurrent with his 'natural' history as if that history could be considered as at least initially complete in itself without the relation it bears to the eternal Son. Jesus's human history is exhausted in the fact that it is the form of the divine descent into the world, acting out in time (but not, as it were, constituting for the first time) the eternal relation of Father and Son. We can therefore scarcely hope to render the saving human history of the Saviour intelligible without appeal to teaching about Trinity and hypostatic union, by which its reference back to the infinity of God's life is shown; only thus may it be seen as the divine κατάβασις which really does bring life: 'It was his task to swallow up death. Who but life could do this? It was his task to conquer sin. Who but very Righteousness could do this? It was his task to rout the powers of world and air. Who but a power higher than world or air could do this? Now where does life or righteousness, or lordship and authority of heaven lie but with God alone? Therefore, our most merciful God, when he willed that we be redeemed, made himself our Redeemer in the person of his only-begotten Son.'[45]

The special character of Jesus's saving history may be stated by speaking of it as a *commissioned* history, the discharge of an office.[†] This is not to eliminate personal and historical spontaneity, for what is commissioned is precisely a personal history, not an inexorable divine process in which a human life is merely caught up like flotsam. But this personal, historical spontaneity is not that of a lost creature drifting through time, untethered to the divine telos, a mere accumulation of episodes. It is a doing of the works 'which the Father has granted me to accomplish' (John 5.36). The enactment of these works constitutes the office and role of Jesus. But, again, his office and role are not external to his inner person, so that his real identity is somehow anterior to his function. For, like his humanity and divinity, Jesus's 'personal' identity and his 'official' activity are inseparable.[46]

---

[*]The language of '*enhypostatic*' draws on patristic and later post-Reformational Christology where it is affirmed that the human nature of Christ does not ever constitute its own person but lives personally only in the person of the divine Son (thus *en-hypostasis*).
[†]The gospels regularly speak of 'necessity' in ways that go well beyond that of historical or political happenstance. They attest a divine necessity that roots these historical contingencies in an eternal, divine will.

Is it then the case that 'the atoning work of Christ is something which Jesus does as a man towards God?'[47] If the work of the Saviour reinstitutes the covenant between God and creatures from both sides – if he is the high priest of the eternal covenant – then Jesus's human obedience to the will of the Father is intrinsic to the achievement of reconciliation.[48] But a further question must be pressed: is there a man Jesus apart from the being and act of the eternal Word, and so apart from the being and act of God the Father and God the Holy Spirit? Is there a human obedience on the part of the man Jesus which is not a temporal repetition of the Son's active consent to the will of the Father? There is no such one; there is only the human Jesus whose coming is the descent to us of the 'very majesty of God'.[49] And it is as the history of such a one that the human history of the Saviour is to be told: as the accomplishment of the incarnate Son, the servant of God who is exalted and lifted up, and very high.

Notes

1 G. C. Berkouwer, *The Work of Christ* (Grand Rapids: Eerdmans, 1965), p. 10.

2 Commanding examples of this can be found in Aquinas (*Summa theologiae* IIIa.46–52) and Calvin, *Institutes of the Christian Religion* II, especially II.xvi.

3 See D. Ford, *Self and Salvation. Being Transformed* (Cambridge: Cambridge University Press, 1999).

4 See H. Boersma, *Violence, Hospitality and the Cross. Reappropriating the Atonement Tradition* (Grand Rapids: Baker, 2004).

5 From a (repetitive) literature, see T. Gorringe, *God's Just Vengeance. Crime, Violence and the Rhetoric of Salvation* (Cambridge: Cambridge University Press, 1996); J. D. Weaver, *The Nonviolent Atonement* (Grand Rapids: Eerdmans, 2001).

6 W. Pannenberg, *Systematic Theology*, vol. 2, p. 398, n. 1; consequently, Pannenberg notes, soteriology is to be treated 'independently of existing and historically shifting hopes of salvation' (p. 398).

7 *Summa theologiae* Ia.32.1 ad 3; my translation, reading *donum* rather than *dona*.

8 By way of contrast to Richard Swinburne's comment that 'It is possible to discuss redemption without needing to analyse what is meant by the doctrine that God is three persons in one substance' (*Responsibility and Atonement* (Oxford: Clarendon Press, 1989), p. 152), one might consult from the recent literature: V. Brümmer, *Atonement, Christology and the Trinity* (Aldershot: Ashgate, 2005); C. Gunton, *The Actuality of Atonement* (Edinburgh: T&T Clark, 1989), pp. 143–71; idem, 'Atonement: The Sacrifice and the Sacrifices. From Metaphor to Transcendental?', in *Father, Son and Holy Spirit* (London: T&T Clark, 2003), pp. 181–200; M. S. Horton, *Lord and Saviour. A Covenant Christology* (Louisville: WJKP, 2005); R. Jenson, *Systematic Theology*, vol. 1, *The Triune God* (Oxford: Oxford University Press, 1997), pp. 179–93; idem, 'Reconciliation in God', in C. Gunton, ed., *The Theology of Reconciliation* (London: T&T Clark, 2003), pp. 159–66; idem, 'Justification

as Triune Event', *Modern Theology* 11 (1995), pp. 421–7; N. B. MacDonald, *Metaphysics and the God of Israel. Systematic Theology of the Old and New Testaments* (Grand Rapids: Baker, 2006), pp. 225–45; W. Pannenberg, *Systematic Theology* vol. 2, pp. 397–464; C. Schwöbel, 'Die "Botschaft der Versöhnung" (2 Kor. 5,19) und die Versöhnungslehre', in S. Chapman, C. Helmer, C. Landmesser, ed., *Biblischer Texte und theologischer Theoriebildung* (Neukirchen: Neukirchener Verlag, 2001), pp. 163–90; idem, 'Die Trinitätslehre als Rahmentheorie des christlichen Glaubens', in *Gott in Beziehung. Studien zur Dogmatik* (Tübingen: Mohr Siebeck, 2002), pp. 25–51; idem, 'Reconciliation: from Biblical Observations to Dogmatic Reconstruction', in C. Gunton, ed., *The Theology of Reconciliation*, pp. 13–38; R. J. Sherman, *King, Priest and Prophet. A Trinitarian Theology of Atonement* (London: T&T Clark, 2004); A. Spence, *The Promise of Peace. A Unified Theory of Atonement* (London: T&T Clark, 2006).

9   'Die Trinitätslehre als Rahmentheorie des christlichen Glaubens', p. 32.
10 'Die Trinitätslehre als Rahmentheorie des christlichen Glaubens', p. 37.
11 'Die Trinitätslehre als Rahmentheorie des christlichen Glaubens', p. 32.
12 'Die Trinitätslehre als Rahmentheorie des christlichen Glaubens', p. 39; on this, see also C. Gunton, *The Actuality of Atonement*, pp. 143–71.
13 *Summa theologiae* IIaIIae.2.8 resp (my translation).
14 *Summa theologiae* IIaIIae.2.8 resp.
15 J. Edwards, 'God Glorified in Man's Dependence', in *The Works of Jonathan Edwards*, vol. 17, *Sermons and Discourses 1730–1733* (New Haven: Yale University Press, 1999), p. 200.
16 'God Glorified in Man's Dependence', p. 202.
17 'God Glorified in Man's Dependence', p. 202.
18 Basil, *On the Holy Spirit* XVI.38.
19 'God Glorified in Man's Dependence', p. 212.
20 J. Edwards, 'Economy of the Trinity and Covenant of Redemption', in *The Works of Jonathan Edwards*, vol. 20, *The "Miscellanies" 833–1152* (New Haven: Yale University Press, 2002), p. 432.
21 *Systematic Theology*, vol. 1, p. 189.
22 'Reconciliation in God', pp. 159–66.
23 See Horton, *Lord and Servant*, pp. 11–13.
24 See J. Denney, *The Death of Christ* (London: Hodder, 1911), p. 236: 'The Atonement comes to us in the moral world and deals with us there: it is concerned with conscience and the law of God, with sin and grace, with alienation and peace, with death to sin and holiness; it has its being and its efficacy in a world where we can find our footing, and be assured that we are dealing with realities.' But Denney's Ritschlianism betrays itself in his claim that the New Testament is 'ethical, not metaphysical' (p. 237).
25 *Church Dogmatics* IV/1, p. 48.
26 *Church Dogmatics* IV/1, p. 49.
27 Berkouwer, *The Work of Christ*, p. 39.
28 Calvin, *Institutes of the Christian Religion* II.xv.

29 Berkouwer, *The Work of Christ*, p. 40.

30 *Summa Contra Gentiles* II.4.5; on the relation of 'on God' and 'on creatures', see G. Emery, *The Trinitarian Theology of Thomas Aquinas*, pp. 41–3, 413–15.

31 Edwards, 'Economy of the Trinity and Covenant of Redemption', p. 430.

32 Edwards, 'Economy of the Trinity and Covenant of Redemption', p. 430.

33 Edwards, 'Economy of the Trinity and Covenant of Redemption', p. 431.

34 J. Edwards, *Discourse on the Trinity*, in *The Works of Jonathan Edwards*, vol. 21, *Writings on the Trinity, Grace, and Faith* (New Haven: Yale University Press, 2002), p. 135.

35 Edwards, 'Economy of the Trinity and Covenant of Redemption', p. 431.

36 There is certainly a 'new, particular determination' of God with respect to the work of redemption (Edwards, 'Economy of the Trinity and Covenant of Redemption', p. 432); but it is what Edwards calls 'circumstantially new' (p. 440), not God's becoming what he was not; see also Aquinas's statement in *Summa theologiae* Ia.43.2 ad 2: 'The reason that a divine person is present in a new way in anyone or is possessed in time by anyone is not a change in the divine person, but in the creature'.

37 See G. Emery, 'Essentialism or Personalism in the Treatise on God in St. Thomas Aquinas?', in *Trinity in Aquinas*, pp. 165–208.

38 *The Trinitarian Theology of Thomas Aquinas*, p. 368.

39 J. Calvin, *The Gospel according to St. John 11–21 and the First Epistle of John* (Edinburgh: St Andrew Press, 1961), p. 291. See also his comment on 1 Tim. 1.15: 'For although God the Father a thousand times offers us salvation in Christ, and Christ himself proclaims to us his own saving work, yet we do not cease to be afraid or, at any rate, to wonder within ourselves whether it be so. Thus, whenever any doubt about the forgiveness of sins comes into our mind, we should learn to drive it out, using as our shield the fact that it is truth sure and certain and should be received without any controversy or demur': idem, *The Second Epistle of Paul the Apostle to the Corinthians, and the Epistles to Timothy, Titus and Philemon* (Edinburgh: St Andrew Press, 1964), p. 198.

40 J. Calvin, *The Gospel according to St. John 1–10* (Edinburgh: St Andrew Press, 1959), p. 74 (on John 3.16).

41 D. M. MacKinnon, 'Prolegomena to Christology', in *Themes in Theology. The Three-Fold Cord. Essays in Philosophy, Politics and Theology* (Edinburgh: T&T Clark, 1987), p. 180.

42 For a recent argument that Jesus's humanity is so to be regarded, see Spence, *The Promise of Peace*.

43 Calvin, *Institutes of the Christian Religion* II.xiii.2.

44 Calvin, *Institutes of the Christian Religion* II.xii.2.

45 Calvin, *Institutes of the Christian Religion* II.xii.2.

46 On this, see the finely-drawn interpretation of Calvin on Christ's *persona* in J. Edmondson, *Calvin's Christology* (Cambridge: Cambridge University Press, 2004), pp. 182–219, and, more generally, Berkouwer, *The Work of Christ*, pp. 58–87.

47 Spence, *The Promise of Peace*, p. 22.

48 See on this Horton, *Lord and Servant*, pp. 208–41; the covenantal framework which Horton brings to bear upon the topic enables him to integrate the deity and humanity of the Saviour much more tightly than Spence.

49 Calvin, *Institutes of the Christian Religion* II.xii.1.

7

Eschatology and anthropology

EDITOR'S INTRODUCTION

It is not coincidental that Webster's trenchant research in the 1990s and early 2000s into Karl Barth's theology increasingly led him to focus upon the work done in the 1920s when Barth was being prepared for his task as a church dogmatician. First, Webster found in Barth an example of one who felt unprepared for the task at hand by his modern training and who thus set himself to a rigorous program of *ressourcement*. When Jason Byassee and I interviewed him over a decade ago, Webster spoke with explicit regret regarding his training in the world of modern Protestant divinity and philosophy (surely too hard on himself!), and with conviction regarding his decided commitment to immerse himself in lots of biblical exegesis and in the catholic tradition of the fathers, medieval doctors and the early and Orthodox Reformed.* Second, Webster shared Barth's concern that a theocentric focus never forgets the wider circumference where the works of God, in nature and grace, bring about life and blessing in the creaturely realm. His work on Barth's moral ontology was meant to offer a distinctly Christian and theological angle on genuine human being and action. And it was a concern that he never left behind, even as he turned from intensive exposition of Barth to deeper engagement of the Christian tradition.

Though Webster is most known for commending a theological theology, we miss his project's tenor if we fail to see how he also committed himself to developing a theological anthropology. One of the earliest such essays was entitled 'Eschatology, Anthropology, and Postmodernity', later published in *Word and Church* as 'Eschatology and Anthropology'. Why address these three topics together? Most importantly, why talk of postmodernity at all?

Whatever else we may wish to say about the location of church and theology, this, at least, must be said: church and theology stand in the space between Jesus's coming in humiliation and his coming in glory. That space – and not any cultural space, postmodern or otherwise – is determinative of what church and theology may and

---

*Jason Byassee and Mike Allen, 'Being Constructive: An Interview with John Webster', *The Christian Century* 125, no. 11 (June 3, 2008), 32–34.

must be. Put differently: Christian theology, and therefore Christian eschatology and anthropology, is 'responsible in' its context but not in any straightforward way 'responsible to' its context.

In seeking to assess how he spoke 'in' the postmodern context though was not responsible 'to' it, it will be important to recognize Webster's negative judgement about the flourishing of critical methods: '[T]he explanatory success of critical philosophy depended upon the incapacity of Church and theology to deploy doctrinal and exegetical material to meet its challenges.' Webster sought to redeploy concepts culled from Scripture, and this essay sketched two such areas where the postmodern era seemed to be suffering the lack of fundamental Christian concepts. In so doing, he drew together concerns for two areas that I personally had been taught to keep apart: narrative theology and theological metaphysics.

The first loss in the postmodern era is the 'dissolution of teleology'. All is play. Nowhere is there purpose. Responses from Christians have tended to take the form of commending a biblical narrative ending in glory. Webster himself has signalled the importance of a story – the humbled appearance of the Son and his future return in glory – which frames our theological work and the very being of the church. His essays regularly sketched the broad contours of the biblical storyline, considering a theme in light of its key moments. We do well to ask, then, does confession of a 'grand narrative' involve an unavoidable identification of the gospel with the abuse of that narrative as if the future of God's coming were 'to hand'? To do so would, presumably, be to fall into the ills of all metanarratives (so Lyotard and others who are now legion).

Fending off such ills, Webster argues for two needed specifications which render our hope precise and distinctly Christian and, as such, life-giving. 'First, the fundamental content of Christian eschatology is the personal identity of the one who was and is and is to come, and only by derivation is it teleological. Its core is not the elaboration of a scheme of historical purposes, but the coming of Jesus Christ.' Eschatology is ultimately personal and fundamentally about divine presence. 'Second, this coming of Jesus Christ, and thus Christian eschatological talk which tries to indicate his coming, is promissory, not possessive, in character.' The posture of eschatology is prayer, not presumption of immediacy now; the sense of eschatology is faith, not sight of that which might be available already.

The second loss in postmodernity is 'the dissolution of the human subject', that is, of any concept of nature or substance. These terms had fallen into disrepute as totalizing categories taken to be nothing more than the globalizing extension of the preferences of the powerful. 'Ontotheology', or any concern for natures, essences and substances at all, has been a word to be feared.

Though we have seen his employment of redemptive history already, we must note also that Webster breaks with some critics of postmodernism – such as Calvin Schrag – in arguing that a return to narratival development of identity will not be sufficient. Webster invokes the language of 'field' and 'space' for 'moral selfhood and action', quickly specifying what such terms evoke: 'It is an account of the identity of God (the triune creator, reconciler, and perfecter); an account of the identity of the human agent as both a divine gift and a human task; an account of the encounter between this God and his creature; and an account of the differentiated teleology of their actions.' Space is more than story and involves concepts such as nature, not merely narrative. Genuinely theological anthropology must also address metaphysics, specifically, the concept of human nature.

This essay was one of the earliest by Webster that I devoured, when it appeared in *Word and Church*. At a time when I was an undergraduate taking in texts on postmodernity alongside the study of Hebrew and Greek texts and ensuing works in biblical theology, this article commended a way in which the plotline of the Bible might provide orientation to the contemporary in light of the canonical. Still further, it pushed beyond the orbit of most analyses of redemptive history (the ends of eschatology) by pressing to the significance of the metaphysical (the natures of human subjects). In a day when most trained in contexts to attend deeply to the biblical storyline were also warned off against the incursions of Hellenistic or philosophical categories, this essay was a conceptual reminder that the Bible itself commends both a story (narrative) and a setting (metaphysics). Setting without story is empty; story without setting is blind.

I have never regretted my schooling early in the Presbyterian tradition of covenant theology or later in evangelical approaches to the modern discipline of biblical theology. But Webster's wisdom helped me see something of the significance of story and metaphysics. In later years, John would offer a wider frame to his anthropology, starting not only with the narrative history of the eschatological but beginning further back in the inner life of God and the protological. His later essays would unfold in a thicker manner, and he sketched a number of aspects of human being, existence and action along such lines to great effect. They would also flesh out, exegetically and materially, the way in which ends and natures were addressed. In many respects, this essay represents his early work in Christian dogmatics and does not exemplify his mature efforts, which came a decade later. He taught me that a theology oriented by the gospel itself will invariably move from theology proper to theological anthropology and that our thinking about anthropology, like everything else, must always be attentive to God. 'From Him and through Him and to Him are all things.' John never tired of reminding us and exemplifying for us that posture of being theologically alert, so that, we might say in all things, 'To him be glory forever. Amen' (Rom. 11.36).

Suggested readings

'Eschatology, Ontology and Human Action', *Toronto Journal of Theology* 7 (1991): 4–18.

'The Human Person', in K. Vanhoozer (ed.), *The Cambridge Companion to Postmodern Theology* (Cambridge: Cambridge University Press, 2003), pp. 219–34.

'Human Identity in a Postmodern Age', in A. Morrison (ed.), *Tolerance and Truth. The Spirit of God or the Spirit of the Age?* (Edinburgh: Rutherford House, 2007), pp. 75–94.

'The Dignity of Creatures', in P. Middleton (ed.), *The Love of God and Humanity Dignity: Essays in Honour of George M. Newlands* (London: T&T Clark, 2007), pp. 19–33; repr. in GWM 2: 29–48.

Michael Allen, 'Toward Theological Anthropology: Tracing the Anthropological Principles of John Webster', *International Journal of Systematic Theology* 19, no. 1 (2017): 6–29; repr. in Allen and Nelson (eds), *A Companion to the Theology of John Webster* (Grand Rapids, MI: Eerdmans, forthcoming).

ESCHATOLOGY AND ANTHROPOLOGY

Christian theological anthropology is the dogmatic depiction of human identity as it is shaped by the creative, regenerative and glorifying work of the triune God.* Dogmatic portrayal of human identity is thus determined both in its content and its procedures by the church's confession of the gospel, for the gospel constitutes the space within which Christian dogmatics operates. Dogmatics (of which anthropology is a part) is not a free science; although it requires of its practitioners considerable creative powers, it is not simply an imaginative construal of the human situation which draws heavily on Christian religious themes, symbols or practices; although in the accomplishment of its task it will inevitably make use of all manner of language, concepts and patterns of thought, it is not simply the result of a dialogue with whatever philosophical or social-scientific concerns are considered to have resonance with the Christian confession. Dogmatics is the focused, modest and self-critical activity whereby the church seeks reflectively and systematically to give its attention to the gospel as it is announced in Holy Scripture: no more and no less.

Baldly expressed in that way, such an account of dogmatics seems fearfully unfriendly: closed, assertive, very far indeed from the conversational and interrogative mood which might recommend Christian doctrine to those who don't want to be scolded by catechesis. A recent and much heralded work on theological anthropology announces itself as an example of 'how to draw on various theological and other disciplines and genres without becoming stuck in any one', to avoid the way in which 'some theology and religious studies … are inhibited from pursuing fascinating and appropriate questions by the fear of transgressing boundaries which are often quite arbitrary'; and so the book recommends 'the fruitfulness of thinking theologically in dialogue with phenomenological and hermeneutical philosophy'.[1] But *are* the barriers simply arbitrary? Sometimes, indeed, they may be; but I am unconvinced that in the present situation Christian dogmatics will have interesting and fruitful things to say without some quite firm marking out of its territory. In other situations – where, for example, wide familiarity with the traditions of doctrinal thought can be assumed, or where the tradition has become self-obsessed – theology might be able or might need to operate in a different, more extra-mural, way. But in the present situation, where dogmatics in English-speaking circles is at best a fragile enterprise in the academy and has almost completely lost its hold on the life of the mainline churches, what is needed more than anything else is a recovery of theology's exegetical and catechetical

---

*Interestingly, 'identity' is remarkably modern and non-theological language. While there are precursors in the scriptural or classical theological tradition, language of identity arises in twentieth-century psychology (and adjacent disciplines). Webster engages the terminology but seeks to discipline it by reference to distinctly theological categories (i.e. nature, ends).

vocation.* Christian theology will only be worthy of the title 'Christian' if it allows itself to be led all along the line by the witness of Holy Scripture, and if it modestly and humbly, and yet also with courage and astonishment, tries to indicate what it finds there. The essential task of Christian dogmatics, whether in postmodernity, modernity or premodernity, is one of patient, respectful attentiveness to the biblical testimony, allowing itself to be shaped by the hope which is there expressed, and quietly letting that hope disturb, shatter and remake human thought and action.

Christian anthropology is eschatological in two senses, only the second of which I propose to explore in this chapter. It is eschatological, first, in the sense that central to its account of human identity is the regenerative work of God, effected in the life, death and resurrection of Jesus Christ, realized through the work of the Holy Spirit and signified in Christian baptism. Christian anthropology concerns the new creature of God; its ontology of the human is shaped by that eschatological event in which the creature's goal is confirmed even as the creature is put to death and made alive in Christ. Thus Christian anthropology, and especially Christian moral psychology, will be concerned with convertedness, that newness of life bestowed by the Spirit in which true human being is to be found. I am what in Christ through the Spirit I become.[2] However, it is a second sense of 'eschatological' which I want to take up here. Christian anthropology is eschatological in the sense that its account of human identity is possessed of a distinct teleology.† It sets what it has to say about human identity in the context of the gospel's announcement of a comprehensive account of God's purposes for creation. It is important to stress this second feature of the eschatological character of Christian anthropology in order to prevent the first, more subjective, aspect from expanding to become the totality of what is said about eschatological humanity. The detachment of the eschatological aspects of regeneration from their wider teleological background, and the abeyance of the concept of 'nature' which this often entails, have been common enough in modern theology, especially of the more dramatically existential variety.[3] If these moves are to be resisted, it is because a theology of human identity and action needs to be supported on more than simply the rather narrow base of convertedness, which, however important it may be and however thoroughly it may pervade a Christian ontology of the human, cannot provide the whole scope of Christian anthropology.‡ What is required is an understanding of destiny sufficiently sturdy and expansive to resist being collapsed

---

*In other words, 'conversational theology' might operate more fruitfully when catechesis and Christian theological formation can be assumed; yet Webster deems the present, post-Christian situation in the West to be a time where no such theological assumptions are warranted. Thus, theological theology needs to precede and resource any future conversational efforts to engage 'theology and *x*, *y*, or *z*'.

†An illuminating synonym would be to speak of 'human ends'.

‡In earlier chapters we have seen Webster argue that Christology goes awry when it is reduced to the incarnation (eclipsing pre- and post-existence). Here a parallel move is made. Anthropology goes off-kilter when creation or eschatological teleology is dropped or thinned because of a singular fixation on conversion.

into the psychological or ethical dramas of selfhood. And so a dogmatic account of converted human identity will be closely related to an account of the ends of creation.

How does this understanding of the dogmatic task of Christian anthropology relate to the claim that Christian theology now is undertaken in the context of postmodernity? By way of initial orientation, it is important that 'postmodernity' should not be allowed to become itself an eschatological term, as if the advent of postmodernity were the new age, such that the church and its theology now find themselves in an entirely altered situation, which requires them to rethink the fabric of Christian culture. Such epochal claims are both historically and theologically deficient.* Historically, their weakness is that, far from enabling reflective awareness of our present situation and tasks, they are often little more than (rather specious) philosophical-cum-literary proposals masquerading as historical-cultural analysis. Theologically, their weakness is that they promote an account of the church and its theological responsibilities which are largely unchastened by the discipline of the gospel. Over against such epochal thinking, in which church and theology are simply bit-players in some larger cultural drama, I want to suggest that by the grace of God it is given to the church (and therefore to its theology) to discern the situation of humanity faithfully and truthfully – in faith, not in sight, but nevertheless in truth – and therefore to see the human situation now as that stretch of human history which lies between the first and second advents of Jesus, in whom and for whom all things are created and perfected. Whatever else we may wish to say about the location of church and theology, that, at least, must be said: church and theology stand in the space between Jesus' coming in humiliation and his coming in glory. That space – and not any cultural space, postmodern or otherwise – is determinative of what church and theology may and must be. Put differently: Christian theology, and therefore Christian eschatology and anthropology, is responsible *in* its context but not in any straightforward way responsible *to* its context. For context is not fate; it may not pretend to have a necessary character, to be anything other than a contingent set of cultural arrangements which stands under the judgement of the Christian gospel.† And, moreover, context – despite what we are often instructed – is not transparent or self-interpreting. Truthful understanding of context requires the exercise of discernment, and, for Christian faith and theology, such discernment is a gift of the Holy Spirit, a mode of sanctification and a prophetic task; it is not simply a skill acquired through cultural immersion. We do not by nature know who or where or

---

*Context matters, but biblical reasoning finds creation, fall, redemption and final consummation to be more significant contextual descriptions than anything on offer by way of the 'postmodern condition'.

†To treat context as fate – along the lines of 'you must say that because you're a [insert demographic description]' or 'they couldn't possibly see that because they're [insert a political moniker]' – would be to view the life of the mind and the practice of theology in wholly material terms, in other words, to view theology in a secular fashion. While Christians are neither optimists nor pessimists, however, the gospel prompts us to be hopeful about theology's promise even in the face of what may seem to be contextual limitations.

when we are; and if we are to come to know these things, our knowledge itself must be the Spirit's work, greeted with the obedience of faith.

The question, therefore, for Christian eschatology and anthropology in postmodernity is not what may still be said by Christian theology in the postmodern condition, for there is no such simple condition: 'the possibility of speech about God can be founded on nothing less than God's own speaking'.[4] That means that in one important sense, Christian theology in postmodernity must, as Barth once put it, carry on 'as if nothing had happened'.[5] In Barth's case, this was not because nothing had happened; indeed, what had happened in Barth's context was very grave indeed. But Barth knew better than almost anyone in his context that what that context required more than anything else was the service of a theology which was theological to the bone, which did not allow its context, however stringent, to distract it from the task of clarifying the Christian confession, precisely so that it could indicate to its culture the word of judgement and grace spoken to it by the gospel. Theology's task, in other words, is neither apologetic nor revisionary, but exegetical and dogmatic, busying itself quietly and confidently with its proper concerns, not in order to sidestep the exigencies of whatever its host culture may be, but precisely so as to be able to address them with the right kind of Christian specificity, determination and hope.[*]

Our concern here is with the particular set of exigencies which have come to be termed collectively as postmodernity. The term is notoriously slippery, but can be thought of as a handy way of clustering together diverse ideas and styles of cultural and philosophical analysis which repudiate presence, the given, depth, order, identities and structures in favour of absence, surfaces, dispersal, the non-identical, plurality, play. In theological terms, postmodernity is often proposed as ushering in the end of 'onto-theology' – that is, of the mode of talk about God in which God and being are thought together in the kind of metaphysical mythology of absolute presence which Nietzsche and the genealogists finally scoured out of Western culture. Postmodern theology turns away from the substance metaphysics of selfhood, history and deity which have been considered ingredient within the world-view of Christian faith, replacing them by a style of theology which is non-identical, a historical and atheological. Christian eschatology and anthropology, set as they are within an overarching teleology of time and a particular commitment to the significance of human action in history, are points at which the sharpness of postmodernity can be felt with particular acuteness. Postmodernism is deeply hostile to teleological renderings of history, with their apparently unified trajectories and their emphasis on the preservation of identity. And it is similarly inimical to accounts of moral agency which tie human action to pre-given human identity or to an overarching order within which moral action is possible and meaningful. In short: once onto-theology

---

[*]To operate in the apologetic mode at length is to open oneself to temptation to adopt the concerns and categories of some other discipline (whether it is an ethics or aesthetics or epistemology).

is disposed of, then eschatology, and the framework which eschatology offers for generating and evaluating human action, requires radical reworking. In this paper, I want to explore some of the connections between eschatology and anthropology, suggesting that eschatology furnishes part of the teleological context for dogmatic depiction of human identity. Without such a context, accounts of the identity of human agents are difficult to sustain. In the first section I look at the postmodern dissolution of teleology; in the second at the dissolution of the human subject.

1. Eschatology and the end of history: The dissolution of teleology

One way of characterizing postmodernism would be to view it as a 'radicalization of historical consciousness'.[6] If modernity involves an account of being as time – as historical process rather than as unchanging substance – postmodernism dissolves the notion of history itself. That is, postmodernism characteristically rejects any idea that human existence in time constitutes an ordered whole; history is dispersed into a non-sequential, non-developmental, non-utopian, non-eschatological scatter of elements. History is 'a matter of constant mutability, exhilaratingly multiple and open-ended, a set of conjectures or discontinuities which only some theoretical violence could hammer into the unity of a single narrative'.[7] This, of course, lies behind the rejection of 'grand narratives' in postmodernity, famously enunciated in an essay on the nature of the university institution by Jean-François Lyotard: 'The narrative function', he wrote, 'is losing its great functors, its great hero, its great dangers, its great voyages, its great goal. It is being dispersed in clouds of narrative language elements.'[8] Lyotard's specific target is the emancipatory narrative of modern intellectual institutions, according to which the scientist – the hero of knowledge – is the central character in a story of liberation from myth and opinion into true science. But what Lyotard terms 'incredulity toward metanarratives'[9] has wide application: it signals a turn from any attempt to articulate a coherent shape to human history as having origin, ground or goal, any 'totalization' of history into a single, unidirectional and intelligible whole. Partly what comes to expression here is an attempt to display the link between narrative and the exercise of power: the process of telling a coherent story about history, making history into a whole, is itself an exercise of power – as Lyotard puts it, 'speech acts fall within the domain of a general agonistics'.[10] Totalizing stories erase otherness, by turns absorbing or excluding what is other in order to project a satisfyingly coherent temporal structure. It is important, however, to grasp that this postmodern critique of the narrative function is more than simply a further version of modernity's critique of ideology (contemporary versions of which we find in some kinds of feminist or liberationist thought, for example). Modernity, we might say, responds to the ideological potential of narrative by seeking to construct a better narrative – that is, a narrative of history which does not erase the counter-factual, but offers a better (more liberating, better founded, above all more *critical* and therefore more truthful) story. Postmodernism simply abandons the whole task of making sense: protology and teleology, and agents with stable or developing identities, are renounced, and history is dismantled into a jumble of heterogenous bits.

One obvious casualty of this process of dismantling in postmodern theology is, clearly, eschatology. The point can be seen in a couple of representative works, Mark Taylor's manifesto *Erring*, and John Caputo's more recent reflections on religious themes in Derrida's later work in *The Prayers and Tears of Jacques Derrida*.

Taylor's account of history in *Erring* is a somewhat amateurish attempt to break free of the inheritance of classical Christian theology (which he sketches in rather haphazard fashion from Augustine to Hegel), a tradition which, he believes, was organized around 'the conviction that a temporal course of events is plotted along a single line, which extends from a definite beginning, through an identifiable middle, to an expected end'. Or again: 'Between the "tick" of Genesis and the "tock" of Apocalypse, the history of the West runs its course. The line that joins beginning, middle, and end traces the plot that defines history. History, as well as self, is a theological notion.'[11] All this Taylor expunges from the Christian imagination with appeal to Nietzsche, for whom any such comprehensive schemes are *poiesis*, fabrication, the imposition of comprehensible logic on scattered events, the fashioning of seriality. For the postmodern, Taylor writes,

> [t]he death of Alpha and Omega, the disappearance of the self, and the overcoming of unhappy consciousness combine to fray the fabric of history. When it is impossible to locate a definite beginning and a definite end, the narrative line is lost and the story seems pointless.[12]

On these terms, we should note, there can be no eschatology: destiny is invention, not temporal shape, and so what is left to us is (in the book's title) 'erring', undirected wandering (playful, carnivalesque, but entirely lacking in any point): 'the endlessness of erring discloses its unavoidable purposelessness'.[13]

If Taylor's account makes pretty plain that postmodernism doesn't offer much by way of soil in which eschatology might take root and grow, John Caputo's reflections on Derrida hint in a slightly different direction – namely, that it might be possible to redeem the notion of 'coming', the advent, without falling prey to the spectre of teleology. Caputo finds scattered in Derrida's writings occasional reflections on the theme of 'coming', 'in-coming', 'arrival' and the like which intimate a kind of eschatology which is on the far side of the manageable apocalypse of onto-theology. 'Derrida', he says, 'is dreaming and praying over an "absolute" future, a future sheltered by an absolute secret and absolved from whatever is presentable, programmable, or foreseeable'.[14] Still, however, there is a sort of extreme ascesis here, an extraordinarily scrupulous reluctance to associate coming with history and its goals. Partly this is because Caputo finds in Derrida a distaste for the apocalyptic theme of privileged access or vision; partly it is because the theme of coming has to be detached from the modern 'politics of invention' in which that which comes to us is managed by being integrated into the economics of the same, so that its sheer novelty is suppressed; above all, the reticence is a response to the stringent demand to resist the metaphysics (and the metaphysical theology) of presence. 'Every determinable telos is still "present", has already been anticipated within the horizon of what presently prevails'.[15] What Derrida is gesturing towards, therefore is 'the beyond, *au-delà*, the *tout autre*, *the* impossible, the unimaginable, un-foreseeable, unbelievable, ab-solute surprise, which is absolved from the same'.[16] Over against the metaphysics (and political and cultural economy) of the classical traditions of the West, in short, what is needed (or perhaps what is left to us) is 'an apocalypse without vision, without truth, without revelation'.[17]

Is that all that's left to us? Has postmodernism simply chased from the field those traditions of thought and practice (both Christian and secular) which have struggled with the notion of destiny as an essential backcloth to human identity and action, to meaningful speech and action? To answer that question would be a lengthy business indeed; but we may, perhaps, sample some of the issues if we set ourselves a more restricted task of asking whether the target of the postmodernist's criticism is not so much an authentically Christian eschatology but rather its pathological substitute, sharing some of its outer form but lacking its inner substance.

In pondering this question, we need to bear in mind that in one very important sense Christian theology, spirituality and morals are such that we cannot abandon 'grand narratives'.* The proposal that '[t]he mythos of salvation history, with its logic of triumph and causality, its distinction of planes (profane and sacred), its special sequence of events, its linear teleology, and its supernatural, other-worldly eschatology must be allowed to die out'[18] is one over which we should pause long and hard before accepting. The structure of a single (though complex) line of history of redemption, stretching protologically to the divine act of creation out of nothing and eschatologically to the consummation of all things, with a centre in the life, death and resurrection of Jesus Christ as the ground and manifestation of its teleology, is one so deeply embedded in the canonical texts of the Christian faith that it is almost impossible to envisage forms of Christian belief and practice, forms of theology, prayer and pastoral nurture from which that teleology has been excised. In one sense, the Christian faith is irredeemably positive, singular, comprehensive and purposive. The suggestion that responsible Christian faith and practice can be envisaged without

---

*This claim is not meant to suggest that Christian faith and practice demand a 'grand narrative' understood in just the ways that were defended by moderns or are decried by postmoderns. Webster will do some reconceptualizing work in paragraphs to come, so that language of 'metanarrative' is not applied *as is* to the biblical narrative.

a 'God-given, pre-given order'[19] runs the risk of simply trimming Christianity to the shape of our cultural imagination (or lack of it). Christian faith and practice are or ought to be *responsible*, that is, *responses*, ways of making sense of the world and of acting truthfully in the world which are generated by a sense that reality and history have a nature, that they are not infinitely malleable, or mere projections, and that the economy of desire is not all that there is. Put differently: styles of Christian faith and practice which are purely constructivist are self-defeating, since they exclude from the beginning that whose denial leads them into hopeless self-contradiction, namely that to believe and act Christianly is to be transfigured by a gift of transcendent freedom, goodness and splendour.

But if we are thereby committed to some form of 'grand narrative', we are not thereby committed to the abuse of that narrative as if the future of God's coming were 'to hand', an available telos neatly completing whatever purposes we happen to have arranged for ourselves. In this sense, postmodernism is quite correct to reject what Taylor calls 'the realized eschatology of the system';[20] authentically Christian eschatology needs to be distinguished from what we might call futurism, that is, the elaboration of a satisfyingly coherent narrative scheme on the basis of which we may come to possess and control the outcome of human history, assigning roles and predicting outcomes in what is no more than a kind of eschatological technology. Postmodernists rightly deplore the false homogenization and singularization of history which this entails.[21] But the protection against this predictive abuse of eschatology is not to abandon teleology, but to specify its character with the right kind of Christian precision. Two things above all are of critical significance here.

First, the fundamental content of Christian eschatology is the personal identity of the one who was and is and is to come, and only by derivation is it teleological.* Its core is not the elaboration of a scheme of historical purposes, but the coming of Jesus Christ. His being, his presence and activity, now known in a hidden and yet real way in the activity of the Holy Spirit but to be manifest in the last day, is the content of Christian eschatological belief, and only on the basis of that coming as the transfiguring event of human history may we speak of history's *telos*. It is therefore supremely important that we 'concentrate *on the eschatos rather than on the eschata*: on Jesus Christ as he is described in Revelation 1:17f .... as "the first and the last and the living one"'.[22] Eschatology is the forward expansion of the name of Jesus; it is the confession that he will be, that he will come; only as such is it also a confession of the future of humanity and its history. The object, therefore, of Christian eschatological speech is the perfect, that is, complete and utterly self-sufficient, reality indicated by the name of Jesus. Once this point is quietly laid aside, and the Christological determinacy of eschatology is allowed to recede, the space

---

*All ends follow from God's character. The personal shapes the vocational and the political, provided we understood God's identity and being as the core of 'the personal'.

so vacated is filled with all manner of substitutes. It may be replaced, for example, by large-scale immanent teleologies of human history in which talk of Jesus Christ becomes a mere ornament in what is, in effect, a theory of temporality or an ideology of human achievement. But, as Barth once remarked, '[r]edemption does not mean that the world and we ourselves within it evolve in this or that direction. It means that Jesus Christ is coming again.'[23]

Second, this coming of Jesus Christ, and thus Christian eschatological talk which tries to indicate his coming, is promissory, not possessive, in character.* The centrality of promise for biblical eschatology is what distinguishes it from any kind of predictive futurism. This is not because promise indicates that Christian eschatology is ambivalent or even sceptical, lacking in definiteness or assurance. Quite the opposite: the creedal confession that 'he will come again' is no less assured than the confession that God is the creator of heaven and earth, that God's Son suffered under Pontius Pilate or that on the third day he rose again. But such assurance is the assurance of faith, and therefore quite different from that self-certainty which might be the basis for predictive control. Eschatological certainty takes the form of confidence in the promises of God, a confidence whose certainty cannot be replaced by an act of intellectual or spiritual or political possession of the object of hope. The negative aspect of this promissory character of Christian eschatology is the hiddenness of its object, that is, its unavailability for systematic comprehension and its resistance to be used as an instrument in some project of our own devising. God's promise

> is hidden because God becomes present as himself in his own way and in his own time but remains beyond human grasp. He remains hidden even as he reveals himself. His acts take place *sub contrario* of that which humankind expects of him (instead of waiting for him and hoping in him!).[24]

If this suggests that Christian eschatology is more modest than postmodernism allows, it is not because the Christian shares postmodernism's extreme apophaticism, but because the object of Christian eschatological certainty is Jesus Christ himself, the unfettered risen one who shares in the absolute liberty of God. This divine freedom properly shapes both eschatological speech and eschatological spirituality.

One of the primary modes of eschatological speech is prayer for the coming of God. 'The Spirit and the Bride say, "Come" … Amen. Come, Lord Jesus' (Rev. 22.17, 20); '*Maranatha*, our Lord, come!' (1 Cor. 16.22); 'Thy kingdom come' (Mt. 6.10). This prayerful mode of speech is to be retained with full seriousness, and not

---

*Claims about teaching regarding last things – return, resurrection of the body, judgment, heaven, hell – all must be classified as creedal or confessional claims of faith, not sight. Webster's Burns lectures (now published as *CT*) describe further how the apocalyptic language involved in speaking of these gospel promises is meant to humble our grasp of future life, given that it exists on the far side of divine action that explodes our current experience in various ways.

simply regarded as a liturgical decoration which can be translated without residue into propositional form. What does the idiom of prayer indicate about Christian eschatology? First, it gives expression to the personal specificity of Christian eschatology. Jesus is our hope: come, Lord *Jesus.* Jesus is not merely an emblematic figure in a larger historical canvas; he *is* the future. Second, in praying that he may come, Christian speech indicates that Jesus is not to be handled as an available object, something or someone to hand. As the one who will come, he is other than an object or figure within the horizon of the world. Third, we *pray* that he may come; that is, we look for the action of another, we implore him to take the initiative, to act in an affair where we cannot act. Here, in other words, Christian speech is quite other than some sort of apparatus for controlling destiny; it is supplication. In short: if Christian eschatology has prayer for Jesus' coming as one of its primary modes, then it is not to be confused with projection. If the postmodernist misconstrues Christian faith at this point, it is because of a lack of attention to some of its basic modes of speech, and a consequent misapprehension of the character of God's relation to the world.

Eschatological speech is never far from the language of prayer. An eschatological spirituality is therefore ascetical, eschatology in the desert.[25] That is to say, it involves the rupturing of ties and attachments, separation, processes whereby we are detached from belonging to a comprehensible historical order, on the basis of which we can assign roles to ourselves and others, above all, in which we can be safe. This is not to deny that Christian eschatology indicates a kind of security, even safety. But what kind? In his remarkable book *Expérience et Absolu*, the French theologian Jean-Yves Lacoste suggests a link between the ascetic's refusal of possession and location and the way in which 'the fool' (unlike the person of learning) is dissatisfied with that which is provisional. The person of learning, the sage,

> is satisfied with a happiness which bears every sign of being provisional (since speculative knowledge suggests that God is present other than through the Second Coming, since the promises made at Easter – which the sage is either unaware of or misunderstands – remain unfulfilled, etc.), and on the other hand he does not really try to situate in the present all the eschatological meanings that he may perceive. The fool, because he desires the final state … more deeply than anyone, but can accede only to a fragile degree of anticipation … is thus able to smile at those who hold that the *eschaton* is already here in the present.[26]

Once again, some vigilance is needed here. A spirituality of reticence ought properly to dispossess us of false objects of desire and the satisfactions they afford; it ought not to direct itself against those hopes which are, indeed, given to the saints. But with that caution, we may at least be reminded of the need to build into the fabric of Christian dogmatics the disavowal of those uses of eschatology which annexe it to the fertile processes of idolatry.

We may sum up this first section by reminding ourselves of what Barth once said about the doctrine of providence, and which applies very aptly to the doctrine of the last things. '[T]he Christian belief in providence is faith in the strict sense of the term, and this means ... that it is a hearing and receiving of the Word of God'.[27] Belief in providence is not consent to a narrative projection. It is not 'an opinion, postulate or hypothesis concerning God, the world, man, and other things, an attempt at interpretation, exposition and explanation based upon all kinds of impressions and needs, carried through in the form of a systematic construction'.[28] And it is not this because the movement which the doctrine states begins with God.

> We can and must understand that the knowledge of this lordship of God can be compared only to the category of axiomatic knowledge, and that even in relation to this knowledge it forms a class apart .... It consists in a realisation of the possibility which God gives to man.[29]

In sum: in belief in providence we do not have to do with 'a so-called world view, even a Christian world view. For a world view is an opinion, postulate and hypothesis even when it pretends to be Christian'.[30] In Christian eschatology we do not have to do with a world view but with the confidence of faith, discerned through patient attention to faith's forms of prayer and speech. Yet what such prayer and speech presuppose is that the history over which Jesus Christ presides is directional and purposive, culminating in the day of the Lord. What does this have to say for dogmatic questions of human identity?

2. Eschatology and the end of the subject: The dissolution of ethics and politics

Postmodernism sometimes tells a story which runs something like this. The history of the modern age is the history of the invention of the self. Modernity is self-consciously a process of the emancipation of cognitive and moral selfhood from the encompassing orders of gods, societies, customs and texts, and all their attendant officials. In the course of this emancipation, the self finally emerges into the light as that which is axiomatically real, true and good. Postmodernity announces that this modern drama of emancipation is mere pretence. The transcendent subject is simply a fictive conglomeration of fragments. And so Kant's lonely, severely rational and utterly responsible agent becomes Musil's 'man without qualities' – either an empty space played upon by systems of differences, or an anarchic trickster figure lacking in form or definition. Whereas modernity stands under Montaigne's rubric 'I look within',[31] postmodernism more characteristically says: '[E]ach of us knows that our self does not amount to much'.[32] Like all such stories, the cogency of the postmodern version of the history of anthropology depends on not being too worried about the details and on being harnessed to a strong proposal in the light of which it acquires plausibility. This strong proposal – the so-called 'death of the subject' – is well described by Calvin Schrag at the beginning of one of the very best studies of the topic, *The Self after Postmodernity*:

> For the most part, questions about the self, and particularly questions about the self *as subject*, are deemed anathema. As there is no longer a need for the unification of the diverse culture-spheres, so the problem of the self, at least as traditionally formulated, is seen to evaporate. Questions about self-identity, the unity of consciousness and centralized and goal-directed activity has been displaced in the aftermath of the dissolution of the subject. If one cannot rid oneself of the vocabulary of self, subject, and mind, the most that can be asserted is that the self is multiplicity, heterogeneity, difference, and ceaseless becoming, bereft of origin and purpose. Such is the manifesto of postmodernity on matters of the human subject as self and mind.[33]

Postmodern theology has been especially interested in stressing the connection of onto-theology and subjectivity. In the Western tradition of metaphysics and theology, so the argument goes, God the supreme being is equally the supreme subject, the monadic, substantial, self-possessing bearer of a name. Mark Taylor writes,

> From a monotheistic perspective to be is to be one. In order to be one, the subject cannot err and must always remain proper. By following the straight and narrow course, the self hopes to gain its most precious possession – itself.[34]

Human subjectivity is thus the replication of divine self-possession: 'The self-presence of the self-conscious subject reflects the self-presence of absolute subjectivity'.[35] One could certainly argue that Taylor's pretty monochrome portrait of the Western theological tradition succeeds only by maximalizing certain doctrinal aspects (divine absoluteness, mentalist accounts of human nature) and minimalizing other corrective features within the tradition such as the doctrine of trinitarian relations, or those traditions of ascetical theology which have given weight to dispossession (both spiritual and social) as a mode of authentic humanity. Indeed, to target the whole tradition as resting on 'the repressive logic of identity', or 'the "logic" of oneness [which] implies an economy of ownership',[36] is not much more than a crude pastiche. What it serves, however, is a proposal for a differential structure of human selfhood, which 'subverts the exclusive logic of identity' by seeing the self as 'a function of the intersection of structures and the crossing of forces'.[37] '*Desubstantialized* and *deindividualized*' the self is '*co-relative*' and '*co-dependent*':[38] not the centre of a set of given structures, but a trace, a point at which fluid lines of force play against one another (the link between postmodern theology and process theology is not incidental). 'Fabricated from transecting acentric structures, the deindividualized subject is never centred in itself.'[39]

Selfhood, in other words, shares the same fate as teleology in postmodernism: it is left behind in the migration to the fields of anarchic free play. By way of response, I want to suggest that there is a strong connection between Christian eschatology and a certain understanding of the human person, and that the severing of that link by proposing a strictly non-teleological anthropology does severe damage to our understanding of persons as moral and political agents. In short: postmodern turns from eschatology may constitute a (literally) hopeless amoral and apolitical account of what it means to be human.

Critics of postmodern thought have not been slow in pointing out that, when combined with the evacuation of the category of history, the repudiation of enduring selfhood or identity clearly renders any kind of account of meaningful or purposive moral and political action acutely difficult. At best, human action can only be seen as ungrounded, unattached to any depth, unfastened to any features of the world of history which might evoke, order, evaluate or bring such action to completion. At worst, action is anarchic, erratic, sheerly undirected play (though it hardly deserves the name 'play', since games are ruled, not random, behaviour). Thus Richard Rorty, who has been especially concerned with the political fallout of postmodernism, argues for the retention of some kind of moral teleology for human politics, but only 'as long as the point of doing so is to lift our spirits by utopian fantasy, rather than to gird our loins with metaphysical weapons'.[40] I want to suggest that, far from dealing in utopian fantasy, Christian eschatology furnishes a frame for moral-political action, and thus for that resistance to evil which is part of the Christian's baptismal vocation.

In (rightly) discarding the sovereign, self-enclosed, self-identical subject of modernity, postmodernism 'leaves us with a subject too thin to bear the responsibilities of its narratival involvements': so Calvin Schrag.[41] The reference to narrative there is important: over against the postmodern dispersal of the self into fragments, it is rightly objected that a firm sense of human selfhood and agency requires some sort of account of enduring human identity, embodied in a life-story which moves towards an end in which it will be integrated. Thus Schrag argues for 'narrative self-identity borne by a process of character–formation'.[42] Accepting the demise of substance-oriented accounts of selfhood as changeless and fully formed in advance of the history of the self's performance, Schrag nevertheless affirms 'a species of self-identity' acquired through participation in a narratable history.[43] Crucially, such a temporal – and therefore teleological – self is *agent*, '[t]he who of action' that 'can make a difference in the world of communicative praxis'.[44] In slightly less elevated terms: one crucial requirement for being a self is to be able to see oneself as a purposive participant and agent in story where what one does *matters*.

So far, so good. But Christian theology will want to go a good deal further than this. It will not be sufficient to respond to the postmodern dissolution of the self into unstructurable, utterly discrete moments by pressing, as Schrag does, the logic of narratival achievement of identity. Indeed, there is a real question whether Schrag's account of selfhood can distinguish itself sufficiently sharply from the later Foucault's aesthetics of the 'care of the self'.[45] The crucial difference from Christian anthropology will be this. Christian faith will not articulate the teleology of the self and its actions in terms of that *techne tou biou* recommended by Foucault, that 'intensification of the relation to oneself by which one constitute[s] oneself as the subject of one's acts'.[46] Such nominalism, lacking a sense of human nature as brought into being, sustained and perfected by the creative action of divine love, sits very uneasily with Christian theology. Instead, theology will talk of the self and its agency by offering an account of the 'field' or 'space' of moral selfhood and action. It will set its moral anthropology in the framework of an account of the drama of human nature, origin and destiny, a drama presided over by the triune God who will bring it to its consummation at the appearing of the Lord Jesus.* That drama is the space of our action, the field within which what we do is possible and meaningful.

Postmodernism characteristically resists this kind of spatial or geographical language, since it seems to indicate constraint or closure, the establishment of boundaries which eliminate the heterogenous and eclectic.[47] But much depends on how the idiom of space is used. A Christian theological depiction of the field or space of human moral selfhood is not simply a portrayal of some determinate cultural district. It is an account of the identity of God (the triune creator, reconciler and perfecter); an account of the identity of the human agent as both a divine gift and a human task; an account of the encounter between this God and his creature; and an account of the differentiated teleology of their actions. All Christian language is, directly or indirectly, a depiction of moral space, for what it does is express one or other aspect of God or of God's creatures as agents in relation. This is – emphatically – not to fall into the kind of wearisome ethical reductionism in which doctrines can be decoded into moral imperatives. But it is to say that, because the triune creator is the Lord of the covenant, and because the people of the covenant find themselves in obedience to God's gift and summons, then any talk of God is also talk of the identity of God's creatures. In particular, talk of God (and of humanity *coram deo*) is talk which – because it is talk of *this* God – effects at the same time the ascription of roles and the establishment of standards of role-performance. Precisely because and only because Christian talk of God is talk of God, it is also by derivation moral language. If that general rule holds true, then Christian eschatology is not some futurist projection; it is talk about the coming of Jesus Christ which also talks of the

---

*Webster differentiates the Christian approach from the Foucauldian approach by means of an outward or an inward derivation. Whereas Foucault calls for self-construction of the self, Augustine and other Christian theologians attest the call to receive the self from God.

teleological aspects of the moral field in which human agents find their identity. Two things flow from this.

First, Christian eschatology is practical rather than speculative. It has an ethical character, in that one of its functions is to inform and evaluate the church's practice rather than offer a theory of universal history. Christian eschatology is what Jürgen Moltmann calls 'a theology for combatants, not onlookers'.[48] Eschatology informs moral practice by indicating that the field of human action (including the identity of the human agents in the field) is ordered, and ordered teleologically. Human moral action is therefore neither arbitrary, inconsequential behaviour (which scarcely deserves the title 'moral'), nor an attempt to create a goal for or impose a goal upon our lives. It is action ordered towards the telos of history, which is the coming of Jesus Christ. That telos both relativizes and incites action. It relativizes action, because the end of history is the manifestation of Jesus Christ, the one who was and is and is to come; the end of history is not within the sphere of human competence or responsibility, and is hence a matter of prayer. But it incites action, because the Christian's prayer. *Maranatha*! is an active, not an inactive prayer, a prayer which invites, expects, indeed, commands us to do in our sphere what is fitting in the light of the action of God to whom we pray. And so Christian eschatology is ethical, and Christian ethics are eschatological. The ultimate doctrinal grounds for this are, of course, trinitarian: the Christian is now empowered by the Spirit to act in anticipation of the final coming of the Son of God, in which the creative purpose of the Father will reach its ultimate goal.

Second, if all this is the case, then Christian eschatology, far from being the leaden metaphysics of historical sameness, is in part concerned with the manner in which God's action evokes and sustains patterns of human action. As such, it may, perhaps, furnish what postmodernism has found it acutely difficult to provide, namely an account of reality as the ground for true, good human action. The word 'ground' is deliberate: without a sense that moral-political action corresponds, in however fragmentary a way, to the nature and destiny of the world, then moral action will surely be unable to master its discouragements. Moral action, if it is to be hopeful, courageous and free from anxiety about its own possibility, requires a sense of its ontological depth, its being in accord with what is and will be.* For Christian eschatology, we are able to move ahead and resist only because another – Jesus – has gone before us and has overcome and will manifest his triumph at the last. And we move ahead, we resist, because this one is present in the power of the Holy Spirit in which the future is sealed and the powers of the age to come are given in anticipation.

---

*Christianity shares virtues with other comparative philosophies and religions, but its distinctive approach to some virtues (e.g. humility, self-denial) relates directly to the gospel promises in which it places eschatological hope. For instance, because God promises to vindicate the righteous, Christians turn the other cheek (see Rom. 12.17–20).

If all this sounds curiously antiquated, so be it … in one sense it is. But our age is neither (as Kant thought) the age of criticism nor (as postmodernism suggests) the age of the dispersal of all things. Our age is the present age of reconciliation, in which it is given to the church to taste the Spirit and know the presence and power of the risen Jesus, and therefore it is the space in which we may pray and act hopefully and in truth. 'Since all these things are thus to be dissolved', the writer of 2 Peter asks his audience, 'what sort of persons ought you to be?' His answer is an end to the mythology either of total responsibility or of its negation; in their place, he counsels a kind of passive activity and active passivity, 'waiting for and hastening the coming of the day of God'. And why? Because the truth of our situation is that we are those who occupy that place in history where the most truthful thing to do is this: 'according to his promise [to] wait for new heavens and a new earth in which righteousness dwells' (2 Pet. 3.11–13).

Notes

1 Ford, *Self and Salvation*, pp. 12f.
2 On these themes, see my article 'Eschatology, Ontology and Human Action', *Toronto Journal of Theology* 7 (1991), pp. 4–18.
3 For a representative example, see Jüngel, 'The Emergence of the New'. My essay mentioned above falls into some of the same difficulties.
4 F. C. Bauerschmidt, 'Aesthetics. The theological sublime', in J. Milbank et al., eds., *Radical Orthodoxy. A New Theology* (London: Routledge, 1999), p. 201.
5 K. Barth, *Theological Existence Today! A Plea for Theological Freedom* (London: Hodder & Stoughton, 1933), p. 9.
6 P. C. Hodgson, *God in History. Shapes of Freedom* (Nashville: Abingdon Press, 1989), p. 31.
7 T. Eagleton, *The Illusions of Postmodernism* (Oxford: Blackwell, 1996), p. 46.
8 J.-F. Lyotard, *The Postmodern Condition. A Report on Knowledge* (Manchester: Manchester University Press, 1986), p. xxiv.
9 Ibid.
10 Ibid., p. 10.
11 Taylor, *Erring*, p. 53.
12 Ibid., p. 73.
13 Ibid., p. 157.
14 J. D. Caputo, *The Prayers and Tears of Jacques Derrida. Religion without Religion* (Bloomington: Indiana University Press, 1997), p. 73.
15 Ibid., p. 73.
16 Ibid.
17 J. Derrida, *Raising the Tone of Philosophy* (Baltimore, MD: Johns Hopkins University Press, 1993), p. 167, cited by Caputo, p. 71.

18   Hodgson, *God in History*, p. 235.

19   Caputo, *The Prayers and Tears of Jacques Derrida*, p. 75.

20   M. C. Taylor, *Altarity* (Chicago: University of Chicago Press, 1987), p. 293.

21   See the critique of Moltmann's millenarian strand in M. Volf, 'After Moltmann. Reflections on the Future of Eschatology' in R. Bauckham, ed., *God Will Be All in All. The Eschatology of Jürgen Moltmann* (Edinburgh: T&T Clark, 1999), p. 243.

22   G. Sauter, 'The Concept and Task of Eschatology', *Eschatological Rationality. Theological Issues in Focus* (Grand Rapids: Baker, 1996), p. 146.

23   K. Barth, *Church Dogmatics* II/1 (Edinburgh: T&T Clark, 1957), p. 78.

24   Sauter, 'The Concept and Task of Wschatology'. p. 151.

25   Cf. Volf, 'After Moltmann', p. 255.

26   J.-Y. Lacoste, 'Liturgy and Kenosis', in G. Ward, ed., *The Postmodern God. A Theological Reader* (Oxford: Blackwell, 1997), p. 252.

27   K. Barth, *Church Dogmatics* III/3 (Edinburgh: T&T Clark, 1961), p. 15.

28   Ibid., p. 16.

29   Ibid.

30   Ibid., p. 18.

31   M. de Montaigne, 'On Presumption', *Essays*, 11.17 (Harmondsworth: Penguin, 1958), p. 220.

32   Lyotard, *The Postmodern Condition*, p. 15.

33   C. O. Schrag, *The Self after Postmodernity* (New Haven: Yale University Press, 1997), p. 8.

34   Taylor, *Erring*, pp. 41f.; for further representative works here, see R. P. Scharlemann, *The Reason of Following. Christology and the Ecstatic I* (Chicago: University of Chicago Press, 1991), and C. E. Winquist, *Desiring Theology* (Chicago: University of Chicago Press, 1995), pp. 99–126.

35   Taylor, *Erring*, p. 42.

36   Ibid., p. 130.

37   Ibid., p. 134

38   Ibid., p. 135

39   Ibid., p. 139.

40   R. Rorty, 'Cosmopolitanism without Emancipation', *Objectivity, Relativism and Truth. Philosophical Papers Volume I* (Cambridge: Cambridge University Press, 1991). p. 212.

41   Schrag, *The Self after Postmodernity*, p. 28.

42   Ibid., p. 42. Schrag's account is heavily reliant on P. Ricoeur, *Oneself as Another* (Chicago: University of Chicago Press, 1992), and is also indebted to J. Kristeva (e.g., 'The System and the Speaking Subject' in T. Moi, ed., *The Kristeva Reader* (Oxford: Blackwell, 1986), pp. 24–33), as well as to aspects of the later work of Foucault; see now M. Foucault, *Ethics. Subjectivity and Truth* (London: Allen Lane, 1997).

43   *The Self after Postmodernity*, p. 33.

44   Ibid., p. 71.

45   Schrag himself admits as much: see p. 68.

46 M. Foucault, *The History of Sexuality, volume 3: The Care of the Self* (Harmondsworth: Penguin, 1988), p. 41.

47 Cf. K. Tanner, *Theories of Culture. A New Agenda for Theology* (Minneapolis: Fortress Press, 1997), pp. 93–119.

48 J. Moltmann, *The Coming of God. Christian Eschatology* (London: SCM Press, 1996), p. 146.

8

Christ, church and reconciliation

EDITOR'S INTRODUCTION

The twentieth century was the era for ecclesiology. John Webster engaged in various historical essays with *la nouvelle théologie* in the Roman Catholic Church (perhaps especially the work of Yves Congar and Henri de Lubac), the *communio* ecclesiology, the social trinitarianism that took hold across the mainstream Protestant world (not least the ecumenism of Robert Jenson and Reinhard Hütter), all of which were often conjoined with the emphasis on practices as found in the work of Stanley Hauerwas and many of his students (a result of postliberal concern for viewing doctrine as grammar for church practices). Of these approaches Webster here identifies a shared emphasis:

> It has become something of a commonplace in some now dominant styles of modern theology and theological ethics (especially, but not exclusively Anglo-American) to emphasize the coinherence of the divine work of reconciliation and the church's moral action, in such a way that the work of the ecclesial community can properly be considered an extension (fleshing out, realization, embodiment) of the gospel of God's reconciling act.

In many ways he was the rare Reformed (though Anglican) voice crying in the ecumenical and ecclesiological wilderness. This essay marks an early phase of Webster's writing on the church. Later iterations (such as 'In the Society of God') might be less contrastive in describing divine and human action, but major emphases run straight through his consideration of the topic. What is emphasized about God and God's action with respect to the church? Here election plays a leading role in marking out the church as gift called into being by God; the exalted Christ is also a real and active presence in his own right (not simply in the 'body of Christ', the church). What also of the church's own being and action in this account? The language of a 'creature of the Word' signals the ceaseless dependence of the *ekklesia*, and the ethics of indication or witness plays a defining role in understanding all churchly action, ever pointing away from itself and (like John the Baptizer) gesturing towards the Christ.

Webster did not merely disagree with particular judgements about the church, as if one were called to vote up or down on episcopacy, ecclesial invisibility and so on. Rather he worked to reshuffle the very scope and sequence whereby we think of the church. Before addressing the nature of the church, one had always to begin with addressing the God of the church. This essay is one of the first places where Webster explicitly highlights the need to begin with the immanent life and perfection of God before turning to the economy, lest the economy become construed as something other than the free and thus truly merciful will of God.

Elsewhere Webster explicitly linked the being and behaviour of the church. He spoke first of an 'ontological rule' of the church. 'There is, accordingly, a proper passivity to the being of the Church, for faith – that is, recognition and assent and trust in the word and work of God – and not boasting – that is, self-grounded, proud competence – is the fundamental act of the Church's existence' (*Holiness*, p. 63). A 'moral rule' then follows from this 'ontological rule': 'all the acts of the holy Church must demonstrate a reference to the work of the One who alone is holy: the electing Father who reconciles in the Son and perfects in the Spirit' (*Holiness*, p. 63). This essay on the practice of reconciliation seeks to honour that passivity because it seeks to honour the present tense agency of the exalted Christ. Here Webster is insistent on confessing this gift *ek theou* ('from God'). In confessing this gift, two tasks emerge. 'First, they must draw the right kinds of distinctions between the reconciling work of God and those acts of the church in which that reconciliation is present; and, second, they must achieve a properly theological specificity in their depiction of the acts which are considered to be the expression or consequence of the reconciling work of God.'

'What is all-important is that an ethics, politics and spirituality of reconciliation should not be burdened with the task of doing God's work.' But there is such an ethics and it does possess political and spiritual vigour provided that it does not attempt arrogant or idolatrous tasks. Indeed, he turns immediately to add that 'Action is hopeful and unanxious if it knows itself to be action which is in conformity with how the world is *coram Deo*' (*sic*). Interestingly Webster's ecclesiological essays tended to be written in polemical fashion, in each case responding to postliberalism, the ecumenical movement, papal encyclicals, tendencies in *communio* ecclesiology and the like ('The Holiness of the Church' is the most significant exception, though even there he does begin by shirking two false starts in a very abbreviated polemic). Yet he brought decidedly principled convictions about what a well-ordered ecclesiology ought to look like by returning to first theology, namely, God and the works of the perfect God. Most likely the adversarial character of his writing in this theme manifests a judgement that here contemporary theology has gone and is going about its work in a markedly wrong fashion.

Webster commented from time to time about playing the role of a theological Ishmael, one sent to wander by himself. To be sure, he garnered followers in many respects as he came to have influence upon students and colleagues. Perhaps here, more than elsewhere, his approach to the subject at hand was more idiosyncratic among dominant strands of contemporary theology. Perhaps here his tribe appears to be quite different from that of the mainstream.

Suggested readings

'The Holiness of the Church', in *Holiness* (Grand Rapids, MI: Eerdmans, 2003), 53–76.

'The Church and the Perfection of God' and 'The Visible Attests the Invisible', in Mark Husbands and Daniel J. Treier (eds), *The Community of the Word: Toward an Evangelical Ecclesiology* (Downers Grove: InterVarsity Press, 2005), pp. 75–95, 96–113; repr. as 'On Evangelical Ecclesiology' in CG, 153–94.

'The Church as Witnessing Community', *Scottish Bulletin of Evangelical Theology* 21 (2003): 21–33.

' "In the Society of God": Some Principles of Ecclesiology', in Peter Ward (ed.), *Perspectives on Ecclesiology and Ethnography* (Grand Rapids, MI: Eerdmans, 2011), 200–22; repr. in GWM 1, 177–94.

'Ecclesiocentrism: A Review of *Hauerwas: A (Very) Critical Introduction* by Nicholas Healy', *First Things* (October 2014): 54–5.

Christopher C. Brittain, 'Why Ecclesiology Cannot Live by Doctrine Alone: A Reply to John Webster's "In the Society of God" '. *Ecclesial Practices* 1, no. 1 (2014): 5–30.

Joseph Mangina, 'Church', in Michael Allen and R. David Nelson (eds), *A Companion to the Theology of John Webster* (Grand Rapids, MI: Eerdmans, forthcoming).

CHRIST, CHURCH AND RECONCILIATION

I

What follows is a half-way between a theological essay and a homily; but we should not be particularly troubled by its homiletic tone. The clear distinctions which some members of the academic theological guild draw between proclamation and critical reflection are part of the pathology of modern theology: our forebears would have been distressed by the way in which theology has succumbed to the standardization of discourse in the academy and the consequent exclusion of certain modes of Christian speech, and we should probably worry more about what Bernard or Calvin might think of us than about the way in which *wissenschaftlich* colleagues may shake their heads. Part of what is involved in talking Christianly about reconciliation (as about any other topic) is coming to see that forms of thought and speech, genres of discourse, can themselves alienate us from the matter which must be spoken: thinking and speaking themselves need to be reconciled to God by God. As Stephen Williams has put it in his perceptive analysis of the resistance to the gospel of reconciliation in modernity:

> Those convinced of the fact of divine reconciliation should thereby be convinced that intellectual conviction is not attained in a sort of spiritual vacuum. One must have bared one's soul, even reckoned oneself as some kind of sinner ... [T]alk of such realities as sin and forgiveness may fail to commend itself to us because it cannot discover in us a disposition to receive it.[1]

The main purpose of these remarks is, on the basis of some theological comments on 2 Corinthians 5.18, to ponder what is involved in the church's ministry of reconciliation, most of all in its ethical aspects. It has become something of a commonplace in some now dominant styles of modern theology and theological ethics (especially but not exclusively Anglo-American) to emphasize the coinherence of the divine work of reconciliation and the church's moral action, in such a way that the work of the ecclesial community can properly be considered an extension (fleshing out, realization, embodiment) of the gospel of God's reconciling act.[2] These various attempts to articulate the concrescence of soteriology, ecclesiology and moral theology are by no means necessarily lacking on a theology of divine prevenience, for they are often quite explicitly directed against the individualistic moral heroics of modernity, and often root ecclesiology in considerations of the trinitarian relations in which the church graciously participates through the work of the Holy Spirit. Nevertheless, they are characteristically less drawn to expansive depiction of the sheer gratuity of God's act of reconciliation, and more commonly offer lengthy accounts of the acts of the church, sacramental and moral, often through the idiom of virtues, habits and practices.* The success or otherwise of such proposals, I suggest, will depend in large measure upon the care with which they are able to accomplish two tasks. First, they must draw the right kinds of distinctions between the reconciling work of God and those acts of the church in which that reconciliation is present; and, second, they must achieve a properly theological specificity in their depiction of the acts which are considered to be the expression or consequence of the reconciling work of God. The questions to be asked, roughly phrased, are these: what is the content of the church's ministry of reconciliation, and how is it to be related to and distinguished from the reconciling act of God in Christ?

There is a danger that dogmatic moral theology may be excessively preoccupied with the question of who does what – with identifying the precise demarcations between human and divine action (many contemporary readers of Barth whose theological instincts are shaped by the ethics of ecclesial practice are understandably nervous on precisely this score). The danger of such preoccupation is not only that of forcing distinctions where there are properly none, or of making distinctions appear to be polarizations. It is more that we may fall victim to moral agonistics: in making such distinctions, we may remain trapped within a set of oppositions which derive not from the gospel but from modernity's acute sense that in order to talk of moral dignity we have to talk of human autonomy, and in order to talk of human autonomy we have to counter the thought of divine heteronomy.† The range of Barth's thinking is such that (in my judgement) he only rarely failed to escape the problem of competitive accounts of divine and human action. But he also sounded the alarm about the danger of grounding human moral action in the wrong way and of subverting a proper understanding of the sovereignty of God. And he also, especially in the last two decades of his life, protested (sometimes in rather jaundiced tones) against the over-inflation of ecclesiology and ethics into quasi-independent theological themes. His protests went largely unheeded, and are still routinely passed over, especially by enthusiasts for *koinonia* ecclesiologies who judge him to be a tetchy Zwinglian who could not cope with the thought of any enduring divine action through creaturely media.[3] Part of what I want to open up is the question of whether the recent luxuriant growth of ecclesial ethics has not made it hard for us to see the force of Barth's protest. And this, in turn, may lead us to ask whether ecclesiology

---

*Here Webster is clearly identifying ecumenical discussions related to the Second Vatican Council, the Faith and Order Movement (perhaps reaching its crescendo with the 1983 document, *Baptist, Eucharist, and Ministry*) and, finally, the postliberal theological movement often associated with Yale (a mood with which Webster interacted critically several times in the late 1990s, as he worked alongside a Yale-trained colleague, George Schner, in Toronto).

†These 'moral agonistics' clearly involve a reduction of divine transcendence to something merely quantitative rather than an infinite qualitative distinction in some real sense. Webster's argument here parallels analyses by Kathryn Tanner, David Burrell and William Placher.

is, in fact, not such a self-evidently basic doctrine as it has become in some modern Protestant dogmatics, and take up a comment of Edward Schillebeeckx – who, after all, comes from a tradition with a rather long track record in producing industrial-strength ecclesiologies – suggesting that what we need is not so much an ecclesial ethics of reconciliation but 'a bit of *negative theology*, church theology in a minor key'.[4]

II

All this is from God, who through Christ reconciled us to himself and gave us the ministry of reconciliation; that is, in Christ God was reconciling the world to himself, not counting their trespasses against them, and entrusting to us the message of reconciliation. (2 Cor. 5.18f.)

First, what is 'all this' that is from God? Clearly it is the great divine work of salvation, summed up in verse 17 as the establishment of a 'new creation', a work of God of such generative force that its accomplishment spells the end of one mode of existence (which thereby becomes 'the old') and brings into being 'the new'. And all this is from God, ἐκ τοῦ θεοῦ. This 'from God', of course, is not to be thought of as if it were some statement of distant origin; it does not merely furnish the ultimate backcloth against which other more immediate or available or manageable realities may stand out in relief. It is utterly proximate; 'from God' is directly and presently constitutive of the reality of 'the new' which has come. To put it slightly differently, the little phrase 'from God' has real work to do here, since it is an operative assertion, not merely a remote statement of something at the far end of our description of the present life of the new creation.[*] Indeed, the entire presentation of apostolic ministry and activity in 2 Corinthians, most of all in chapter 4, is predicated on this directly and constitutively present and effective reality of ἐκ τοῦ θεοῦ: 'the transcendent power belongs to God and not to us' (4.7). 'Not to us': because apostolic existence is a matter of the manifestation, the ostensive indication, of 'the life of Jesus' (4.10). Jesus' life, as the embodied actuality of God's transcendent power, cannot be transferred to the apostle in any straightforward way without compromise to its gracious, eschatological character; in one (only one) very real sense the life of the risen one is incommunicable. 'To God': because at the heart of apostolic existence is new creation, which is by its very nature *ex nihilo* and therefore on the other side of creaturely competence or capacity. 'All this', therefore, 'is from God'.

---

[*]'From God' cannot be reduced to foundational origins, but continues to have 'operative' or – we might say – ongoing relational and moral consequence. Christ is not mere founder; he is presently active as the 'great shepherd of the sheep' (Heb. 13.20).

What are the consequences here for the way in which we approach a theological ethics of reconciliation? Two remarks are in order, one material or dogmatic, and one more formal in character.

The material remark is that an operative notion of ἐκ τοῦ θεοῦ will require us to invest a great deal of theological energy in the depiction of the person and work of the reconciling God. Most of all, what will be required will be a rich description of divine aseity as it is manifest in the work of redemption. The chief task, of course, will be a trinitarian theology, above all, one which is able to talk of the purposiveness of the life and activity of Father, Son and Spirit without thereby collapsing the life of God into the economy of salvation. This is not to set 'immanent' and 'economic' against one another; but it is to claim that there is a proper order in which immanent has soteriological priority over economic, because the economy of salvation is the sphere of the *free* mercy of God. And it is also to lodge a protest against the kinds of elision of the distinction between the triune life of God and the moral community of God's creatures which can result from making *koinonia* a common term between the Trinity and the church.* Finally, it is also to suggest that one test of the adequacy of an ethics of reconciliation will be the seriousness (and the joy) with which it pauses over this descriptive task, and the vigilance which it demonstrates to the possibility of an ecclesial ethics which has ceased to make its appeal all along the line to Trinity, election and grace.

The second, more formal remark, is that ἐκ τοῦ θεοῦ is to be the dominating feature of a Christian ethical geography, of a theological depiction of the space for the church's endeavour which is established by the action of the triune God, and which it is the chief task of Christian moral theology to map. Human moral action is subordinate to divine saving action; the church is subordinate to the Holy Trinity; and therefore the sociology of morals is strictly subservient to moral ontology. To see the point at work, we may pause to consider a couple of examples.

First, in Professor Timothy Gorringe's book *God's Just Vengeance*, an approach is made to the ethics of reconciliation (Gorringe has in mind especially the reconciliation of criminal offenders) in which the church is envisaged as an 'imagined community', that is, as a group held together by a commonly held image of social communion which may provide resources through which different modes of social relation can be envisaged and practised.[5] 'The Christian Church', he writes, 'was from the beginning ... an "imagined community" ... whose purpose was to provide a messianic "home", or rooting, to human beings';[6] 'the community called "church" contributes to that struggle and negotiation for forms of social life properly called human by faithfulness to and proclamation of [its] tradition, and ... by the creation of such communities'.[7]

---

*The reference to elision here points to those such as Robert W. Jenson who looked to Vatican 2 ecclesiology for inspiration and, in so doing, adopted a model that used *koinonia* or 'communio' as a bridge term for speaking of triune life and ecclesiastical life.

To the obvious question which this provokes – 'Do we need to talk about the church at all?',[8] since many strategies of reconciliation are secular – Gorringe replies:

> the community of reconciliation (not the church, but the church sacramentally) is the means through which atonement is effected, which is the reason, presumably, Christ bequeathed to us not a set of doctrines or truths, but a community founded on betrayal and the survival of betrayal.[9]

What this opposition of 'truths' and 'community' signals is simply the absence of a metaphysics of morals, a theological ontology of the church's acts of reconciling. In the absence of such a dogmatic underpinning to morals, what rushes in to fill the gap is a strong sense of churchly causality: it is the church which is (sacramentally) 'the means through which atonement is effected'. The moral force of the Christological ἐφάπαξ is simply lost.

A second example, initially at least much more companionable with what I am proposing here, is Miroslav Volf's theological-ethical study *Exclusion and Embrace*, whose central proposal is that 'God's reception of hostile humanity into divine communion is a model for how human beings should relate to the other'.[10] Volf is entirely correct to urge the priority of reconciliation over liberation, and to suggest that, because of its orientation to freedom, the theology and ethics of liberation may often betray a 'tendency to ideologize relations of social agents and perpetuate their antagonisms'.[11] Hence the book's proposal that the primary need is for a 'theology of embrace'.[12] Yet there is a disabling slenderness to the Christology and soteriology which undergird this theology; whilst the book does not lack a theology of grace, it rarely succeeds in portraying grace with much vividness, and often does so as a concession rather than as a major preoccupation. Problems emerge initially with Volf's insistence that 'final reconciliation' is prospective, and that, therefore, a 'grand narrative' of reconciliation is not available to us: the right question, he argues, 'is not how to achieve the final reconciliation, but *what resources are needed to live in peace in the absence of final reconciliation*'.[13] This is well taken, if it simply means that we are to 'renounce all attempts at the final reconciliation: otherwise, we will end up perpetrating oppression'.[14] But there is a real loss here: the loss of a vigorously operative sense that human, churchly reconciling action is not only prospective but also, crucially, *retrospective*, looking *back* to a final reconciliation which – τετέλεσται – has already taken place. 'Both the modern project of emancipation and its postmodern critique suggest that a *nonfinal reconciliation in the midst of the struggle against oppression* is what a responsible theology must be designed to facilitate.'[15] But eschatological relativization of human action now must not be allowed to undermine the achieved sufficiency of the reconciling work of God; if it does, then human action once again threatens to become omnicompetent or omniresponsible.

Anxieties are not eased by the underlying account of the relation of God's action to that of creatures. Volf commends a life of 'self-giving modelled on the life of the triune God',[16] and urges engagement in 'the struggle for *a nonfinal reconciliation based on a vision of reconciliation that cannot be undone*'.[17] With 'model' and 'vision' we are in the sphere of *imitatio*: a useable concept, certainly, but only if it is grounded in a transcendental Christology. Yet it is just this sort of Christology which seems not to be at work, as Volf's account of repentance shows. The account is almost entirely immanentist and instrumentalist,[18] reduced to the task of removing psycho-social barriers to reconciled community. 'To repent means to resist the seductiveness of the sinful values and practices and to let the new order of God's reign be established in one's heart.'[19] Is not this too voluntarist, lacking in the backward reference of repentance? Is not repentance an act in face of an achieved act of divine mercy which has already abolished the condition of hostility and guilt and rendered its continuance absurd? Or again, repentance is a matter of 'creation of the kinds of social agents that are shaped by the values of God's kingdom and therefore capable of participating in the project of authentic social transformation'.[20] But how can repentance 'create'? And what is 'capacity' in these matters? And does not such a statement run the risk of reducing repentance to a useful instrument in a process of social engineering? Volf's appeal to the notion of the Christian as 'catholic personality' ('personal microcosm of the eschatological new creation') brings the same problems to the surface as it runs together Trinity, soteriology and eucharist in an alarmingly Hegelian manner.

> In the Eucharist ... we celebrate the giving of the self to the other and the receiving of the other into the self that the triune God has undertaken in the passion of Christ, and that we are called and empowered to live such giving and receiving out in a conflict-ridden world.[21]

This is a generalized and moralized account of the eucharist which says little of Jesus and his death.[22] 'Much of the meaning of the death and resurrection of Christ is summed up in the injunction, "Let us embrace each other"'. It is, accordingly, entirely characteristic that 'the drama of embrace'[23] is not a Christological drama; it is a phenomenology of human activities of embracing diversity and reconciling differences, *illustrated* at the end by the parable of the prodigal, but left Christologically unspecific.

Attempts at an ethics of reconciliation of this kind, with their basic conceptual equipment of community, education, embracing, vision and so forth,[24] are at best accounts of the moral application of the benefits of Christ in the social sphere; but without a robust theology of the *opus Christi*, they can scarcely resist the drift into immanence.

Over against this stands Paul's ἐκ τοῦ θεοῦ, the determinative divine action which generates the community of reconciliation. In verse 19, this determinative divine action is expanded in two ways: as incarnation ('in Christ God was reconciling the world to himself') and as justification ('not counting their trespasses against them') – the latter act being what Calvin finely calls the 'foundation and cause' of reconciliation.[25] Christian moral theology is required to give a vivid and sustained depiction of these realities: of the atoning work of the incarnate Son as the condition of possibility for human action. 'Whereas God had been before far distant from us,' Calvin remarks, 'He has drawn near to us in Christ, and so Christ has been made to us the true Emmanuel and His advent is the drawing near of God to men.'[26] More than anything else, a Christian depiction of the field in which human acts of reconciliation take place will want to insist on the wholly unique and perfect action of God in Christ.* This act, as Barth puts it in a comment on 2 Corinthians 5.19, 'was a definitive and self-contained event'.[27] It is not just an incitement to human moral activity, still less a kind of cipher for what is properly a mode of human engagement; it is that without which reconciliation is groundless, lacking in any purchase on reality. Because this act was done by this one, there and then, acts of reconciliation are more than an attempt to create reality by establishing imagined communities which offer a different sort of social space from that of the world's routine violence. Human acts of reconciliation are in accordance with the structure of reality which God in Christ creates and to the existence of which the gospel testifies; and therefore they are acts which tend towards the true end of creation which God's reconciling act establishes once and for all in Christ's person and work.[28] In sum: because of the ἐκ τοῦ θεοῦ, expounded here as incarnation and sin-bearing, there is an unbridgeable gulf between the reconciling activity of God and the church's ethical endeavour: his action forgives sin, the church's does not.[29] The church's acts of reconciling are no more than the repetition of the judgment of God which is established at the cross and resurrection from which the new creation comes: he reconciled us to himself.[30]

III

What, then, of the church's ministry of reconciliation? It is that which God *gave*. That is to say, it is a matter of election or appointment. It does not spring into being as an activity of a busy imagined community with a lively sense of the need for alternatives to oppression and marginalization. 'Reconciliation' is not a reality which is generally well known and understood, something to which the church also makes its particular contribution and lends its authority, but whose content is not strictly derivable from the content of the church's proclamation of salvation. The church is not simply as it were a volunteer, willing to spend itself in a task for which others are also suited but in which they decline to involve themselves. The church engages in actions which

---

*'Wholly unique' picks out its singularity (and thus divine or heavenly source), while 'perfect' marks its completeness or wholeness (and therefore warns against its narrowing to some segment of Christ's work, as in incarnation *or* atonement instead of, rightly, incarnation *and* atonement).

are given to it to do by its constitution as that gathering of humanity which confesses that in Christ God has reconciled the world to himself.* No less than in the depiction of the moral space of the church, there is need also in our discussion of the moral διακονία of reconciliation to root what we have to say in divine election.

If the origin of this διακονια of reconciliation is the divine appointment, its content is primarily *speech*. What God has entrusted to the church is (in verse 19) the 'message (λόγος) of reconciliation'; we are 'ambassadors' through whom God 'makes his appeal'. Crucially, this emphasis on speech as primary in the church's ministry of reconciliation helps retain a sense of the proper transcendence and uniqueness of the divine act of reconciliation. Speech is in contrast here to 'ethical realization'. It helps counter the notion that through the moral life of the church reconciliation is first introduced into the anthropological sphere, first made real in the world. For apostolic speech is not a making real of the gospel of reconciliation, but a testifying to the fact that in Christ and Spirit it is already realized. The word of reconciliation is a word which witnesses to that reality which lies on the other side of our speech, which it may indicate or gesture towards but which it can never embody or present or realize in our midst.† The apostolic word *indicates*, and that indication is the first great act of the ethics of reconciliation. What is the apostolic ministry? Barth puts it thus:

> It is a request for the openness, the attention and obedience which are needed to acknowledge that what has happened in Christ has really happened, to enter the only sphere which is now left to man, that of the new, that of the conversion to God which has taken place in Christ. The ministry of reconciliation which consists in this entreaty is not of itself self-contained, but it begins only with this self-continued and completed event. This ministry is its first concrete result. The world … needs this ministry. But reconciliation in itself and as such is not a process which has to be kept in motion towards some goal which is still far distant. It does not need to be repeated or extended or perfected. It is a unique history, but as such – because God in Christ was its subject – it is present in all its fulness in every age … As this completed and perfectly completed turning, reconciliation makes necessary the ministry of reconciliation, giving to it a weight and a power to arouse and edify which no other ministry and indeed no other human activity can ever emulate.[31]

There is, of course, an objection near to hand: is not such an assertion of a 'perfectly completed turning' of human history merely ideological, a cloak for the self-evidently unreconciled state of human history? But the objection misses the real nature of the reconciliation which has been established and which is the content of

---

*Not merely message but also means are a gift of Christ (and thus normed and limited by him, which brings freedom to Christians who have learned to delight in living dependently in God's provision).
†Like Barth, Webster speaks in a way that evokes the image of John the Baptist who speaks of decreasing that another might increase (Jn. 3.30).

the apostolic ministry. To see the point we might set these verses from 2 Corinthians 5 alongside Ephesians 2.14ff.:

> He is our peace, who has made us both one, and has broken down our dividing wall of hostility, by abolishing in his flesh the law of commandments and ordinances, that he might create in himself one new man in place of the two, so making peace, and might reconcile us both to God in one body through the cross, thereby bringing the hostility to an end. (cf. Colossians 1.20–2)

These verses, we might say, offer a description of what Markus Barth called 'the political result of the Messiah's mission and work'.[32] We may try to put the matter thus. What the apostolic ministry of reconciliation indicates is the *existence* (not simply the *potentiality*)[33] of the 'one new man'. This new man, this reconciled existence in which human division and hostility have been put away, is not present to us simply as an imperatival goal. It is a divine creation, already made, already established as part of the new creation. The new creation establishes a form of human fellowship in which the dividing wall is broken down, and in which there is common 'access in one Spirit to the Father' (Eph. 2.18) through the Son; thereby, strangers become fellow-citizens. *Where* is this reality? In is *in him*; *he* is it; he does not simply figure it to us, or call us to fulfil what he initiates or instances: he *is* our peace.[*]

But again, the question comes: if this is the doctrinal space of the church's life, what room is left for the activity of reconciliation? What kind of peace-*making* is left to us? Pannenberg asks: 'Do we not have to regard not merely God's reconciling act but also its human acceptance as constitutive of the event?'[34] A response might go along these lines: Human action is not constitutive of the event of reconciliation in the sense that the Christological 'once-for-all' is dependent for its completion upon those human acts through which reconciliation is accepted and lived out; in this sense, the event of reconciliation is closed. But that event is not closed in the sense that it eliminates all subsequent reconciling activity. It is an event charged with force to expand itself and establish conformity with itself, for it is an event one of whose agents is the Holy Spirit. And this expansion takes place as the risen Christ in the Spirit's power generates those human acts which seek to demonstrate conformity between achieved divine reconciliation and patterns of human life, and which refuse to act as if reconciliation had not, in fact, taken place. Truthful human action is action which is in conformity with the reality which is established in the resurrection of Jesus from the dead. It is 'truthful' because it presupposes that its *ratio essendi* (and therefore its *ratio cognoscendi*) lies outside itself in a reality to which it is conformed, but which it does not establish or actualize. The church, therefore, lives in that sphere of reality in which it is proper to acknowledge and testify to reconciliation because we have

---

[*]The blessings or kingdom of Christ cannot be had apart from Christ himself; he is not a mere instrument or tool, but the King himself.

been reconciled; in which it is fitting to make peace because peace has already been made; in which it is truthful to speak to and welcome strangers because we ourselves have been spoken to and welcomed by God, and so have become no longer strangers but fellow-citizens. What is all-important is that an ethics, politics and spirituality of reconciliation should not be burdened with the task of doing God's work. Action is hopeful and unanxious if it knows itself to be action which is in conformity with how the world is *coram deo*.

All this should give us pause before deploying too swiftly the language of human action as a 'mediation' of the divine work of reconciliation. It would be superfluous here to rehearse in detail the constituents of the characteristic Protestant nervousness concerning ecclesial mediation: its apparent failure to state the sheer gratuity of the gospel; its potential compromise of the sole mediatorship of the risen Christ and of the Spirit's presentation of the *beneficia Christi*; its weakening of the backward reference of ecclesial action to the Christological 'once for all'; the danger that mediating agencies quickly become interesting in their own right; the assumption that the bridge between the 'objective' reality of the gospel and its 'subjective' realization must be built through human activity.* It is, of course, more than ever an open question whether anxieties along these lines are well-founded, or whether they simply highlight the need for careful theological specification and refinement of language about ecclesial mediation. But behind the anxieties lies a fear that any account of ecclesial mediation can scarcely avoid becoming too dense, too humanly solid, and therefore insufficiently transparent towards – ostensive of – the self-presentation of God. The Western Catholic tradition developed its understanding of mediation in particular relation to questions concerning the significance of matter in sacraments and concerning the significance of institutional office in ministry. One result of such preoccupations (shared in many respects by the Reformers even as they struggled against this part of their heritage) was a strongly *kataphatic* theology of mediation. Later theologians, especially some strands of nineteenth- and twentieth-century Roman Catholic and Anglican theology, took up these developments and justified them by appealing to an 'incarnational' principle in which Christ, church, sacrament and ministry (and sometimes culture and ethos) threatened to become points on a continuum of God's 'embodied' saving activity. Contemporary ecclesial ethics often stands within this tradition, even if sometimes in a less dogmatic form owing as much to Hegelian theory of history as to theology.

By way of contrast, I suggest that the Christological ἐφάπαξ† and its drastic curtailment of the *soteriological* significance of human ecclesial activity may best

---

*Webster frequently pushed back against theological fads that he deemed to negate the Creator–creature distinction. 'Mediation' here is an ecclesiastical parallel to 'participation' in the realm of soteriology; in both cases, he regularly worried that contemporary accounts (unlike their classical or premodern exponents) failed to form them in ways that began with and honoured the perfection of God in an abiding, operative manner.
†'Once-for-all'.

be safeguarded by a theology of mediation which is more *apophatic* in character. This is – emphatically – not grounded in a general principle of apophasis, whether philosophically or religiously derived; apophasis does not secure freedom from idolatry, and, indeed, may be itself a form of idolatrous resistance to the human vocation to positive speech and action.[35] Rather, an apophatic account of mediation draws attention, not so much to creaturely incapacity as to the utter capacity of God's self-communicative presence in Christ and Spirit, thereby entirely reorienting the task of creaturely witness. Apophatic mediation is at heart *indicative*, the mediating reality – object, activity, person, word – does not replace or embody or even 'represent' that which is mediated, but is as it were an empty space in which that which is mediated is left free to be and act. Such mediation is not *wirksame Handeln* but *darstellende Handeln*:[36] a 'showing' which does not effect but indicate and celebrate God's most proper effectiveness. Human mediation is not spontaneous; it is at its deepest level an ontological *passivum*. And the ontology of such mediation is therefore to be spelled out – over against the Western Catholic tradition – not in terms of an ontology of presence,[37] but in terms of what might be called an ontology of indication. Mediating realities have their being in the action of indicating that whose utter plenitude lies wholly beyond them. Once again, the grounds for this do not lie in general repudiations of the metaphysics of presence, but in a specifically theological critique which extends into ontology the force of the exclusive particles *solus Christus, solo verbo, sola gratia, sola fide*, behind all of which lies the great trinitarian principle of all dogmatics and ethics: *solus Deus*.

From this, two consequences of importance for an ecclesial ethics of reconciliation might be noted. The first concerns the concepts of virtue, habit and practice which of late have enjoyed much authority in theological ethics. In *Embodying Forgiveness*, Greg Jones writes that God's

> healing and re-creating is not God acting wholly without us. They also invite, and require, our practices, which – by the guiding, judging, and consoling work of the Spirit – enable us to witness to God's forgiving, re-creating work and to be transformed into holy people. To be involved in such practices is to engage the narrative of the triune God's creative and re-creative work as Father, Son, and Spirit; likewise, to believe faithfully in the Triune God is to have our lives formed and transformed through participation in Christian practices.[38]

Almost right; but the potential moral immanence of the language of practice may be troubling; talk of crafting forgiveness may run counter to its sheerly unassimilable character as the gift and work of God. Put differently: the region of Christian faith and practice is eschatological, and therefore notions such as practice can only be used if we allow that they will suffer some very considerable strain if they are to be bent to serve in a Christian moral psychology. The rule here, as for all ethics, is: *non nostri sumus, sed Domini*.[39]

The second is to suggest, accordingly, that before we need to speak of the church as a community characterized by reconciling practices, or by learned habits of peacemaking, we need to talk of the church as the creature of the Word, in order to retain the fundamental asymmetry between divine and human action.[40] To talk of the church in these terms is to insist that at its heart the church is passive, a community whose life has as its core activity the listening to the apostolic Word of reconciliation.[41] Ecclesiologies which centre on Word customarily have greater success in articulating the transcendent freedom of the object of Christian faith, and are customarily more resistant to moralization of the gospel, in which God's reconciling deed takes up residence in institutional forms or patterns of moral practice. If it was an assertion of the centrality of Word for church which drove much of the Reformers' unease about the structures of sacramental reconciliation in later mediaeval Christianity in the West, such an assertion may equally render us rather uneasy with an ecclesial ethics of reconciliation in which the task of indicating the gospel has been in some measure nudged to the sidelines.* This is not, of course, to deny that the practice of the ecclesial community is of importance, nor to fall into the error of ethical nominalism in which human action *cannot* refer to divine action. It is simply to urge that what holds the ecclesial community together is not common moral activity but attention to the gospel in which existing reconciliation is set before us both as – shocking, revolutionary, unpossessable – reality, and also as task. In morals, too, the figure of Jesus the present one can be eclipsed and his work of self-demonstration be quietly assumed by others. But: he is present and self-communicative, and needs no acts or speeches of ours to do what is his to do.

> It might be asked, 'Where is Christ the peacemaker between God and men now? How far from us does He dwell?' He says that as He once suffered, so now every day He offers the fruit of His suffering to us through the Gospel which he has given to the world as a sure and certain record of His completed work of reconciliation.[42]

IV

'[O]nly in the sphere of the ethico-religious life, viewed from the standpoint of the Kingdom of God, does the God-man find His place, because that Kingdom, and nothing else, is the direct correlate of the Divine self-end.'[43] Thus Ritschl. If he is wrong, it is not only because of his near-identification of the Kingdom of God and 'the sphere of ethico-religious life', but because that near-identification corrodes Christ's transcendence of moral community, the sheer freedom of his presence to the church,

---

*Another way to say this would be to say that faith marks all ecclesiastical existence and action, for faith is the creaturely moral posture that befits reception of that divine Word of Christ.

and leads to a fundamentally non-dramatic Christology, a Christology in which the sharp contours of the identity and action of Jesus are not given adequate delineation because they serve as little more than an ultimate whence of human life and action.* If an ecclesial ethics of reconciliation is to commend itself as genuinely eschatological, and therefore genuinely hopeful, it will have to demonstrate its concern to resist what Ritschl failed to resist, in part by remembering the dire fate of Protestant dogmatics and ethics when it adopted 'the *ethical apprehension of Jesus*'.[44] But modern theology has a very short memory.

Notes

1 Williams, *Revelation and Reconciliation*, pp. 146f.
2 Some (varied) examples: T. Gorringe, *God's Just Vengeance. Crime, Violence and the Rhetoric of Salvation* (Cambridge: Cambridge University Press, 1996), esp. pp. 248–71; M. Grey, *Redeeming the Dream. Feminism, Redemption and Christian Tradition* (London: SPCK, 1989); idem, *From Barriers to Community. The Challenge of the Gospel for a Divided Society* (London: HarperCollins, 1991); G. Jones, *Embodying Forgiveness. A Theological Analysis* (Grand Rapids: Eerdmans, 1995); M. Volf, *Exclusion and Embrace. A Theological Exploration of Identity, Otherness, and Reconciliation* (Nashville: Abingdon Press, 1996); R. Williams, *Resurrection. Interpreting the Easter Gospel* (London: Darton, Longman & Todd, 1982); idem, *The Truce of God* (London: Fount, 1983); idem, '*Resurrection and Peace. More On New Testament Ethics*', *On Christian Theology*, pp. 265–75; W. Wink, *When the Powers Fall. Reconciliation in the Healing of Nations* (Minneapolis: Fortress Press, 1998).
3 One of the most recent (and very sophisticated) version of this critique is that by R. Hütter, *Evangelische Ethik als kirchliches Zeugnis. Interpretationen zu Schlüsselfragen theologischer Ethik in der Gegenwart* (Neukirchen-Vluyn: Neukirchener Verlag, 1993) For a milder account, see J. Mangina, 'The Stranger as Sacrament. Karl Barth and the Ethics of Ecclesial Practice', *International Journal of Systematic Theology* 1 (1999), pp. 322–39.
4 Schillebeeckx, *Church*, p. xix.
5 Gorringe, *God's Just Vengeance*, p. 263. The notion is adopted from B. Anderson, *Imagined Communities* (London: Verso, 1991).
6 Gorringe, *God's Just Vengeance*, p. 263.
7 Ibid., p. 264.
8 Ibid.
9 Ibid., p. 268.
10 Volf, Exclusion and Embrace, p. 100.

---

*The warning here is to resist treating Jesus as an exclusively historical prompt for human and ecclesiastical moral response and, in so doing, to miss the continuing agency of the exalted Christ, the Lord of his Church.

11   Ibid., p. 105.

12   Ibid.

13   Ibid., p. 109.

14   Ibid.

15   Ibid. Responsible to whom? And can a truly responsible theology be 'designed'? Only if its task is reduced to that of 'facilitating' action (which is why, of course, Marx – correctly – perceived much theology to be ideology).

16   Ibid., p. 101.

17   Ibid., p. 110.

18   'Almost', because he does concede (p. 119) that '[f]or good reasons, Christian tradition thinks of genuine repentance not as a human possibility but as a gift of God'.

19   Ibid., p. 116.

20   Ibid., p. 118.

21   Ibid., p. 130.

22   Ibid.

23   See ibid., pp. 140–7.

24   Or 'facing' the other, as in David Ford's *Self and Salvation*, a book which in the end does not escape from moralizing the gospel.

25   J. Calvin, *The Second Epistle of St Paul to the Corinthians and the Epistles to Timothy, Titus and Philemon* (Edinburg: Oliver & Boyd, 1964), p. 79.

26   Ibid., p. 78. It is one of the strengths of Pannenberg's treatment of reconciliation in volume II of his *Systematic Theology* (Grand Rapids: Eerdmans, 1994),

27   Barth, *Church Dogmatics* IV/1, p. 76

28   For a magisterial depiction of this theme, see T. F. Torrance, 'Ecumenism. A Reappraisal of Its Significance, Past, Present and Future', *Theology in Reconciliation*, pp. 25–81.

29   On this, see the brilliantly suggestive essay by G. Outka, 'Following at a Distance. Ethics and the Identity of Jesus', in G. Green, ed., *Scriptural Authority and Narrative Interpretation* (Philadelphia: Fortress Press, 1987), pp. 144–60, which offers an acute analysis of the correspondences and differences between the acts of Christ and the acts of the Christian, especially in relation to being 'for' others. Attention should also be given to the distinction drawn between Christ as sacrament and Christ as example by Eberhard Jüngel in 'The Sacrifice of Jesus Christ as Sacrament and Example', *Theological Essays II*, pp. 163–190.

30   Here, at least, E. Käsemann was correct to protest against the way in which the notion of reconciliation can be expounded in such a way that Christology and soteriology are subordinated to ecclesiology: see 'Some Thoughts on the Theme "The Doctrine of Reconciliation in the New Testament"', in J. M. Robinson, ed., *The Future of Our Religious Past* (London: SCM Press, 1971), pp. 49–64.

31   *Church Dogmatics* IV/1, pp. 76f.

32   M. Barth, *Ephesians 1–3* (Garden City: Doubleday, 1974), p. 266.

33   The priority of actuality over potentiality in ecclesiology is (rightly) emphasized by D. Bonhoeffer, *Sanctorum Communio. A Theological Study of the Sociology of the Church* (Minneapolis: Fortress Press, 1998), p. 144.

34   *Systematic Theology*, II, p. 415.

35 On this last point, see two essays by Louis Dupré: 'From Silence to Speech. Negative Theology and Trinitarian Spirituality', *The Common Life. The Origins of Trinitarian Mysticism and Its Development by Jan Ruusbroec* (New York: Crossroad, 1984), and 'Negative Theology and Religious Symbols', *Religious Mystery and Rational Reflection* (Grand Rapids: Eerdmans, 1998), pp. 92–103, along with F. J. van Beeck, 'Apophaticism, Liturgy and Theology', in D. Cunningham et al., eds., *Ecumenical Theology in Worship, Doctrine and Life* (Oxford: Oxford University Press,

36 For this distinction (taken from Schleiermacher) see E. Jüngel, 'Der Gottesdienst als Fest der Freiheit', and 'Der evangelisch verstandene Gottesdienst', *Wertlose Wahrheit. Zur Identität und Relevanz des christlichen Glaubens. Theologische Erörterungen III* (Munich: Kaiser, 1990), pp. 283–310.

37 For theological critique of the application of the metaphysics of presence to the reality of God, see Jüngel, *God as the Mystery of the World*, for example pp. 182–4. I am not sure if the ontology in J.-L. Marion's *God Without Being* (Chicago: University of Chicago Press, 1991) is theologically derived

38 Jones, *Embodying Forgiveness*, p. 163.

39 On this, see my article 'Habits. Cultivating the Theologian's Soul', *Stimulus* 7/1 (1999), pp. 15–20.

40 See Schwöbel, 'The Creature of the Word'

41 For a pungent recent reminder of this, see E. Jüngel, *Das Evangelium von der Rechtfertigung des Gottlosen als Zentrum des christlichen Glaubens* (Tübingen: Mohr, 1998).

42 Calvin, *The Second Epistle of St. Paul to the Corinthians*, p. 79.

43 A. Ritschl, *The Christian Doctrine of Justification and Reconciliation*, III (Edinburgh: T&T Clark, 1900), p. 465

44 Ibid., p. 442.

9

Evangelical freedom

EDITOR'S INTRODUCTION

John Webster came to international prominence – for instance, attaining his post as Lady Margaret Professor of Divinity at Oxford or his invitations to give a number of major lecture series – as he emerged as a leading interpreter of Karl Barth. By this time, he had already shown his historical–theological prowess in analysing the work of Eberhard Jüngel in successive works. It has been overly easy for friend and foe alike to glibly categorize Webster's own constructive theology (or at least a phase of it) as 'Barthian', and such judgements have never quite fit or at least do so with severe restrictions. He has always respected Barth, frequently drawn directly upon Barth, sometimes sounded rhetorically like Barth and yet always (not just at the end) diverged in ways small and (sometimes) big. Nonetheless, there are some notable parallels between his own theological vocation and development and the way in which he focused upon Barth's theology, especially as it developed in the 1920s. We have already considered the parallel between Webster and Barth's experience upon his appointment to an academic post in 1922, needing to familiarize himself with classical resources for a job for which he found himself underprepared. Now we consider a more thematic parallel.

Webster's main area of expertise in Barth studies, at least initially, pertained to the Swiss theologian's ethics. His first monograph, *Barth's Ethics of Reconciliation*, looked at his final writings on ethics, while his next book, *Barth's Moral Theology*, ranged much more broadly across his moral teaching. In a variety of ways, Webster's own ethical writings would diverge from Barth. Yet one crucial area where he mimicked or patterned his approach after Barth was in the move to locate all moral judgement within a particular space or frame. Early in his career, Webster would describe that frame one way; in his 1991 essay 'Eschatology, Ontology, and Human Action', he would look eschatologically to a moral ontology determined in hope by what new things emerged in the end. By the end of his life, he was addressing the matter of ontology in a rather different approach (as evidenced by the various essays found in volume 2 of *God without Measure*). Consistently throughout his work, though, he was insistent that doctrinal – that is, biblical – concepts needed to frame out the matrix within which moral determinations could be analysed. Whether that scriptural frame was eschatological or took a fuller scope and sequence ranging all the way from God's own immanent life through election, creation, fall, reconciliation and redemption, he sought to discipline moral thought by approaching it in a distinctly Christian manner. Over time, he grew not only to seek a distinctively Christian canon but also to pursue a broadly canonical rubric (i.e. attuned to the scope and proportions of the whole counsel of God). In this essay, that approach that looks to the wider moral order cuts against the grain of recent trends to address human freedom.

As with many such essays (not least 'Theological Theology'), Webster noted that his approach was out of step with mainstream trends in the modern academy and wider culture, so he offered a 'sketch of some of the constitutive features of modern understandings and practices'. In his genealogy of freedom, he describes how the concept was radicalized such that 'freedom is turned into the very root of human authenticity and dignity'. Alongside this privileging of freedom has come a definition of freedom as 'self-constitution'. This sort of 'constructivist' approach has significant contrast with classical Christian approaches: today, 'Being human is not a matter of having a certain nature or being placed within an ordered reality of which I am not the originator; rather, the distinguishing feature of humankind is, at least resort, the will.' Indeed, Webster later suggests this secular notion developed as certain theological concepts ceased to be operative in the work of theologians as well as the wider culture: 'this misperception is a consequence of the retraction of a specifically Christian understanding of God and God's freedom, and the replacement of that specifically Christian understanding by something much more abstract, as well as much more threatening, namely, an idea of God as impersonal causal force, mere absolute power'.

Webster asks and answers: 'What is evangelical freedom? Evangelical freedom is the freedom announced in the gospel.' To clarify that very compact statement, Webster offers something of a conceptual anatomy by considering its 'origins,' 'establishment' and 'ends'. Over against the pagan notion that 'the agent is characterized, above all, not as a sort of substance, but as enacted intention', Webster describes the human agent in terms of divine gift. 'Far from protecting human authenticity, freedom as self-governance is the expression of alienation from God, and therefore inhumane.' His constructive proposal offers a sketch of both a dogmatics and ethics of human freedom; however, it begins by specifying the identity of God and the nature of this God's freedom. When we look to Scripture, we see God reveal himself not as an oppressive power, related to us only causally and thus oppressively, but we observe God's being as that which turns to us in love and in pursuit of covenant fellowship. Webster unpacks this divine freedom with respect to each triune person, so that he can then define human freedom fittingly as that which is given space and invited to live into this fellowship with God.

This essay was originally written for a 2003 volume addressing 'homosexuality in the church' from within the Anglican context in Canada. While the essay does not explicitly address that topic, it does model the approach to providing a theological frame to a given question: in this case, Webster seeks to define rightly the notion of freedom, so that Christian freedom can be related then to controverted matters of human sexuality. Yet we should catch the way that he does conclude by addressing 'the assumption around which so much of our economic, political and sexual identity is organized, namely the assumption that freedom is autonomy'. He says we must 'lay aside the assumption', for '[f]reedom is, rather, the capacity to realize what one is' and 'to be what I have been made to be, to fulfil my vocation as a creature of God, and so (and only so) to exist in authenticity'. Hence, he concludes by noting, first, that 'human freedom is given' and, second, that 'human freedom is freedom within situations, and not sheerly transcendent'. Indeed, he goes further: 'freedom is thus not some property or potency which I have in myself anterior to all relations and to the givenness of nature and situation; nor is it something which is necessarily constricted or compromised by relations and situations'. Surely this does have something to say rather directly to debates about human sexuality (and a whole range of other ethical issues to boot).

Suggested readings

Barth's Ethics of Reconciliation (Cambridge: Cambridge University Press, 1995).

Barth's Moral Theology. Human Action in Barth's Thought (Edinburgh: T&T Clark; Grand Rapids, MI: Eerdmans, 1998).

'Eschatology, Ontology and Human Action', *Toronto Journal of Theology* 7 (1991): 4–18.

'The Ethics of Reconciliation', in C. Gunton (ed.), *The Theology of Reconciliation* (London: T&T Clark, 2003), pp. 109–24.

'Discipleship and Calling', *Scottish Bulletin of Evangelical Theology* 23 (2005): 133–47.

'Discipleship and Obedience', *Scottish Bulletin of Evangelical Theology* 24 (2006): 4–18.

'Communion with Christ: Mortification and Vivification', in Kent Eilers and Kyle Strobel, eds, *Sanctified By Grace: A Theology of the Christian Life* (London: T&T Clark, 2014), pp. 121–38; repr. in GWM 2, pp. 103–22.

Oliver O'Donovan, 'John Webster on Dogmatics and Ethics', *International Journal of Systematic Theology* 21, no. 1 (2019): 78–92.

Paul Nimmo, 'Ethics', in Michael Allen and R. David Nelson (eds), *A Companion to the Theology of John Webster* (Grand Rapids, MI: Eerdmans, forthcoming).

EVANGELICAL FREEDOM

I

We are schooled by cultural convention to believe that freedom is self-determination. The convention is long-standing and pervasive. Its origins, largely hidden from us within our everyday dealings with the world until retrieved by critical historical reflection, lie in some deep mutations in the West's traditions of religious, philosophical and political thought and practice from the early modern period. Its presence is made known in a complex set of images of human selfhood which form our civic, economic and moral accounts of ourselves. Among its most enduring and culturally successful corollaries is the assumption that the existence of God and human freedom are necessarily antithetical.

One of the primary tasks of a theology of evangelical freedom is to bring that cultural convention to consciousness, and to show that it is both contingent and inhumane. That is, a theology of evangelical freedom has to demonstrate that the conventional conception of freedom as self-government is precisely that – a *convention*, an intellectual and practical strategy for negotiating certain problems which arose in the course of the history of the West's religious and political life. And it has also to demonstrate that the convention's claim to promote human well-being is untruthful, that it is, in fact, destructive of the very reality of liberty which it seeks to uphold and defend.

But this critical or polemical task of Christian theology can only be a secondary undertaking. Its primary task in the matter is descriptive, indeed celebratory: that is, the task of loving and joyful depiction of evangelical freedom. It is the claim of the Christian faith that the understanding and experience of evangelical freedom alone can illuminate, chasten and heal us of the convention which holds us in thrall and which is destructive of the peace and good order of our culture. What is evangelical freedom? Evangelical freedom is the freedom announced in the gospel. The gospel is the proclamation that in Jesus Christ, the risen one who is now present in the power of the Holy Spirit, God the Father's eternal decision to live in fellowship with his human creatures has been unshakeably secured. In fellowship with this God, creator, reconciler and perfecter, we have our freedom as the creatures of God's mercy. Evangelical freedom is the freedom which God bestows on the creatures who, in seeking freedom apart from God, have ruined themselves and fallen into slavery. Its origins lie in the Father's grace, in the omnipotent goodness of God in which he secures the creaturely freedom which he purposes. Its establishment is in the person and work of the Son of God, who is the embodied act of God's liberating of sinners from bondage to decay and death. Its end is in the Spirit's reconstitution of creaturely life and liberty in company with the triune God. In what follows, we offer, first, a sketch of some of the constitutive features of modern understandings and practices of freedom, and, second, the briefest of Christian dogmatics and ethics of freedom as the freedom for which we have been set free.[*]

II

Modern understandings and practices of freedom are a central feature in one of the most important shifts in Western culture which began before the Renaissance and Reformation in the rise of nominalist philosophy and which continues to shape our socioeconomic and political order as well as our reflective images of ourselves. The shift is one in which human selfhood comes to be morally, politically and metaphysically fundamental. As part of this transition to an anthropocentric culture, freedom is radicalized; that is to say, freedom is turned into the very root of human authenticity and dignity.[†] Freedom comes to be constitutive of that which is inalienably human; its inhibition comes to signal the destruction of the humane.

What we might call 'fundamental freedom' – freedom as the basis and distinguishing property of humankind – consists in self-constitution or self-government. Freedom is, first, the distinctively human capacity for self-constitution through action. A human person is human in so far as she is free; and she is free in so far as she can properly be identified as the originator of purposive action. For to be is to act, and to act is intentionally (voluntarily, without overwhelming external constraints) to realize oneself. Truly human action, that is, is a matter of the human agent's self-constitution. In free action, the human agent puts into effect her intentions and so makes herself in a way which is fundamental to her being. The agent's action is not merely to be conceived as the externalizing or 'acting out' of what that agent finds herself to be. Authentically human action is not mere action in accordance with a pre-given human nature (such action is judged to be 'mere' role playing, neither intentional nor free), but rather a making of the agent's nature by free action. Tucked inside this concept of freedom, then, is the notion that the human person is best understood, not as substance but as voluntary subject and agent. Being human is not a matter of having a certain nature or being placed within an ordered reality of which I am not the originator; rather, the distinguishing feature of humankind is, at last resort, the will. The agent is characterized, above all, not as a sort of substance,

---

[*]The outline follows that of 'Theological Theology', first by describing a pathology and giving diagnosis and second by charting a distinctly theological (here: 'evangelical') approach by way of counter-proposal.

[†]'Radicalized' is here a qualitative, not a quantitative, statement. It is not a matter of talking more of freedom or of a more extreme use of it, but of treating freedom as a fundamental ('radical' from *radix* or root) matter, a basic concept not sourced in something anterior to it.

but as enacted intention.* The subject is agent, and in her action is demonstrated her capacity for the self-determination which is freedom: in free action, the human subject is self-positing.

Making self-constitution humanly fundamental is, in the end, radically constructivist. Accordingly, freedom is inseparable from self-government. The freedom which the agent realizes in voluntary acts of self-constitution is to be understood as autonomy. The agent is free in so far as she is autonomous, literally, a law to herself. 'Law' – that is to say, the norms by which we govern action, make discriminations between policies and hold up practices for evaluation – is thus radically internalized.† Classically conceived, law is the structure of given reality ('nature'), and the imperative force of that reality. To say that reality is law is to say that it presents itself to us as an order which requires me to be shaped by and to act in accordance with its given character. On a modern (and a postmodern) account of freedom, by contrast, 'law' is not an externally derived norm, but rather a corollary of my most fundamental activity of self-projection or self-constitution. It bears upon me only as the object of my choice (political, economic, religious, sexual). And so only as a self-legislator can I be said to be free.

One centrally significant feature of this constructivist understanding of freedom as self-constitution and self-government is that freedom is often construed in oppositional terms. Freedom, that is, comes to be portrayed as an opposing of the self to forces which seek to inhibit, contain or envelop the self and rob it of its authenticity, its self-constituted and self-legislated identity. The dynamic of freedom is thus one of acting against a countervailing force, whether that force be nature, custom, law, society or God. Thus, for example, freedom may be set over against nature. To be free is precisely to stand apart from the supposedly given. The experience of freedom (like the self-consciousness to which it is closely allied) is only conceivable if there is a space between the free self and that which is given: the space of freedom. Nature – metaphysical, material, political, legal, moral – is always that to which freedom is opposed and that which may quickly become an object of resentment. By its very givenness, nature constitutes an order of reality which is an obstacle to free self-constitution, a blockage in the path of self-government which must be overcome or transcended. The goal of free selfhood is thus not self-fulfilment in accordance with the order of nature, but self-shaping, a making of the self by struggling free from nature.

Similarly, freedom is to be set over against situation. Freedom is antithetical to the particular sets of circumstances in which agents find themselves, which present

---

*Recent discussions on gender identity surely bear out this approach to characterizing identity (enacted intention takes precedence over some notion of nature or 'ordered reality'). This essay was originally published in a volume that dealt with sexual ethics, so the connection is not accidental or immaterial.
†Note that internalization of law is not equivalent to removal of law. A redefinition and relocation is involved here, not a repudiation of the concept in every form.

themselves as an obligation to undertake certain tasks or a call to certain kinds of responsive (and therefore responsible) action. Like nature, situation is oppressive and must be cleared away by the assertion of liberty. In particular, freedom is real over against social situatedness – over against the way in which human existence is determined and limited by entanglements with others. For if freedom is fundamental to identity, and if identity is achieved by self-constitution and self-government, then other persons cannot be intrinsic to my freedom, but must – like nature – be that which I have to negotiate in order to be free. Society is heteronomy, and therefore erodes the autonomy in which my freedom consists.

A sketch like this cannot pretend to be anything other than a rough-and-ready portrayal of a cultural convention in which nearly all of us are implicated; a full account of the matter would require a massively ramified history of the intellectual and civic traditions by which freedom as autonomy is carried. From a theological point of view, one of the most indispensable components in an understanding of that history is the way in which modern conceptions and practices of human freedom both trade upon and reinforce misperceptions of divine freedom. Indeed, it is at least arguable that *the* determinative feature of the moral and spiritual landscape which had to be conquered and obliterated in the establishment of freedom as self-determination was the existence and freedom of God.* It is often noted that modern conceptions of human autonomy assume a competitive understanding of divine and human freedom. That is, into the idea of freedom as self-determination is built a presumption that God's freedom is intrinsically a limitation upon human liberty, since our freedom and God's are inversely proportional. In so far as God is free agent, his presence and activity will inevitably annexe the space in which human freedom operates; that space must properly be retrieved for humankind if we are to be freely self-constituting agents. More simply: God's freedom will always interfere.

From the point of view of a theology of evangelical freedom, this misperception is a consequence of the retraction of a specifically Christian understanding of God and God's freedom, and the replacement of that specifically Christian understanding by something much more abstract, as well as much more threatening, namely, an idea of God as impersonal causal force, mere absolute power. The retraction of a Christian understanding of God is partly to be explained by the priority accorded to philosophical theism, in which a generic idea of God as transcendent ground of all things is deployed, first as a preliminary to Christian theology and then as a replacement for positive Christian trinitarian and incarnational teaching about the nature of God and of God's relation to the world. But the retraction is not without its theological roots; more than one strand of the history of theology in modernity

---

*A particular definition or identification of God is presupposed in this and the prior reference to the existence of God as threat to human freedom (as moderns construe it). A range of gods – for instance, of a process sort – would not be a threat to human freedom construed as such.

has failed to appeal to positive Christian teaching in its response to philosophical criticism, at cost to the internal structure of Christian doctrine, and with the result that trinitarian teaching in particular drifted towards the margins of theology, with little real work to do.

Because of this, a theology of evangelical freedom will respond to conceptions of freedom as self-determination by returning to the inner structure and content of Christian teaching, seeking to show that the spectre of an absolutely free deity who is by definition the enemy of human freedom is just that: a *spectre*, and one which has to be exorcized by careful and loving attention to what the gospel announces concerning the nature and purposes of God. In making the character of God's freedom its first concern, theology will seek to exhibit that the construal of human freedom as self-determination is rooted in a misconception of God, one which issues in a misconception of human freedom. Indeed, theology will suggest that to think of the world as the kind of place where human freedom can only be maintained if we think of that freedom as self-governance is to think of the world untruthfully.* Far from protecting human authenticity, freedom as self-governance is the expression of alienation from God, and therefore inhumane.

What is required of the church and its theology, therefore, is a dogmatics and an ethics of freedom. Dogmatics and ethics are the church's attempts to submit its mind to the gospel; they are part of the struggle by which the church's thinking and speaking are sanctified as they are taken into the service of the gospel. In its dogmatics, the church orders its thinking towards the gospel as an *indicative*, as a claim to truth. Part of the gospel's claim to truth is a claim about the nature of God's freedom and the nature of the freedom proper to the creatures of God. A dogmatics of freedom is thus an attempt to spell out the character of the free God in his directedness to his free creatures. In its ethics, the church orders its thinking towards the gospel as an *imperative*, as a call to action. For the gospel is not only the announcement of how we are to think aright about God and humankind. It is also a summons to freedom. And so a theology of evangelical freedom will include an ethics of freedom. Dogmatics and ethics are not speculative; they are part of the church's endeavour to orient its life by the truth about God and the human situation, and to discern the shape of truthful human action. Only on the basis of a Christian specification of the freedom of God in relation to the freedom of the creature can a theology of evangelical freedom proceed; and, moreover, only on such a basis can Christian faith

---

*Again, a shift regarding the way in which divine and human action is construed lies at the heart of this perceived problem. Because God is now construed as an agent among other like agents, God's law externally communicated to humans is a threat to human autonomy. But Webster returns our attention to the fact that Christians have not construed God as an agent among other agents but have emphasized his holy transcendence of all creaturely existence and action. He can rule sovereignly without displacing human integrity and agency. Webster's historical work on Barth's ethics (e.g. in *BER* and *BMT*) seeks to show that Barth's emphasis on divine agency and sovereignty does not remove space for human moral responsibility; clearly he takes this to be a commendable and needful Christian argument in its own right, not merely a historical aside.

offer any attempt to heal us of the hurtful axioms which have so deeply embedded themselves into modern practices of freedom, both inside and outside the church. If the church has been largely tongue-tied or concessionary in bearing witness over the matter of freedom, it is in part because of a reluctance to engage in the kind of theological clarifications by which the gospel shapes the church. What is required is a gospel-derived account of freedom as that which creatures discover in fellowship with the free, self-bestowing God made known in Christ and in the Spirit. Above all, we must set aside the bad habit of polarizing divine and human freedom, and must attempt to display how the gospel concerns their integration.

The task, then, of a theology of evangelical freedom is that of letting our thinking be guided by the account of the nature of God and of God's creatures which is set before us in the history of God's fellowship with us. In that history are enacted the identities of the free God and of the creatures of his grace whom he reconciles and perfects. The theological thinking of the church must not be led by abstract conceptions of freedom (human or divine) taken over from its cultural settings, but rather by the gospel's answers to the questions: 'Who is God?' and 'Who is the free creature whom God reconciles and perfects for fellowship with himself?'

III

As with all matters concerning God, so in the matter of God's freedom: the primary question is not 'What is God?' but 'Who is God?' The former – abstract – question invites answers which determine God's essence in advance of any specific considerations of the mode or manner of God's existence. By contrast, the latter – concrete – question is answered by beginning from the given reality of God's self-manifesting existence and only on that basis moving on to determine the essence of God. Because a Christian theology of the freedom of God is a thinking in the wake of God's revelation, it addresses itself to this latter question. For revelation is of all things the most concrete and particular. It is the communicative presence of God, vouchsafed to us in God's works of creation, reconciliation and perfection as Father, Son and Holy Spirit. In those works God sets before us his identity as *this one*, the triune creator who has reconciled his fallen creature and is now bringing it to its final fulfilment. His freedom is the freedom of the one who does this work, and in so doing manifests that his freedom is freedom to be God for us and with us. In short: if we are to think truthfully of God's freedom, avoiding the abstract antitheses which have so ruined the modern conception of freedom, we must grasp that God's freedom is the freedom of the triune God.*

---

*As in 'Immensity and Ubiquity of God', here Webster locates all discussion of nature after examination of divine identity. Because God is unique, his nature cannot be probed without first picking him out from among other beings (who are in distinct metaphysical categories, creatures rather than the Creator).

God's freedom is his freedom as God the Father, creator of heaven and earth. God's freedom is not simply arbitrary power or unfocused will. Rather, because God's freedom is made known in the act of creation, it is a freedom which is actual in his purposive bringing into being of another reality to exist alongside himself. God's freedom is not an infinite reserve of potency which could be actualized in ways other than those which he determines for himself as creator; it is rather the undeflected energy with which God follows the direction in which he determines to be himself. His freedom is thus freedom for fellowship with the creature. As creator, *God is free* – standing under no necessity, having no external claims upon himself, in no need of the creature; as free Lord, God the Father is and creates *ex nihilo*. But because God is free *as creator*, his freedom is not a merely empty or formal idea but a very definite direction and act of relation. And, moreover, as an act of relation, God's freedom is teleological – it involves not simply an initial act of making heaven and earth, but also the preservation and governance of the creaturely realm. As creator, that is, God's freedom is the grace in which he promises himself or commits himself to the creature. The free creator is the free Lord of the covenant, the origin and sustainer of fellowship with himself.

God's freedom is his freedom as God the Son, the reconciler of all things. God's freedom as Father involves the grace with which he pledges to maintain fellowship. That pledge is enacted in God the Son, who restores the covenant between God and his creatures after it has been broken by the creature's wicked and false attempt to be free from God. The creature seeks to be apart from God; only in that way, the creature believes, can real freedom be exercised. This attempt to master its own destiny becomes the creature's ruin and misery, because it strikes at the root of the fellowship with God in which alone the creature has its being. In this situation of the absolute jeopardy of the creature, God's freedom demonstrates itself, not as freedom to withdraw from fellowship, but precisely as an utter determination to maintain fellowship (whatever else it may mean, this is part of what is set before us in the story of Noah). And God's maintenance of fellowship culminates in the person and work of the Son who, as God in the flesh, is reconciliation embodied and effective. He *is* Emmanuel, the fulfilment of the free divine resolve and promise: I will be your God, you will be my people. The fulfilment of this resolve is, of course, entirely gratuitous – God fulfils his freedom in that 'the Word *became* flesh'. But, as in the Father's work of creation, so here in the Son's work of reconciliation: God's freedom is freedom for and with, not freedom apart from or against.

God's freedom is his freedom as God the Holy Spirit, who brings all things to their perfection. In the work of the Holy Spirit, the reconciliation of the creature which has been willed by the Father and accomplished in the person and work of the Son becomes real as the creature's own history. By the power of the free Spirit, God sanctifies the creature, completing his purpose for it and so finally establishing the work begun in creation and maintained in reconciliation. It is the Spirit who thus consummates the purpose of God, not the creature itself. The perfecting of the creature by the Spirit is no less a free work of divine sovereignty than any other of God's works. But the Spirit's freedom is known in the work of making real the relation to God in which the creature has life. The Spirit is Lord, sovereignly free, majestic and unfettered; but as Lord the Spirit is also the life-giver, bestowing upon the creature the life (and therefore the freedom) forfeited in the creature's betrayal of the covenant. As free Spirit, God directs his ways to the final realization of fellowship with those whom he has created and redeemed for life with himself.

What may we draw from this trinitarian sketch of the freedom of God? Two things. First, God's freedom is his aseity – his being from himself. God is the sovereign originator and accomplisher of all that he is and does. Second, we can only grasp what it is for God to be thus eternally and majestically self-moved when we attend to the direction of the divine movement, which is towards us in his work as Father, Son and Spirit.* God's freedom is the glorious spontaneity, reliability and effectiveness in which he is the Holy One in our midst.

IV

What of the freedom of the creature? For Christian theology, that question can only rightly be answered after the question of God's identity as the free creator, reconciler and perfecter has received an answer. To begin by determining the conditions of creaturely freedom in advance of an understanding of God, and then inquiring into the compatibility of human freedom with God's freedom, is simply to remain captive to the destructive convention of human freedom as self-government. A theology of evangelical freedom will work from an understanding of God's freedom towards an anthropology of freedom. God's triune freedom, we have seen, is the sovereign purposiveness with which he establishes fellowship. Human history is the 'space' – arena, setting – in which that fellowship is realized. For the Christian gospel, moreover, the history of God with us is definitive of what it means to be human. It is not a mere modulation or particular form of a more general human history, but is ontologically definitive: to be human is to be the reconciled creature of God pointed by God to perfection. Our freedom, therefore, is the capacity bestowed on us by God to take an active part in the history of fellowship with our creator, reconciler and perfecter.

To understand this, we need to lay aside the assumption around which so much of our economic, political and sexual identity is organized, namely the assumption that freedom is autonomy. Freedom is, rather, the capacity to realize what one is. What we

---

*Elsewhere he will make these two points by speaking of perfection, not just aseity, and by speaking of the processions being made manifest in the divine missions. The conceptual register can shift somewhat at times, although the dogmatic judgements are largely synonymous.

are is reconciled creatures, those set free for true humanness by the work of the triune God. To be free is not to exercise the false freedom to invent myself by my actions, nor to be creator, reconciler and perfecter to myself. Nor is it mere unrestricted will. It is, rather, to be what I have been made to be, to fulfil my vocation as a creature of God, and so (and only so) to exist in authenticity.* Two things flow from this.

First, human freedom is *given*. Because it is the freedom of creatures, it cannot be wholly self-originating. But the contingency of human freedom, its dependence upon the agency of another, is not a restriction but a specification, a way of characterizing its particular nature. In the same way that our life is no less life for being the gift of God, so our freedom is no less freedom for its dependence upon the free grace of God. Or, we might say, given freedom only seems a lesser reality if we cling to the decision that only absolute freedom is real freedom, and that nothing but autonomy can guarantee our authenticity.

Second, therefore, human freedom is freedom within situations, and not sheerly transcendent.† The modern ideal of freedom idealizes freedom as independence, thereby mirroring the degenerate idea of divine freedom which it was designed to negate. But evangelical freedom is not my removal from the realm of contingency and relation; it is, rather, the character of my relations with that which is other than me. Freedom emerges in my occupancy of the space of the material and social world and, above all, of the reality of God as my origin and end. I am not free in abstraction from these relations, nor simply when those relations are a function of my will and exist solely by my sovereign choice. Rather, I become free when I become myself in the space of relations in which I exist. Those relations are the occasions of my freedom when they quicken me to fulfil my nature as creature of God and fellow-creature with others. Freedom is thus not some property or potency which I have in myself anterior to all relations and to the givenness of nature and situation; nor is it something which is necessarily constricted or compromised by relations and situations. Freedom is that which I come to exercise as I exist in freedom-granting fellowship.

Evangelical freedom cannot therefore be conceived or practised as a single spasm, an act of defiance or protest against the fact that I find myself within an order of reality which is not of my invention. Such accounts of freedom, however deeply ingrained they may be, are too thin to furnish a persuasive account of free human selfhood, above all because they reduce all relations to hostile and oppressive determinations. It is certainly true that not all aspects of our situation do quicken freedom: some

---

*The doctrine of creation is crucial, then, for understanding humanity. As in other essays (e.g. 'Eschatology and Anthropology'), natures and ends (or 'vocations' here) are crucial for unpacking creational teaching. Also, creation, reconciliation and eschatology must all be considered to grasp the human creature in the full range of biblical or theological description.

†Interestingly, Webster wants to call even postmodernists back to the reality of context, though chastened. The Scriptural context is, as he also says elsewhere, the most significant context (with creation, fall, redemption being more definitive than race, gender or class). And yet he here also warns that self-determination can never occur as though humans exist apart from or irrespective of situations at a human and social level.

relations can be life-denying, robbing us of authenticity. But these diminutions of freedom are overcome, not by abstracting selfhood from the dependencies which are fundamental to what it means to be human, but by the restoration of the human self to the space in which freedom can be received and acted out.

Human freedom is, in short, that which we are given as we live in the space of fellowship which is made by God's free acts of setting us free. In that space we are met by God as the maker, rescuer and preserver of our freedom, and by those others to whom we have been bound as fellow-recipients of grace. What is the form of this freedom for which, according to the gospel, we have been set free?

Evangelical freedom is a form of life which acts out the fact that I have been set free from 'the law of sin and death' (Rom. 8.2). Sin tyrannizes and limits God's creatures as they act out the falsehood that in order to be human they must make themselves. Such self-making is self-destruction, because it breaks the human side of fellowship with God. Since it is only in fellowship with the creator that we can have life, sin and death are inseparable; together they form the despotic principle ('law') which enslaves humankind. For the gospel, however, that tyranny has been overcome by 'the law of the Spirit of life in Christ Jesus' (Rom. 8.2): in what 'God has done' (Rom. 8.3) in Christ and in the effective presence of that achievement in the Holy Spirit, sin and its entailments – death and bondage – have been condemned (Rom. 8.3), and life and freedom have been irreversibly established as the condition by which we are governed.

Evangelical freedom, emerging from our being put to death and made alive in Christ and the Spirit, is thus freedom from the *care of self* which so harasses and afflicts the lost creatures of God. My freedom is in part my freedom from final responsibility for maintaining myself, a freedom which is the fruit of my having been liberated from the anxious toil of having to be my own creator and preserver.* Evangelical freedom is rooted in a security given to me – not dreamed, imagined or effected by stringent acts of self-realization. That security is such that in Christ I am inviolable, and so free from concern for my own preservation. Such inviolability is not expressed as self-defensive closure of myself against all transgression from without, but as a profound lack of self-preoccupation, a confidence which has its roots in the sheer objectivity of my condition as one set free by God. The compromise of my liberty which I have made by seeking to be my own liberator has been overcome; because by the Spirit I am in Christ, having my centre not in myself and my own acts but in Jesus Christ who has set me free, then all other bonds are set aside. I no longer need to cultivate my freedom; and so I am free. A particular mode of this freedom is the freedom to pray. Prayer is an act of evangelical freedom because in it is expressed

---

*As elsewhere, he does not use the language of 'faith' as often as he might, but this notion of being freed from 'final responsibility for maintaining myself' is bound up with living by faith in the triune God and that God's gospel.

our liberation from anxiety and self-responsibility, and our freedom to live on the basis of fellowship with God and trust in the divine promise. Prayer thus expresses the fact that, as we have been set free by God, so we have had taken from us the evil custody of ourselves which we thought ensured our safety but which in fact fastened us to sin and death. Prayer, indeed, is at the centre of the fellowship with God which is determinative of whatever is authentically humane.

Free for fellowship with God, I am thus free also for human fellowship. If freedom is self-governance, it is the end of love; if, however, freedom is the restoration of my identity in company with my fellows, then I am free to act in support of my neighbour's cause. 'Let no one seek his own good, but the good of his neighbour' (1 Cor. 10.24). Far from being a compromise of freedom, such a rule guides us towards the practice of freedom. To 'seek one's own good' is not to realize one's true nature but to mobilize all one's forces in living out of oneself, making oneself by choices; and so it is to place oneself in the hands of death. To seek that which is one's neighbour's is, by contrast, to be free for life. Looking to the neighbour's cause is not mere self-abandonment; it is rather to exist in the human fellowship by which, precisely by not striving to realize ourselves, we attain to the liberty of the children of God.

Such, then, is a sketch of evangelical freedom, for which we have been set free by the gloriously free God, our maker, redeemer and end. Whether such an account of freedom can commend itself to modern culture is not easy to know. Its persuasiveness depends on many factors: on a willingness to stand apart from dominant conventions; on the existence of forms of Christian common life which exemplify the practice of a freedom which is beyond autonomy or heteronomy; but above all on the coming of the Holy Spirit who is the agent of all persuasion in the matter of the gospel. To understand and practice freedom we need to become different people. It is the office of the Spirit to make us such; the office of the church to bear witness in word and action to the Spirit's convincing work; and the office of the church's theology to assist that witness by trying to speak the gospel well.

10

Intellectual patience[1]

EDITOR'S INTRODUCTION

John Webster had addressed the significance of virtue long ago. In the sixth and final of his 1998 Burns Lectures on 'The Culture of Theology', he spoke of habits and of character formation. In this lecture, titled "Habits: Cultivating the Theologian's Soul", he addressed virtue, trying to affirm the significance of moral psychology, virtue ethics and communal formation, all the while avoiding the immanentist tendencies of postliberalism. In other words, he wanted to think about how virtue could still be construed as a divine gift, not merely the achievement of inwardness. In so doing he was pushing against the way in which some strands of social anthropology were being applied to Christian ethics, particularly among students of the Yale School (as mediated by Stanley Hauerwas and George Lindbeck).

Virtues were an early priority, but that's not the same as saying that Webster was well known for his teaching on the virtues. In his early constructive work (e.g. that collected in *Word and Church* and *Confessing God*), he was known for his teaching on canon and Scripture, or on God's perfection and the church's confession. But he was not yet known for the place of virtue in his moral theology. Notably, however, *God without Measure*, volume two, includes a number of essays on virtues and others still can be added to those few. Webster made virtue and vice a major area of concern in his last decade, expressing more fully that commitment first addressed in the 1998 Burns Lectures.

Likely the most central essay on virtue in Webster's corpus was this inaugural lecture delivered in May 2014 upon his appointment as Chair of Divinity at the University of St Andrews. He plainly intended the lecture and essay to serve as a programmatic statement of his vocation and of his perceived judgement about not merely his own personal service to the university but that of divinity as a distinct discipline, indeed as queen of the sciences. Here virtue met intellect, bringing together two areas of his concern (namely, moral theology and a theology of and for the university). Webster says that 'one of the chief parts of divinity's apostolic office in the university is the articulation of a metaphysics and morals of intellectual inquiry, presenting and enacting a version of the good intellectual life'.

'A virtue is a stable property of character which disposes its possessor to operate well in some realm of human activity. Virtues are principles of the reliably excellent functioning which is required of practitioners in that realm.' One such realm is the intellect or the life of the mind, so 'intellectual virtues underlie intellectual faculties, powers, skills and practices, and animate excellent intellectual performance'. Such intellectual virtues are parsed into four groups: (1) those relating to the search for knowledge, (2) those relating to the reception of knowledge, (3) those relating to the shared pursuit of that knowledge and (4) those relating to difficulties in that pursuit of knowledge. Intellectual patience fits in this fourth category.

In each of his analyses of particular virtues, Webster first searches out the place of that moral good in God himself. He then expounds the way in which God elects that this moral good is communicated to human creatures throughout the course of the divine economy of God's works in creation and new creation. In this case he leans on a range of patristic texts (Cyprian, Tertullian and Augustine) to speak of God's patience as the source of any and all human patience. In so doing he is making good on that early inclination in his 1999 essay on 'Habits', namely, to present a particular virtue or element of moral character as not merely a social achievement or inward performance but ultimately – in and through such connections – as a divine gift of grace. While Webster has clearly gained comfort and ease in speaking about the particularities of moral theology (drawing intensively in these essays on patristic, medieval and Puritan essays on the virtues and vices as well as the underlying moral psychology), he remains a Reformed moral theologian concerned at every point to confess the theme as owing to God's grace.

Webster relates patience to its opposites and its imposters. He relates it thereby to other moral excellencies, showing that human virtues cannot be parcelled out discretely even if they must be spoken of particularly. In so doing, they witness (imperfectly) the simple nature of the ever-patient God, for whom patience cannot be separated from any of his other perfections. Perhaps more notably, Webster also relates patience to its contexts; he shows how a theological frame of reference reorients not merely one's stratagems for success but also one's perceptions of difficulty. In this case finitude and fallenness are the two dire realities to which patience is a necessary moral posture. In so doing he pushes back against predominantly inward or socio-political definitions of difficulty as guiding lights (though they may play contributing or ancillary roles).

Suggested readings

'Courage', in M. Barnes (ed.), *A Man of the Church: Honoring the Theology, Life, and Witness of Ralph Del Colle* (Eugene: Wipf and Stock, 2012), pp. 40–55; repr. in GWM 2, pp. 87–102.

'Curiosity', in M. Higton et al. (eds), *Theology and Human Flourishing: Essays in Honour of Timothy J. Gorringe* (Eugene: Cascade, 2011), pp. 212–23; repr. in DW, pp. 193–202.

'Habits', *Stimulus* 7, no. 1 (February 1999), 17 (15–20; repr. in John Webster, *The Culture of Theology* [intro. and ed. Ivor J. Davidson and Alden McCray; Grand Rapids: Eerdmans, 2019]).

'Sins of Speech', *Studies in Christian Ethics* 28, no. 1 (2015): 35–48; repr. in GWM 2, pp. 123–40.

'Sorrow', in R. Song and B. Waters (eds), *The Authority of the Gospel: Explorations in Moral and Political Theology in Honour of Oliver O'Donovan* (Grand Rapids, MI: Eerdmans, 2014); repr. in GWM 2, pp. 67–86.

Especially helpful are a sequence of five, brief essays on the fruit of the Spirit (from Gal. 5) which appeared in sequence on the Reformation21 blog. Titles include 'Walk by the Spirit', 'Love', 'Joy', 'Peace', and 'Patience'. See links here: http://www.reformation21.org/john-webster-/ (accessed 22 April 2019). Unfortunately, the series was not completed prior to his death. He had intended to bring the essays together as a small book on moral theology.

Matthew Levering, 'Humility', *International Journal of Systematic Theology* 19, no. 4 (2017): 1–29.

INTELLECTUAL PATIENCE

I

What follows is an anatomy and commendation of an intellectual virtue whose presence contributes much to common pursuit of intellectual goods and whose absence inhibits their acquisition. It arises from persuasion that one of the chief parts of divinity's apostolic office in the university is the articulation of a metaphysics and morals of intellectual inquiry, presenting and enacting a version of the good intellectual life. Alongside and in the course of pursuing their other scholarly tasks, divines are charged with inquiry into inquiry – with giving an account of the origin, nature, settings and ends of intellectual activity and of the ways in which that activity is fittingly and fruitfully to be undertaken.* Such matters are, of course, also treated by other disciplines from time to time; but in divinity they have an especial salience, because of divinity's often ambiguous and sometimes conflicted relation to the university since the middle of the eighteenth century. Alone of the four mediaeval faculties, divinity had to struggle to find acceptance in the modern university as it was reconceived in the wake of the German Enlightenment. The struggle may be read in a number of ways, but one of the foremost matters of contention concerned the nature of intellectual inquiry: is divinity to be numbered among the sciences, or is it simply the domestic thought of the ecclesial community? Often enough in the last two centuries, divinity has secured acceptance in the university by compliance, assenting, whether enthusiastically or half-heartedly, to one or other version of a naturalist metaphysics of inquiry, and reinventing itself as the historical and literary science of religious phenomena. The magnificence of the scholarly harvest from such an arrangement can scarcely be over-estimated, though it came at a heavy cost. But another stance has been and still is possible, one less immediately accommodating but ultimately more generous, and one, moreover, which regards the conception of intellectual inquiry in classical Christian thought, not as a liability to be shaken off but as an asset to be shared. Precisely in its unconventionality, a theological metaphysics and morals of inquiry will try to illuminate the life of the mind and provide intelligibility to natural experience and action. This it will do by tracing intellectual life to its source in divine benevolence, by which alone its nature and duties are disclosed. Alongside this, theology will also seek to diagnose inherited or deliberate disorders of our rational nature which prevent that nature's full flourishing, and to suggest how they may be overcome. The cogency of such illumination, pathology and therapy of the intellect

---

* 'Theological Theology' had commented on how theology ought to provoke study elsewhere in the wider academy, and this exploration of an intellectual virtue on Christian terms serves as one such prompt.

will be compromised, however, if divinity fails to govern itself by the metaphysics and morals of inquiry which derive from its proper subject-matter.* Divinity's modern history in this matter is, with significant exceptions, an unhappy one, commonly lacking in the large-spirited confidence and munificence which arise from the knowledge of being in possession of an immense store of riches. Part of that store is a theology of the intellectual virtues, to reflection upon one of which we now turn.

II

The prospering of intellectual life and institutions requires the exercise of certain virtues. The life of the mind is natural, that is, inherent in our nature and faculties as the kind of beings that we are. But, though natural, it is not instinctive but intentional, the result not of simple innate prompting but of deliberate, active cultivation of a potentiality of our nature. Because this is so, it may go well or badly, and, if it is to go well, it requires not only superior innate capacities but also traits of character which dispose us to intellectual excellence. Intellectual life requires intellectual virtue.

A virtue is a stable property of character which disposes its possessor to operate well in some realm of human activity. Virtues are principles of the reliably excellent functioning which is required of practitioners in that realm. Moral virtues are those qualities of person which incline us to moral excellence; intellectual virtues are virtues exercised in relation to intellectual activities and goods. What may be said by way of further description?

Some differentiations are worth noting. Intellectual virtues are different from intellectual faculties such as memory or reason. Faculties are innate, and their operation is generally not deliberate; intellectual virtues, by contrast, are acquired over time and require intentional exercise.† Virtues direct the operation of faculties. Similarly, intellectual virtues are different from intellectual powers, that is, the set of capacities possessed by some person which make possible talented performance in a particular intellectual sphere. Virtues, once again, enable powers to be exercised in an optimal way. Intellectual virtues are different from intellectual skills, that is, the capability to perform specific intellectual tasks in expert fashion (read the score of Bach's Goldberg Variations, translate the text of *Beowulf*). Intellectual virtues, by contrast, enable the cultivation, enhancement and use of skills. Lastly, intellectual virtues are different from intellectual practices. Intellectual practices are

---

*Any intellectual virtues need to be examined in specifically Christian terms, not merely taken on loan from some adjacent line of inquiry (e.g. Aristotelian virtue theory or Frankfurt-style critical theory).

†The distinction is not airtight, as powers or faculties can be expanded or diminished with use and practice (either good or bad). But the distinction remains important, nonetheless, between character traits (dispositions) and powers. It should also be noted that Webster makes the distinction to emphasize the importance of both categories, not to somehow suggest that virtue renders powers or faculties insignificant.

the operations in which intellectual faculties, powers and skills are put to work to accomplish intellectual tasks and so to acquire intellectual goods. Practices may be primarily individual – such as reading – or social and public – such as teaching and debating. Intellectual virtues, once again, are the qualities of person which enable discriminating, fitting engagement in intellectual practices.

In short: intellectual virtues underlie intellectual faculties, powers, skills and practices, and animate excellent intellectual performance. 'Excellent' here refers not simply to technical proficiency, but to intellectual performance which moves in estimable ways to worthy intellectual ends: it is this which intellectual virtues empower.

The supreme intellectual virtue, and the source and moving power of other intellectual virtues, is well-formed love of knowledge, desire for intellectual goods which are worthy of praise. Intellectual life takes its rise in the appetite and the will. We desire intellectual goods – to understand the commanding moral and literary power of Balzac's *Human Comedy*, or some such good – and we experience the satisfaction of that appetite when we attain such understanding. This attraction to knowledge and its rewards engages the will to pursue intellectual ends, subordinating or eliminating competing desires – if you want to figure out Balzac, don't get too fascinated with Stendhal or Zola – and driving us into intellectual activity. Yet in itself love of knowledge does not suffice for intellectual excellence. Our desire to know may be prurient, attaching itself to unworthy goods; or it may attach itself to worthy goods for unworthy reasons such as self-advancement or desire for celebrity. Desire for the goods of knowledge must be discriminating. Such discrimination is the fruit of the *formation* of desire; it arises from the right ordering of love of knowledge, so that love is set on fitting objects and pursues them in well-tempered ways. Where such formation is lacking, love of knowledge risks becoming vicious – a greedy ungoverned appetite bent on the satisfactions of intellectual consumption. Rightly formed love, by contrast, is the root of the other virtues of the intellect. Formation is in large part a social process. We learn what constitutes an intellectual good, and how to pursue it fittingly, by being schooled, observing others who love truth and live the intellectual life in an excellent manner, appropriating the desires, intentions and behaviours of eminent practitioners of the arts of the mind, and so acquiring the habits which dispose us to similar excellence.* The fruit of the formation of intellectual character is possession and prudent exercise of intellectual virtues.

Enumerations and classifications of the intellectual virtues vary quite widely; here is a relatively simple arrangement. (1) There are those virtues which dispose us to

---

*The social dimension of learning these virtues – otherwise put, of learning how intellectual love involves the formation of desire for knowledge – highlights the flaw in autonomy as an essential human descriptor. See 'Eschatology and Anthropology' and 'Evangelical Freedom' for further critique of autonomy as a basic human description and an exposition of creatureliness that involves situation, both socially and theologically, crucial to human being and maturing.

labour to acquire intellectual goods. The principal virtue here is love of knowledge, the animating and directive power of intellectual life. The chief ancillary virtue is studiousness – assiduous, open-minded, objective, consistent and well-tempered application to the pursuit of new knowledge. Studiousness is earnest, ardent deployment of intellectual faculties, powers and talents, resisting premature satisfaction of intellectual appetite, and continuing to study until the desired goods are acquired. (2) There are those virtues which dispose us to receive the intellectual goods. These virtues include attentiveness (steady, observant direction of the mind to that which lies beyond ourselves); humility (awareness and acceptance of intellectual limitations); modesty (temperate estimation of one's own excellence and resistance to the desire to be conspicuous); and docility or teachableness. (3) There are those virtues which fit us to contribute to and profit from common intellectual life: intellectual benevolence (the disposition to promote the intellectual good of others); intellectual generosity (sharing intellectual goods); affability (friendliness and approachability in intellectual exchange); impartiality (justice in intellectual conduct towards others); and gratitude (glad recognition of intellectual indebtedness). (4) There are those virtues which ready us to deal with difficulty in the pursuit of intellectual goods. These include magnanimity (the largeness of purpose which causes us to attempt demanding tasks); intellectual courage (firmness of mind in enduring what is outstandingly difficult); and, finally, intellectual patience, the analysis of which is our next task.

III

We may begin with an anatomy of patience generally considered.

Patience is that excellence of character by which, for the sake of some good end, we tolerate difficulties, and encounter obstacles to present happiness with equanimity, collectedness and steadiness of purpose. It is the quality of mind which overcomes aversion to extended labour and lack of fulfilment by composure and readiness to endure prolonged misfortune in order not to lose or desert good things.

Patience has a secure place in the table of Christian virtues, appearing routinely in apostolic and early Christian paraenesis: patience enables believers to endure the interval before the promised return of Christ and the completion of history, to face present affliction, and to maintain peaceful common life. 'Be patient . . . until the coming of the Lord' . . . 'may you be strengthened with all power. . . for all endurance and patience'. . . 'be patient with them all' (Jas 5.7; Col. 1.11; 1 Thess. 5.14). In the Latin patristic tradition, patience is the subject of three widely-influential treatises – those of Tertullian, Cyprian and Augustine[2] – and exhortation to patience is scattered throughout its exegetical, homiletical and ascetical texts. Though not a cardinal virtue, it is one of the principal moral entailments of Christian teaching, and an integral element in the present framing of life before God. Gregory the Great spoke of it as the 'root and guardian of all virtues'[3] – though others accord it a more minor status, subordinating it to courage: Aquinas is a case in point. Patience is also a common theme in the moral and spiritual literature of the Reformation and post-Reformation periods; affecting treatments of it may be found in English Puritan writers such as John Owen[4] and Thomas Goodwin.[5]

Texts on Christian patience often address the question of what it is that marks out distinctively Christian patience, 'the patience of the saints' (Rev. 13.10; 14.12).* Classical treatments of the virtue, aware of the overlaps between their moral world and that of late antique paganism, are nevertheless often insistent on this distinctiveness. Here, for example, is Cyprian, writing in Carthage in the middle of the third century: 'Philosophers also profess that they pursue this virtue; but in their case the patience is as false as their wisdom also is. For whence can he be either wise or patient, who has known neither the wisdom nor the patience of God?'[6] True patience, on the other hand, is on Cyprian's account an excellence only of the 'servants and worshippers of God', those who give 'spiritual obedience' and so demonstrate 'the patience which we learn from heavenly teachings'.[7] Cyprian's point is not merely a bit of moral one-upmanship; it is more that for the servant and worshipper of God and the recipient of divine instruction, the world is a different place, one which requires and makes possible a distinct manner of life of which patience is a part.

We might elaborate this point along the following lines. Patience is, primordially, an excellence of reconciled creatures. It is an excellence of *creatures*, that is, of those who owe their being and movement to the creator's goodness in communicating life, causing them to be, bestowing on them a specific nature and summoning them to its enactment. Yet that nature is ruined, because of creaturely defiance of both nature and its maker; knowledge of it is available to us only in fragments, intermittently glimpsed but nothing more; its full enactment would demand resources which no longer remain in our possession. Full knowledge and activation of our nature are therefore dependent upon its rescue. The rescue is effected in the works of divine benevolence: in acts of providence which preserve our damaged nature by preventing its collapse and preparing it for completion, and, supremely, in the acts of the divine Word and Spirit which bestow and direct a new creaturely nature. Christian moral teaching, including teaching about virtues, concerns the ways in which the renovation of our nature is appropriated, made a matter of active consent.

If this is so, then to make Christian sense of a virtue we need to grasp its setting in the history of creation and reconciliation.† Reflection upon that history generates

---

*Some virtues are distinctive to Christianity in that they are not otherwise prized in the classical world (e.g. humility), but some, such as patience, are distinctive in their material content (which can be easily misperceived because they seem nominally identical).

†Creation and reconciliation each contribute, and neither can fully unfold the shape of human patience apart from the other. Dogmatics makes distinctions to keep one alert of the full breadth of theological material.

not simply incentives to neglected duties but a metaphysics and an anthropology of morals. These articulate the principles of attitudes and actions which are not to be confounded with attitudes and actions of similar appearance but possessing quite different grounds. Understanding patience, in short, requires attention to what Tertullian, in the first great Latin treatise on patience, called 'the divine disposition of a living and celestial discipline'.[8]

We may briefly set out some of the constitutive differences of a Christian metaphysics and anthropology of patience, before moving to reflect on patience in relation to intellectual life.

Patience Christianly understood has distinct causes and acting subjects. It is not a straightforward effect of human nature. This is because, on the one hand we are creatures and so only live and move through another's love, and, on the other hand our created nature has suffered such depredation that, though some aptitude for patience remains as a residue of our integral state, its completion is out of our reach. Of necessity, therefore, human patience is an effect of a divine cause.

This means, most basically, that God is the 'author' of patience: 'from him patience begins; from him its glory and its dignity take their rise'.[9] But patience is a divine effect because it is a divine property: God is the source of patience because he is patient in himself. Divine patience allows creatures time to enact their lives; in the face of creaturely rejection, it does not terminate the creature but continues to grant to the creature further opportunities and possibilities. This divine patience is not suffering but long-suffering, longanimity: not passive waiting upon creaturely purpose but the enduring exercise of government.[10] Within this patient divine order, creatures enact their lives: 'Where God is' says Tertullian 'there too is . . . patience'.[11] Patience, then, is a divine property and a 'gift of God',[12] generative of, and exemplary for, human conduct. Its exemplary force is known supremely in the life of Christ in which it is embodied and commended. Cyprian, for example, looks at the entire course of the incarnation from heavenly descent through passion to exaltation as divine-human illustration and pattern of the excellence of patience. '[H]e maintained the patience of his Father in the constancy of his endurance';[13] and so, 'let us walk by the example of Christ'.[14]

God's authorship of patience is both creative and exemplary, making possible and in this way evoking creaturely patience.* Divine causality is not simply efficient, propelling our moral lives from outside (how then would they be *moral*?): God moves by love and so does not stifle but bestow life. In patience, as in all things, God so moves us so that we live and move. Yet – precisely because they are moved by God – our life and movement are not some instinctive abundance original in us. Human patience is not innate strength but what Augustine calls 'the patience of the poor',

---

*Luther uses the language of 'gift' and 'example' in making this point repeatedly.

received from the 'Rich One' who is its giver.[15] From the Spirit comes love of God, and with it the ordering and formation of right desire, from which, by the Spirit's further grace, patience arises: 'of whom cometh in us love, of him cometh patience.'[16]

Such are the causes of patience. What of its objects, the matters about which we need to be patient? Patience is endurance of difficulties and resistance to the dejection which those difficulties generate. Classical Christian moral literature picks out four related kinds of difficulty to which patience directs itself: (1) the active presence of hostility and persecution, and the possibility of martyrdom; (2) the deprivations encountered in pursuing monastic and ascetical vocation; (3) the demands of social relations in the Christian community; (4) Christian experience of distress, arising either from our fallen natural existence or from the unresolved and contested condition of the Christian pilgrim. Christian patience reads these afflictions in a distinct way. Sorrow persuades us that adversity is an eruption of disorder, the onslaught of malignant fortune. Patience suffers the same sorrow, but sees the afflictions which give rise to sorrow as contained within the divine providence. Afflictions, that is, are purposive occasions for divine goodness, instruction, correction and consolation, as well as opportunities for the enactment of virtue. Patience is not resignation to calamity, because calamity is not a Christian category; patience is, rather, composure in adversity derived from knowledge of divine order and protection.

This, in turn, is because Christian patience has a specific end. Its goal is a good deal more than preservation of equanimity in tribulation, for patience directs itself to the cessation of tribulation and the completion of our nature – in simple terms, heaven. Christian patience arises from knowledge of and trust in a future good already secured but at present not enjoyed. Patience, on Augustine's definition, is 'that by which we tolerate evil things with an even mind, that we may not with a mind uneven desert good things through which we may arrive at better'.[17]

What of the operation of Christian patience? Having this cause, these objects, this end, in what attitudes and behaviours is it displayed? Much might be gleaned from the literature of moral analysis and pastoral exhortation: about conformity to Christ's patience; about *willing* endurance of affliction as discipline; about composure and joy in tribulation; about tolerance of and gentleness towards others whom we find troublesome. Activities and behaviours such as these arise not simply from diligent application of natural capacities but from knowledge of the new nature and from affection for the good to which it directs us. The point may be illustrated by a contrast which Calvin draws between Christian patience and insensibility or resignation. Patience is not, on Calvin's account, a refusal to allow 'the natural feeling of sorrow'[18] when met by outrageous fortune; if we 'make patience into insensibility and a valiant and constant person into a stock', then 'we renounce the pursuit of patience'.[19] Facing affliction, truly patient persons feel bitterness and apprehension, but, instead of suppressing these emotions, incline to a certain forbearance. This forbearance is grounded in a condition in which patient persons find themselves, one which, even in contrary circumstances, displays the fact that God 'does nothing except with a well-ordered justice'.[20] To suffer patiently is thus much more than to 'yield to necessity'; it is, rather, to 'consent [to our] own good'[21] – and this, once again, because Christian patience reads the world differently.

What of the vices which stand opposed to patience? Most obviously, impatience, refusal to endure affliction with composure. Impatience is manifest as restlessness: feverish excitement, frenzy, distraction, instability, irritability, those attitudes and behaviours which erode steadiness of spirit and longanimity.[22] Impatience harms us more than any affliction to which it responds intemperately. This is because its fury so fills us that we become incapable of following suffering to its term, and we forsake the good in which affliction issues: 'the impatient', Augustine tells us, 'while they will not suffer ills, effect no deliverance from ills, but only the suffering of heavier ills'.[23]

Lastly, what of precepts of Christian patience, injunctions to its exercise? Precepts have their origin and force in conceptions of the way the world is; they are the imperative force of being. Christian precepts to patience rest on and give expression to all that has been said so far about the causes, agents, operations and ends of patience: because there is this God and this world of his making and remaking, because there are these creatures, then act in these ways, strive for these excellences, including the excellence of patience. Precepts to patience seek to elicit and direct the exercise of our renewed nature, status and calling. And, more than anything, they are precepts of divine grace, accompanied by promises of divine assistance and consolation.

This portrayal of Christian patience may perhaps strike some as isolationist. But to draw attention to what differentiates moral worlds and practices is not to betray a sectarian mentality. Rather, it is to recognize that all accounts of virtue, theological or non-theological, necessarily rest upon a reading of the world. If this is so, then to describe a moral act is not simply to describe an occurrence to which a certain value is ascribed, but to indicate a whole anterior realm of moral nature and culture, of goods and intentions, to which the moral act gives practical assent and expression. The interesting – and contested – questions are these: Whose patience? Patience with what causes and objects? Patience for what ends? Patience out of what resources?

Yet difference is not the end of the matter. The moral worlds of believer and unbeliever, divergent though they may be, are not wholly discrete. This is not because they are simply different brands of the same thing; it is more that they exist at different stages in the history of human renovation. A Christian theology of virtue does not treat pagan virtue as wholly devoid of worth. It tries rather to give it intelligibility by seeing it as enfolded within the history of divine judgement and renewal of creaturely life. Unhindered exercise of a virtue like patience requires piety and attraction to worthy goods, which are the fruit of conversion from self-absorption to love of God.

But even in its damaged state and its resistance to the end to which it was appointed, natural human life contains anticipations of its conversion, common graces which, however haltingly, stretch out to its completeness. Intellectual patience is one such anticipation. How may it be described?

Intellectual patience is patience exercised in relation to intellectual goods; the occasions for its exercise are those afflictions which attend pursuit of these goods, inhibiting their acquisition and enjoyment. Intellectual patience is closely affiliated with intellectual courage. Intellectual courage faces the fears which arise when we seek to obtain intellectual goods – criticism, loss of honour, isolation from prestige, and so on – and does not allow the fears to paralyse us. Courage is not recklessness: the threats are real, and mere bravado is of no avail. Rather, courage is prudent, evaluating threats and determining when to be bold, when to exercise caution, when to withdraw from the field. Courage presupposes magnanimity, in which we aspire to undertake great endeavours and extend ourselves to an end which moves us to operate at full capacity. The pusillanimous person attempts little, content to contract and retreat rather than face vexation. By contrast, the magnanimous person – not the presumptive or over-ambitious or vainglorious person – expands and advances. Yet in so doing, such a person finds the path strewn with obstacles; patience is an element in preventing collapse of intellectual purpose in the face of possible injury or loss, and in pressing ahead to completion.

Exercise of intellectual patience is demanding, because in varying degrees we are alienated from our created nature in its integrity, and our customary condition is intellectual impatience. Why is impatience so close at hand? Because we have become covetous, seeking to treat intellectual goods as something other than a divine gift. Covetousness fails to acknowledge that, because we are creatures, 'nothing is ours'[24] – everything is received but not owned. Assent to the condition of being a creature involves coming to see that the fragility and indigence of our being are not a matter of dishonour or peril; they are intrinsic to the way in which we come to enjoy the good things of divine provision. Dissent from the creaturely condition fails to see our intrinsic poverty against the backdrop of God's infinite generosity; it does not understand that the economy of our lives, including our intellectual lives, is characterized by what Tertullian calls 'bestowing and communicating';[25] it prefers to think that only possessed goods are stable and satisfying. When in the course of intellectual activity we meet afflictions with this framing of our affections, the result is impatience: agitation, defensiveness, discomposure. Patience is part of the ascetics of intelligence, necessary for the repair of intellectual nature and the rectification of intellectual appetite. Intellectual patience is a distributed virtue which encompasses both the individual and the social domains of intellectual life, in each of which affliction may be encountered. We look at each in turn.

1. Two elements of individual intellectual life are the objects of intellectual patience. First, patience is required in view of the temporal character of created intellect. Our knowledge is discursive, acquired over time, rather than innate or intuitive. We come to know by learning, and our learning is never complete. Not so divine knowledge, which knows all things in a simple comprehensive act of intuition. Intrinsic to the creaturely intellectual condition is the necessity of *suffering* the process of coming-to-know: human intellectual activity takes time. Because of this, intellectual life requires the virtues of longanimity and patience. Longanimity is the excellence which perseveres long as we direct ourselves to some future good; it is, Aquinas notes, 'that quality by which we have the spirit to strive for a distant aim'.[26] Patience is the excellence which deals with the reality that, in the damaged condition of our nature, the temporal remoteness of the fulfilment of our intellectual appetite is a source of a double misery. First, the injuries which our nature has sustained include loss of powers, making the acquisition of intellectual goods and the satisfaction of intellectual appetite much more laborious (one – crucial – episode apart, Adam thought more quickly than his heirs). Second, we chafe at these labours, and at the delays by which they are exacerbated. Intellectual patience is that part of fortitude which enables us to retain a proper focus, which preserves us from looking for shortcuts to effect deliverance, and which keeps us in a sedate and hopeful temper, in anticipation of the perfect intellectual rest which awaits us.

Patience is also required in view of creaturely insufficiency and dependence. To be a creature – to exist out of nothing – is to be other than self-sufficient, complete in oneself.* We are contingent beings whose nature only flourishes by way of dependence: in receiving from and giving to other creatures, and, most of all, in relying upon infinite divine generosity. The human intellectual condition always involves *pathos*, being subject to constitution from outside.[27] Our intellectual life is by nature and operation always an undergoing, even a surrender, as much as it is an acting.[28] And our injured nature, forgetful of the infinite abundance of love of which pathos bears the impress, treats pathos as something threatening, revealing not only the limitation and incalculability of our intellectual undertakings but also, more deeply, our 'hanging upon' and subjection to another reality.

Intellectual patience is acknowledgement and embrace of this condition. Yet it is not abandonment of responsibility for aiming our intellectual lives: no one can know for me, no one can think on my behalf.† Patience is a condition for intellectual operation, not its relinquishment. Patience is *trustful* bearing of intellectual insufficiency, sheltering our intellectual lives from the malign identification of dignity and autonomy. In this way, patience liberates creatures from the ideal of entire intellectual adequacy: we know in part, but we may still know well.

---

*In this sense, human patience is markedly different from divine patience (which is exercised by one who is *a se* and self-sufficiently perfect).

†That it is metaphysically or soteriologically passive does not mean that it is equated with existential or psychological passivity. Human inactivity is not required to make space for God's provision or agency.

Such intellectual patience is formed and directed by the two fundamental enactments of creaturely dependence: attention to divine instruction and prayer. Much modern intellectual culture despises these acts as evasions or corrosions of responsibility. In distorted and debased forms, of course, they may be. But they may be much more: acts in which the repair of our intellectual nature takes present form, exercises in which we recall our integral state and anticipate our coming completion.

2. What of intellectual patience as a social virtue? Intellectual life, though often individual, is never purely private. Even in its most extreme introversion, it is a mode of life in society. At every point it involves the communication of intellectual goods, and it is almost unthinkable without public, institutional forms – schools, funding arrangements, systems for assessing and rewarding intellectual performance. Excellent engagement in these public realms requires a set of interlaced virtues: charity, generosity, humility, tolerance, docility, and patience. Consider a couple of social extensions of intellectual patience.

Patience is exercised in teachableness, disposing us to readiness for learning. Most immediately, this means learning from our contemporary intellectual neighbours and companions. A little more distantly, patience involves deference to traditions of inquiry, the remains and echoes of companions long gone. Both involve the chastening of self-sufficiency, a certain loss of autonomy, as we come to terms with the fact that the intellectual life is neither from itself or *de novo*. Others are already here, still others have been here in the past. Coming to see that inquiry is a social practice, and learning the difference between intellectual originality and untutored spontaneity, requires a mortification of the affections away from self-command and their renewal through patience, because impatient persons learn little, having cut themselves off from sources of learning. 'Through this vice of impatience . . . instruction, the nurse of virtues, is dissipated . . . Everyone is shown to be by so much less instructed as they are convicted of being less patient.'[29]

Patience is further exercised in the exchange of intellectual goods, especially in practices of public speech and debate. From its inception, Christian faith entailed new rhetorical practices and new modes of intellectual communication which set aside those which enjoyed cultural prestige: 'Where is the debater of this age?' (1 Cor. 1.20 – divines have often been lamentably reluctant to take the point). Patience in public communication of intellectual goods arises from acknowledgement that those goods are not property to be grasped, defended or consumed but gifts. Property confers status and generates competition and conflict, and status, competition and conflict threaten peaceful, generous and friendly pursuit of truth in common. Patience faces these threats and disorders with composure, knowing that tranquil speech serves to commend the truth, and with prudent forbearance, having a well-formed understanding of occasion and opportunity which knows when to withdraw and when to continue. Patience in view of the irritability and hastiness of public speech has a three-fold source. Its first fountain is deep attachment to intellectual goods, which are of such desirableness and splendour that we may not allow ourselves or others to desert them in strife. Second, it springs from humble recognition that we ourselves not only suffer but also inflict suffering. And third, in its Christian modulation, public intellectual patience is sustained by remembrance of divine forbearance, the 'perfect patience' (1 Tim. 1.16) which has set an end to contests and established peace as our proper condition.

IV

By way of conclusion . . . Lament at the threats faced by university institutions is a well-established genre of academic writing; sometimes the results are perceptive, at other times self-indulgent registering of complaints. That universities face externally-imposed inhibitions to their full flourishing is indisputable, though hardly a novel state of affairs. However, such vexations are a sub-set of the perennial vexations of the intellectual life. Two things are required by individuals and institutions if those vexations are not to clog the performance of our intellectual nature.

First, it is necessary to interpret these threats by an act of intelligence, for to know and understand a threat to the best of our abilities is already to contain and move against it. Coming to understand threats to intellectual well-being, however, requires more than a reaction to the surface elements or phenomena which cause anxiety or distress; we need to understand their causes.* We require, in other words, some sort of well-ordered, coherent and plausible account of the first principles of intellectual life and activity; if we would make sense of our troubles, we require a metaphysics of the intellect and its undertakings. One test of the vitality of an intellectual institution is whether it has the appetite to think about and discuss such matters, and sufficient freedom from distraction to do so fruitfully. Divinity is well placed to encourage and participate in such conversations, because it is able to draw upon a long tradition of thought about the inescapably moral and spiritual character of pursuit of intellectual goods, and because it has access to a fund of concepts and arguments about the intellectual life possessed of remarkable illuminative and explanatory power. A theology of the intellectual virtues is part of that store.

Second, engaging threats to the pursuit of any good, intellectual or otherwise, requires understanding and practice of the virtues. Talk of virtues, however, presupposes that there is such a thing as human nature, and that it brings with it a good which beings having that nature are to pursue in order to flourish. Modern political, economic and sometimes intellectual regimes regard such a presupposition

---

*Other disciplines will name intellectual problems in the academy. Theology can uniquely serve the university and the wider life of the mind by tracing those problems to ultimate causes (hence fulfilling a goal charted in 'Theological Theology').

as at best primitive, at worst an obstacle to pure spontaneous self-creation. Once again, divines find themselves under a particular obligation here: to explicate how it is that the intellectual life is part of the good life, and how the good life is that life in which our given nature comes to be realized. To grasp that nature, to observe and understand its inherent direction and to follow the vocation which it carries within itself, we need to grasp its creatureliness, its absolutely conditioned character. To be human is in every element of our being to be referred to a source of life; and that reference is not dark heteronomy but the deeply happy reality that, though we might not have been, by divine generosity we *are* and *live*. It is this which makes intellectual life possible, and which sustains it when harassed by difficulty. Action and emotion are rightly ordered when they follow being or nature; virtues are excellences which direct and preserve this following of nature. Patience is the virtue which directs and preserves by checking distress at adversity as we wait for and persevere towards nature's completion, and so imparts quiet vigour to our often harassed undertakings.

Notes

1   An inaugural lecture as Professor of Divinity at the University of St Andrews, May 2014.
2   Tertullian, *Of Patience* (ANF 3); Cyprian, *On the Advantage of Patience* (ANF 5); Augustine, *De patientia* (NPNF 1.3).
3   Gregory the Great, *Homiliae in evangelia* 35, in *Gregory the Great. Forty Gospel Homilies* (Piscataway: Gorgias Press, 2009).
4   See, for example, Owen's treatment of Hebrews 6.12 in *An Exposition of the Epistle to the Hebrews*, vol. 3 (London: Tegg, 1840), pp. 330–5.
5   T. Goodwin, Patience and Its Perfect Work, in *The Works of Thomas Goodwin*, vol. 2 (Edinburgh: James Nichol, 1861), pp. 429–67.
6   Cyprian, *On the Advantage of Patience* 2.
7   Cyprian, *On the Advantage of Patience* 2.
8   Tertullian, *Of Patience* 2.
9   Cyprian, *On the Advantage of Patience* 3.
10   See K. Barth, *Church Dogmatics* II/1, pp. 410–14; Augustine, *De patientia* I.1.
11   Tertullian, *Of Patience* 15.
12   Augustine, *De patientia* I.1.
13   Cyprian, *On the Advantage of Patience* 6.
14   Cyprian, *On the Advantage of Patience* 9.
15   Augustine, *De patientia* XV.12. In this connection, much may be learned from A. MacIntyre's attention to vulnerability as basic to the human condition in *Dependent Rational Animals*, esp. pp. x–xii, 4–8.
16   Augustine, *De patientia* XXIII.20.

17　Augustine, *De patientia* II.2.

18　Calvin, *Institutes of the Christian Religion* III.viii.10.

19　Calvin, *Institutes of the Christian Religion* III.viii.10 (ET altered).

20　Calvin, *Institutes of the Christian Religion* III.viii.11.

21　Calvin, *Institutes of the Christian Religion* III.viii.11.

22　See, for example, the contrast of patience with frenzy in *Shepherd of Hermas* II.5.ii, and Gregory the Great's admonition to the impatient (*Pastoral Rule* III.9):

> 'The impatient are to be told that . . . while they neglect to bridle their spirit, they are hurried through many steep places of iniquity which they seek not after, inasmuch as fury drives the mind whither desire draws it not, and, when perturbed, it does, not knowing, what it afterwards grieves for when it knows.'

23　Augustine, *De patientia* II.2.

24　Tertullian, *Of Patience* 7.

25　Tertullian, *Of Patience* 7.

26　Aquinas, *Summa theologiae* IIaIIae.136.5 resp.

27　On this, see R. Hütter, *Suffering Divine Things. Theology as Church Practice* (Grand Rapids: Eerdmans, 2000), especially pp. 29–34, 124f.

28　See M. Heidegger's meditation on *Gelassenheit* in 'Conversation on a Country Path about Thinking', in *Discourse on Thinking* (New York: Harper and Row, 1966), pp. 58–90.

29　Gregory the Great, *Pastoral Rule* III.9.

John B. Webster – Chronology of publications

Monographs

1980   *Rudolf Bultmann: An Introductory Interpretation*. Leicester: Religious and Theological Studies Fellowship.

1983   *God Is Here: Believing in the Incarnation Today*. Hampshire: Marshall Morgan and Scott.

1986   *Eberhard Jüngel: An Introduction to His Theology*. Cambridge: Cambridge University Press.

1995   *Barth's Ethics of Reconciliation*. Cambridge: Cambridge University Press.

1998   *Barth's Moral Theology: Human Action in Barth's Thought*. Edinburgh: T&T Clark.

2000   *Barth* (1st edn). London: Continuum.

2001   *Word and Church: Essays in Christian Dogmatics*. Edinburgh: T&T Clark.

2003   *Holiness*. London: SCM.
      Holy Scripture: A Dogmatic Sketch. Cambridge: Cambridge University Press.

2004   *Barth* (2nd edn). London: Continuum.

2005   *Barth's Earlier Theology: Four Studies*. London: T&T Clark.
      Confessing God: Essays in Christian Dogmatics II. London: T&T Clark.

2011   *The Grace of Truth*. Ed. Daniel Bush and Brannon Ellis. Farmington, MI: Oil Lamp.

2012   *The Domain of the Word: Scripture and Theological Reason*. London: T&T Clark.

2015   *God without Measure: Working Papers in Christian Doctrine*. Volume One: *God and the Works of God*. London: T&T Clark.

2015   *God without Measure: Working Papers in Christian Doctrine*. Volume Two: *Virtue and Intellect*. London: T&T Clark.

2019   *The Culture of Theology*. Introduced and Edited by Ivor J. Davidson and Alden McCray. Grand Rapids, MI: Baker.

Editorial work

1994   *The Possibilities of Theology: Studies in the Theology of Eberhard Jüngel in His Sixtieth Year*. Edinburgh: T&T Clark.

2000   *The Cambridge Companion to Karl Barth.* Cambridge: Cambridge
University Press.
Theology after Liberalism: A Reader (with George P. Schner). Oxford: Blackwell.

2007   *The Oxford Handbook of Systematic Theology* (with Kathryn Tanner and Iain
R. Torrance). Oxford: Oxford University Press.

Doctoral thesis

1982   'Distinguishing between God and Man: Aspects of the Theology of Eberhard
Jüngel'. PhD Thesis. University of Cambridge.

Translations

1989   Eberhard Jüngel. *Theological Essays.* Edinburgh: T&T Clark.

1995   Eberhard Jüngel. *Theological Essays II.* Edinburgh: T&T Clark.

1999   Eberhard Jüngel. 'On the Doctrine of Justification'. *International Journal of
Systematic Theology* 1: 24–52.

2001   Eberhard Jüngel. *God's Being Is in Becoming: The Trinitarian Being of God in the
Theology of Karl Barth: A Paraphrase.* Edinburgh: T&T Clark.

Chapters in books

1988   'Althaus', 'Aulen', 'von Balthasar', 'Barth', 'Berkhof', 'Bonhoeffer', 'Bultmann',
'Contemporary Theological Trends', 'Cremer', 'Doctrinal Criticism', 'Heim',
'von Hugel', 'Jüngel', 'MacKinnon', 'Macquarrie', 'Metz', 'Moehler', 'Nygren',
'Schleiermacher', 'Richardson', 'Wingren'. In *Dictionary of Theology.* Ed. David
F. Wright. Leicester: InterVarsity.
'The Christian in Revolt: Some Reflections on *The Christian Life*'. In *Reckoning
with Barth: Essays in Commemoration of the Centenary of Karl Barth's Birth.* Ed.
Nigel Biggar. London: Mowbray.
'Ministry and Priesthood'. In *The Study of Anglicanism.* Ed. Stephen Sykes and
John E. Booty. Philadelphia, PA: Fortress.

1989   'Eberhard Jüngel'. In *The Modern Theologians: An Introduction to Christian
Theology in the Twentieth Century.* Vol. 1. Ed. David F. Ford. Oxford: Blackwell.

1993   'BCP and BAS: Some Thoughts on a Theological Shift'. In *Thinking about the Book
of Alternative Services.* Toronto: Anglican Book Centre.

'Creation, Doctrine of', 'Faith', 'Revelation, Concept of'. In *The Blackwell Encyclopaedia of Modern Christian Thought*. Ed. A. E. McGrath. Oxford: Blackwell.

1994 'Justification, Analogy and Action: Passivity and Activity in Jüngel's Anthropology'. In *The Possibilities of Theology: Essays on the Theology of Eberhard Jüngel in his Sixtieth Year*. Ed. John Webster. Edinburgh: T&T Clark.

1995 'God', 'Authority', 'Bonhoeffer', 'Obligation', 'Original Sin'. In *A New Dictionary of Christian Ethics and Pastoral Theology*. Ed. David J. Atkinson and David F. Field. Leicester: InterVarsity.

'Jesus – God for Us'. In *Anglican Essentials: Reclaiming Faith within the Anglican Church of Canada*. Ed. George W. Egerton. Toronto: Anglican Book Centre.

1997 'Eberhard Jüngel'. In *The Modern Theologians: An Introduction to Christian Theology in the Twentieth Century*, 2nd edn. Oxford: Blackwell.

1998 'Anhypostasis and Enhypostasis in Barth and Jüngel'. In *Anhypostasis and Enhypostasis: An Essay across the Patristic and Reformed Centuries of the Church* (with Companion Essay by G. O. Mazur). New York: Holy Trinity.

'Conscience'. In *Dictionnaire critique de théologie*. Ed. J.-Y. Lacoste. Paris: Presses Universitaires de France.

'George Bell', 'F.W. Dillistone', 'Eugene Fairweather'. In *The SPCK Handbook of Anglican Theologians*. Ed. Alister E. McGrath. London: SPCK.

'What Is the Gospel?' In *Grace and Truth in a Secular Age*. Ed. Timothy Bradshaw. Grand Rapids, MI: Eerdmans.

1999 'Chalcedonian Christology after Berdyaev in Barth and Jüngel'. In *Fifty Year Commemoration to the Life of Nicolai Berdyaev (1877–1948)*. Ed. G. O. Mazur. New York: Semenenko Foundation.

'England, Theology of'. In *Die Religion in Geschichte und Gegenwart: Handwörterbuch für Theologie und Religionswissenschaft*, 4th edn. Vol. 2. Tübingen: J.C.B. Mohr (Paul Siebeck).

'Scripture, Reading and the Rhetoric of Theology'. In *Ten Year Commemoration to the Life of Hans Frei 1922–1988*. Ed. G. Olegovich. New York: Semenenko Foundation.

2000 'Introducing Barth'. In *The Cambridge Companion to Karl Barth*. Ed. John Webster. Cambridge: Cambridge University Press.

'Barth and Postmodern Theology: A Fruitful Confrontation?' In *Karl Barth: A Future for Postmodern Theology?* Ed. Geoff Thompson and Christiaan Mostert. Hindmarsh: Australian Theological Forum.

2001 'Confession and Confessions'. In *Nicene Christianity: The Future of a New Ecumenism*. Ed. Christopher R. Seitz. Grand Rapids: Brazos.

'Güte (Gottes) II. Dogmatisch'. In *Die Religion in Geschichte und Gegenwart: Handwörterbuch für Theologie und Religionswissenschaft*, 4th edn. Vol. 3. Tübingen: J.C.B. Mohr (Paul Siebeck).

'Introduction'. In *Justification: The Heart of the Christian Faith*. Eberhard Jüngel. Edinburgh: T&T Clark.

'Kenotische Christologie'. In *Die Religion in Geschichte und Gegenwart: Handwörterbuch für Theologie und Religionswissenschaft*, 4th edn. Vol. 4. Tübingen: J.C.B. Mohr (Paul Siebeck).

2002   'Discovering Dogmatics'. In *Shaping a Theological Mind: Theological Context and Methodology*. Ed. Darren C. Marks. Aldershot: Ashgate.

'The "Self-Organizing" Power of the Gospel: Episcopacy and Community Formation'. In *Community Formation in the Early Church and the Church Today*. Ed. Richard N. Longenecker. Peabody, MA: Hendrickson.

'What's Evangelical about Evangelical Soteriology?' In *What Does It Mean to Be Saved? Expanding Evangelical Horizons of Salvation*. Ed. John G. Stackhouse. Grand Rapids, MI: Baker.

2003   'Barth, Karl (1886–1968)'. In *Jesus in History, Thought, and Culture: An Encyclopedia*. Vol. 1. Ed. L. Houlden. Santa Barbara: ABC-CLIO.

' "A Great and Meritorious Act of the Church?" The Dogmatic Location of the Canon'. In *Die Einheit der Schrift und die Vielfalt des Kanons; The Unity of Scripture and the Diversity of the Canon*. Ed. John Barton and Michael Wolter. Berlin: Walter de Gruyter.

'The Ethics of Reconciliation'. In *The Theology of Reconciliation*. Ed. Colin Gunton. London: T&T Clark.

'Evangelical Freedom'. In *The Homosexuality Debate: Faith Seeking Understanding Fidelity Essays*. Ed. C. Sider-Hamilton. Toronto: Anglican Book Centre.

'The Human Person'. In *The Cambridge Companion to Postmodern Theology*. Ed. Kevin J. Vanhoozer. Cambridge: Cambridge University Press.

'Introduction: Philosophy and the Practices of Christianity'. In G. Schner. *Essays Catholic and Critical*. Ed. Philip G. Ziegler and Mark Husbands. Aldershot: Ashgate.

'Reading Scripture Eschatologically (1)'. In *Reading Texts, Seeking Wisdom: Scripture and Theology*. Ed. David F. Ford and Graham Stanton. London: SCM.

2004   'Balthasar and Karl Barth'. In *The Cambridge Companion to Hans Urs von Balthasar*. Ed. Edward T. Oakes and David Moss. Cambridge: Cambridge University Press.

'Biblical Theology and the Clarity of Scripture'. In *Out of Egypt: Biblical Theology and Biblical Interpretation*. Ed. Craig Bartholomew, Mark Healy, Karl Möller and Robin Parry. Milton Keynes: Paternoster.

'Forward'. In William H. Brackney. *A Genetic History of Baptist Thought*. Macon: Mercer University Press.

'The Goals of Ecumenism'. In *Paths to Unity: Explorations in Ecumenical Method*. Ed. Paul Avis. London: Church House.

'The Immensity and Ubiquity of God'. In *Denkwürdiges Geheimnis: Beiträge zur Gotteslehre: Festschrift für Eberhard Jüngel zum 70. Geburtstag*. Ed. Ingolf Dalferth, Johannes Fischer and Hans-Peter Grosshans. Tübingen: Mohr Siebeck.

'Incarnation'. *The Blackwell Companion to Modern Theology*. Ed. Gareth Jones. Oxford: Blackwell.

'Response to "What Wondrous Love Is This?"' In *For the Sake of the World: Karl Barth and Ecclesial Theology*. Ed. George Hunsinger. Grand Rapids, MI: Eerdmans.

'Shapers of Protestantism: Karl Barth'. In *The Blackwell Companion to Protestantism*. Ed. Alister E. McGrath and Darren C. Marks. Oxford: Blackwell.

'"There Is No Past in the Church, so There Is No Past in Theology": Barth on the History of Modern Protestant Theology'. In *Conversing with Barth*. Ed. John C. McDowell and Mike Higton. Aldershot: Ashgate.

2005 'The Church and the Perfection of God'. In *The Community of the Word: Toward an Evangelical Ecclesiology*. Ed. Mark Husbands and Daniel J. Treier. Downers Grove, IL: InterVarsity.

'Hope'. In *The Oxford Handbook of Theological Ethics*. Ed. Gilbert Meilaender and William Werpehowski. Oxford: Oxford University Press.

'Karl Barth'. In *Reading Romans through the Centuries: From the Early Church to Karl Barth*. Ed. Jeffrey P. Greenman and Timothy Larsen. Grand Rapids: Brazos.

'Macquarrie, John'. In *Dictionary of Twentieth-Century British Philosophers*. Ed. A. P. F. Sell. Bristol: Thoemmes.

'Prolegomena to Christology: Four Theses'. In *The Person of Christ*. Ed. Stephen R. Holmes and Murray A. Rae. London: T&T Clark.

'Purity and Plenitude: Evangelical Reflections on Congar's *Tradition and Traditions*'. In *Yves Congar: Theologian of the Church*. Ed. Gabriel Flynn. Louvain: Peeters; Grand Rapids, MI: Eerdmans.

'Systematic Theology after Barth: Jüngel, Jenson, and Gunton'. In *The Modern Theologians: An Introduction to Christian Theology since 1918*, 3rd edn. Ed. David Ford with Rachel Muers. Oxford: Blackwell.

'Versöhnung V. Theologiegeschichtlich', 'Wunder VII. Dogmatisch'. In *Die Religion in Geschichte und Gegenwart: Handwörterbuch für Theologie und Religionswissenschaft*, 4th edn. Vol. 8. Tübingen: Mohr Siebeck.

'The Visible Attests the Invisible'. In *The Community of the Word: Toward an Evangelical Ecclesiology*. Ed. Mark Husbands and Daniel J. Treier. Downers Grove, IL: InterVarsity.

2006 'God and Conscience'. In *The Doctrine of God and Theological Ethics*. Ed. Alan J. Torrance and Michael C. Banner. London: T&T Clark.

'God's Perfect Life'. In *God's Life in Trinity*. Ed. Miroslav Volf and Michael Welker. Minneapolis, MN: Fortress.

'Karl Barth's Lectures on the Gospel of John'. In *What Is It That the Scripture Says? Essays on Biblical Interpretation, Translation and Reception in Honour of Henry Wansborough OSB*. Ed. Philip McCosker. London: T&T Clark.

'Principles of Christian Theology'. In *In Search of Humanity and Deity: A Celebration of John Macquarrie's Theology*. Ed. Robert Morgan. London: SCM.

2007 'The Dignity of Creatures'. In *The God of Love and Human Dignity: Essays in Honour of George M. Newlands*. Ed. Paul Middleton. London: T&T Clark.

'God's Aseity'. In *Realism and Religion: Philosophical and Theological Perspectives*. Ed. Andrew Moore and Michael Scott. Aldershot: Ashgate.

'Human Identity in a Postmodern Age'. In *Tolerance and Truth: The Spirit of God or the Spirit of the Age?* Ed. Angus Morrison. Edinburgh: Rutherford House.

'Introduction: Systematic Theology'. In *The Oxford Handbook of Systematic Theology*. Ed. John Webster, Kathryn Tanner and Iain Torrance. Oxford: Oxford University Press.

'Jesus Christ'. In *The Cambridge Companion to Evangelical Theology*. Ed. Timothy Larsen and Daniel J. Treier. Cambridge: Cambridge University Press.

'Pureté et plenitude: reflexions protestantes sur "La tradition et les Traditions" de Congar'. In *Yves Congar, Théologien de l'Eglise*. Ed. Gabriel Flynn. Paris: Cerf.

'Resurrection and Scripture'. In *Christology and Scripture: Interdisciplinary Perspectives*. Ed. Andrew T. Lincoln and Angus Paddison. London: T&T Clark.

'Theologies of Retrieval'. In *The Oxford Handbook of Systematic Theology*. Ed. John Webster, Kathryn Tanner and Iain Torrance. Oxford: Oxford University Press.

2008 'Life in and of Himself: Reflections on God's Aseity'. In *Engaging the Doctrine of God: Contemporary Protestant Perspectives*. Ed. Bruce L. McCormack. Grand Rapids, MI: Baker.

'Rowan Williams on Scripture'. In *Scripture's Doctrine and Theology's Bible: How the New Testament Shapes Christian Dogmatics*. Ed. Markus Bockmuehl and Alan J. Torrance. Grand Rapids, MI: Baker.

'*Ut Unum Sint*: Some Cross-bench Anglican Reflections.' In *Ecumenism Today: The Universal Church in the 21st Century*. Ed. Francesca Aran Murphy and Christopher Asprey. Aldershot: Ashgate.

2009 'On the Theology of Providence'. In *The Providence of God:* Deus Habet Consilium. Ed. Francesca Aran Murphy and Philip G. Ziegler. London: T&T Clark.

'One Who Is Son: Theological Reflections on the Exordium to the Epistle to the Hebrews'. In *The Epistle to the Hebrews and Christian Theology*. Ed. Richard Bauckham, Daniel R. Driver, Trevor A. Hart and Nathan MacDonald. Grand Rapids, MI: Eerdmans.

'*Rector et iudex super Omnia genera doctrinarum?* The Place of the Doctrine of Justification'. In *What Is Justification about? Reformed Contributions to an Ecumenical Theme*. Ed. Michael Weinrich and John P. Burgess. Grand Rapids, MI: Eerdmans.

2010 'Attributes, Divine'. In *The Cambridge Dictionary of Christian Theology*. Ed. David Fergusson, Karen Kilby, Ian McFarland and Iain Torrance. Cambridge: Cambridge University Press.

'Gunton and Barth'. In *The Theology of Colin Gunton*. Ed. Lincoln Harvey. London: T&T Clark.

'"Where Christ Is": Christology and Ethics'. In *Christology and Ethics*. Ed. F. LeRon Schults and Brent Waters. Grand Rapids, MI: Eerdmans.

2011 'Curiosity'. In *Theology and Human Flourishing: Essays in Honour of Timothy J. Gorringe*. Ed. Mike Higton, Jeremy Law and Christopher Rowland. Eugene, OR: Cascade.

'"In the Society of God": Some Principles of Ecclesiology'. In *Perspectives on Ecclesiology and Ethnography*. Ed. Pete Ward. Grand Rapids, MI: Eerdmans.

'Introduction'. In *Trinitarian Theology after Barth*. Ed. Myk Habets and Phillip W. Tolliday. Eugene, OR: Pickwick.

'It Was the Will of the Lord to Bruise Him: Soteriology and the Doctrine of God'. In *God of Salvation: Soteriology in Theological Perspective*. Ed. Ivor J. Davidson and Murray A. Rae. Farnham: Ashgate.

'Perfection and Participation'. In *The Analogy of Being: Invention of the Antichrist or the Wisdom of God?* Ed. Thomas Joseph White. Grand Rapids, MI: Eerdmans.

'*Regina artium:* Theology and the Humanities'. In *Theology, University, Humanities:* Initum Sapientiae Timor Domini. Ed. Christopher Craig Brittain and Francesca Aran Murphy. Eugene, OR: Cascade.

2012 'Barth's Lectures on the Gospel of John'. In *Thy Word Is Truth: Barth on Scripture*. Ed. George Hunsinger. Grand Rapids, MI: Eerdmans.

'Courage'. In *A Man of the Church: Honoring the Theology, Life, and Witness of Ralph Del Colle*. Ed. Michel René Barnes. Eugene, OR: Pickwick.

'Providence'. In *Mapping Modern Theology: A Thematic and Historical Introduction*. Ed. Kelly M. Kapic and Bruce L. McCormack. Grand Rapids, MI: Baker.

'Ressourcement Theology and Protestantism'. In *Ressourcement: A Movement for Renewal in Twentieth-century Catholic Theology*. Ed. Gabriel Flynn and Paul D. Murray. Oxford: Oxford University Press.

2013 'On the Theology of the Intellectual Life'. In *Christ across the Disciplines: Past, Present, Future*. Ed. Roger Lundin. Grand Rapids, MI: Eerdmans.

2014 'Preface'. In *On Religion. The Revelation of God as the Sublimation of Religion*. Ed. K. Barth. London: Bloomsbury, pp. vi–viii.

'Reformed Tradition'. In *The Westminster Handbook to Karl Barth*. Ed. R. E. Burnett. Louisville: Westminster John Knox, pp. 178–80.

'Communion with Christ: Mortification and Vivification'. In *Sanctified By Grace. A Theology of the Christian Life*. Ed. K. Eilers and K. Strobel. London: T&T Clark, pp. 121–38.

'Holy Scripture'. In *Between the Lectern and the Pulpit. Essays in Honour of Victor A. Shepherd*. Ed. R. Clements, D. Ngien. Vancouver: Regent College Publishing, pp. 173–81.

'Sorrow'. In *The Authority of the Gospel: Explorations in Moral and Political Theology in Honour of Oliver O'Donovan*. Ed. R. Song, B. Waters. Grand Rapids, MI: Eerdmans, pp. 250–67.

'God, Theology, Universities'. In *Indicative of Grace – Imperative of Freedom. Essays in Honour of Eberhard Jüngel in His Eightieth Year*. Ed. D. Nelson. London: T&T Clark, pp. 241–54.

'*Non ex aequo*: God's Relation to Creatures'. In *Within the Love of God. Essays in Dialogue with Paul Fiddes*. Ed. A. Moore, A. Clarke. Oxford: Oxford University Press, pp. 95–107.

'Thomas Forsyth Torrance, 1913–2007'. *Biographical Memoirs of Fellows of the British Academy* 13 (2014): 417–36.

2015'Creation Out of Nothing'. In *Christian Dogmatics: Reformed Theology for the Church Catholic*. Ed. M. Allen, S. Swain. Grand Rapids, MI: Baker, pp. 126–47.

'Providence'. In *Christian Dogmatics: Reformed Theology for the Church Catholic*. Ed. M. Allen, S. Swain. Grand Rapids, MI: Baker, pp. 148–64.

'The Place of Christology within Systematic Theology'. In *The Oxford Handbook of Christology*. Ed. F. A. Murphy. Oxford: Oxford University Press, pp. 611–27.

'ὑπὸ πνεύματος ἁγίου φερόμενοι ἐλάλησαν ἀπὸ θεοῦ ἄνθρωποι': On the Inspiration of Holy Scripture'. In *Conception, Reception and the Spirit: Essays in Honor of Andrew T. Lincoln*. Ed. J. G. McConville, L. K.Pietersen. Eugene, OR: Cascade, pp. 236–51.

2017 ' "A Relation beyond All Relations": God and Creatures in Barth'sLectures on Ephesians, 1921–22'. In Karl Barth, *The Epistle to the Ephesians*. Ed. R. David Nelson. Grand Rapids, MI: Baker, pp.31–49.

Journal articles

1983 'The Identity of the Holy Spirit: A Problem in Trinitarian Theology'. *Themelios* 9.1: 4–7.

1985 'Eberhard Jüngel on the Language of Faith'. *Modern Theology* 1: 253–76.

1986 'Atonement, History and Narrative'. *Theologische Zeitschrift* 42: 115–131.

'Bibliography: The Theology of Eberhard Jüngel'. *Modern Churchman* 28: 41–4.

'Christology, Imitability and Ethics'. *Scottish Journal of Theology* 39: 309–26.

'Eberhard Jüngel: God as the Mystery of the World. On the Foundation of the Theology of the Crucified One in the Dispute between Theism and Atheism'. (Review Article) *Scottish Journal of Theology* 39: 551–6.

'The Humanity of God and Man: An Introduction to Eberhard Jüngel'. *Evangelical Review of Theology* 10: 239–46.

'The Imitation of Christ'. *Tyndale Bulletin* 37: 95–120.

1987 ' "On the Frontiers of What Is Observable": Barth's *Römerbrief* and Negative Theology'. *Downside Review* 105: 169–80.

1988 'Books of Interest: Theological'. *Toronto Journal of Theology* 4: 281–3.

'The Firmest Grasp of the Real: Barth on Original Sin.' *Toronto Journal of Theology* 4: 19–29.

'Some Notes on the Theology of Power'. *Modern Churchman* 30: 17–25.

1990 'Education for a Global Theology' (with Marsha Hewitt et al.) *Theological Education* 26, Supplement (1990): 86–112.

1991 'Eschatology, Ontology and Human Action'. *Toronto Journal of Theology* 7: 4–18.

'Thoughts on *Prometheus Rebound: The Irony of Atheism*'. *Toronto Journal of Theology* 7: 226–9.

1992 'Locality and Catholicity: Reflections on Theology and the Church'. *Scottish Journal of Theology* 45: 1–17.

'Response to George Hunsinger'. *Modern Theology* 8: 129–32.

1993 'The Church as Theological Community'. *Anglican Theological Review* 75: 102–15.

1994 '"Assured and Patient and Cheerful Expectation": Barth on Christian Hope as the Church's Task'. *Toronto Journal of Theology* 10: 35–52.

1995 'Jesus' Speech, God's Word: An Introduction to Eberhard Jüngel (I)'. *Christian Century* 112.35: 1174–8.

'Jesus' Speech, God's Word: An Introduction to Eberhard Jüngel (II)'. *Christian Century* 112.36: 1217–20.

1997 'Jesus in the Theology of Eberhard Jüngel'. *Calvin Theological Journal* 32: 43–71.

'Reading Theology'. *Toronto Journal of Theology* 13: 53–63.

1998 'God and Conscience'. *Calvin Theological Journal* 33: 104–24.

'Hermeneutics in Modern Theology: Some Doctrinal Reflections'. *Scottish Journal of Theology* 51: 307–41.

1999 'The Good News of God'. *Stimulus* 7: 21–6.

'Habits: Cultivating the Theologian's Soul'. *Stimulus* 7: 15–20.

'Criticism: Revelation and Disturbance'. *Stimulus* 7: 9–14.

'Conversations: Engaging the Difference.' *Stimulus* 7: 2–8.

'Traditions: Theology and the Public Covenant'. *Stimulus* 6: 17–23.

'Texts: Scripture, Reading, and the Rhetoric of Theology'. *Stimulus* 6: 10–16.

'Culture: The Shape of Theological Practice'. *Stimulus* 6: 2–9.

'Lambeth: A Comment'. *Pro Ecclesia* 8: 143–6.

'Postmodern Eschatology?' *Toronto Journal of Theology* 15: 167–81.

2000 'A Reply to Tom Weinandy'. *New Blackfriars* 81: 236–7.

'Eschatology, Anthropology, and Postmodernity'. *International Journal of Systematic Theology* 2: 13–28.

'Fides et Ratio, articles 64–79'. *New Blackfriars* 81: 68–76.

'Theologische Theologie'. *Zeitschrift für Theologie und Kirche* 97: 238–58.

2001 'Article Review: David F. Ford: *Self and Salvation*'. *Scottish Journal of Theology* 54: 548–59.

'Canon and Criterion: Some Reflections on a Recent Proposal'. *Scottish Journal of Theology* 54: 221–37.

'The Dogmatic Location of the Canon'. *Neue Zeitschrift für systematische Theologie und Religionsphilosophie* 43: 17–43.

'"In the Shadow of Biblical Work": Barth and Bonhoeffer on Reading the Bible'. *Toronto Journal of Theology* 17: 75–91.

'The Self-Organizing Power of the Gospel of Christ: Episcopacy and Community Formation'. *International Journal of Systematic Theology* 3: 69–82.

2002 'Confession and Confessions'. *Toronto Journal of Theology* 18: 167–79.

2003 'The Church as Witnessing Community'. *Scottish Bulletin of Evangelical Theology* 21: 21–33.

2004 'The Holiness and Love of God'. *Scottish Journal of Theology* 57: 249–68.

'On Evangelical Ecclesiology'. *Ecclesiology* 1: 9–35.

2005   'Barth, Karl', 'Canon', 'Gospel', 'Scripture, Authority of'. In *Dictionary for Theological Interpretation of the Bible*. Ed. Kevin J. Vanhoozer. Grand Rapids, MI: Baker.

'Barth and the Reformed Confessions'. *Zeitschrift für Dialektische Theologie* 21: 6–33.

'Discipleship and Calling'. *Scottish Bulletin of Evangelical Theology* 23: 133–47.

'Purity and Plenitude: Evangelical Reflections on Congar's *Tradition and Traditions*.' *International Journal of Systematic Theology* 7: 399–413.

2006   'Discipleship and Obedience'. *Scottish Bulletin of Evangelical Theology* 24: 1–18.

2007   '*Wie Geschöpfe leben*: Some Dogmatic Reflections'. *Studies in Christian Ethics* 20: 273–85.

2008   'Biblical Reasoning'. *Anglican Theological Review* 90: 733–51.

2009   'Principles of Systematic Theology'. *International Journal of Systematic Theology* 11: 56–71.

'Webster's Response to Alyssa Lyra Pitstick, *Light in Darkness*'. *Scottish Journal of Theology* 62: 202–10.

2010   'Trinity and Creation'. *International Journal of Systematic Theology* 12: 4–19.

2011   'Illumination'. *Journal of Reformed Theology* 5: 324–39.

2012   'T.F. Torrance on Scripture'. *Scottish Journal of Theology* 65: 34–63.

2013   ' "Love Is also a Lover of Life": *Creatio ex nihilo* and Creaturely Goodness'. *Modern Theology* 29: 156–71.

'*Sub ratione Dei*: Zum Verhältnis von Theologie und Universität'. *Communio Internationale Katholische Zeitschrift* 42: 151–69.

2015   'What Makes Theology Theological?', *Journal of Analytic Theology* 3.1: 17–28.

Interview

2008   'Being Constructive: An Interview with John Webster'. *Christian Century* 125: 32–4.

Index

affability 201
afflictions 204
alienation from God 182
Anselm 68
anthropology 35, 56
    fixation on conversion 146n.
'anthropology of enquiry' 26–8, 33, 35, 44
anthropology of freedom 191
apophatic theology 78, 176
ascetical vocation 204
ascetics of intelligence 206
ascetic theology 37n., 154
'aspatiality' 83
assurance 134, 153
Athanasian Creed 72
atonement theory 131
attentiveness 201
Augustine 66, 68, 78, 107, 196, 201
    on impatience 205
    on patience 203–4
    on reason 55
Aulén, G. 79
authenticity 185, 186, 192, 193
authoritative tradition 27
autonomy 183, 186–7, 191, 194, 200n.

Baconian rationality 57
baptism 14
Barth, Karl 1–2, 3, 27n., 70, 85, 88, 181
    on the atonement 131
    Christocentrism 101
    on Christology and Trinity 102
    on divine and human action 167
    ethics of 188n.
    on First Commandment 122
    on providence 155

    on reconciliation 172, 173
    and theology in context 148
Barth, Markus 174
Bavinck, Herman 71
being and time 132
Berkhof, H. 82n. 19
biblical commentary 31, 32
biblical interpretation, debates 47
biblical reasoning
    and soteriology 125
    and whole counsel of God 121
biblical theology 110n., 143
bibliology 47
Bildung 21, 27, 28
Bonhoeffer, Dietrich 27n., 58
Bourdieu, P. 33
Buckley, Michael 29
Bullinger, Heinrich 52

Calvin, John 31–2, 66, 77, 122, 131
    on assurance 136
    on Christian patience 204
    on reconciliation 171–2
    on revelation 30
    on trinitarian source of salvation 134
    on Word 50
canon 28
canon of theology 31
Caputo, John 150–1
catechesis 12, 16, 145–6
character formation 195
charity 208
Chemnitz, Martin 70
choice 186
Christian eschatology 159–60
Christian faith, and intellectual inquiry 37

Christian life, contingency of 92
Christian patience 202–5
Christian theology
    as biblical reasoning 44, 46–7, 59
    contribution to modern university 34–9
    discipline of 24
    object, parts, and sources of 90
    self-alienation of 47
Christocentrism 70n., 86, 101
Christology 85
    collapses into soteriology 101
    connects incarnation to immanent
        Trinity 92
    considers eternal Word and Word's temporal
        mission 92
    as distributed doctrine 85, 86, 93, 103
    as division of doctrine of the Trinity 93
    economy as second domain 97–102
    location, role, and rank in systematic
        theology 91
    primacy of theology over economy 91–2, 93
    reduced to incarnational narratives 124n.
    in systematic theology 88–9
    theology as first domain 94–7
    and Trinity 96
church
    as creature of the Word 163, 177
    ministry of reconciliation 166–7, 173–7
    'ontological rule' 164
    passivity of 164
    subordinate to Holy Trinity 169
citation vs. enquiry 28, 31
Clarke, Samuel 69
classics of Christian tradition 2, 8, 12
Coakley, Sarah 37n.
Colet, John 24
commentarial reason 60–1
communion of saints 13
Congar, Yves 163
contemplation 54
context, not fate 147
conversational theology 146n.
coram Deo 13
courage 202, 206

covenant 102, 122, 124, 128, 131, 137, 143
    and freedom of God 190
    and identity of God 158
covenant of grace 132
covenant of redemption 122
covetousness 206
creation
    distributed doctrine 109
    as effusion 57
    ex nihilo 73, 79, 98, 112–13, 190
    and freedom of God 190
    and patience 202, 207
    and reason 57–8
    spacious theology of 107, 109
    wholly benevolent and beneficent 117
    work of nature 98, 108
creational metaphysics 105
creator and creature, continuity of 57
Creator-creature distinction 43, 58, 175n.
creatures
    contingency 79, 113
    dependence and derivation 118
    endowed with reason 54–5
    natures and ends 127
    ontological deficiency apart from
        creator 113
    procession from God 111
    real relation with the creator 114–15
    redemption and perfection 98
critical methods 142
critical theology 7
critical theory 43, 199n.
cursive representation 61
Cyprian 196, 201, 202, 203

Dalferth, Ingolf 66
Davies, Oliver 43, 56–8
deism 51
de Margerie, B. 76
Denney, J. 138n. 24
derivation 88, 93, 97n., 112, 126, 158
Derrida, Jacques 150–1
Descartes, Rene 5–6, 8, 29
destiny, as invention 150–1

distributed doctrine 86, 106, 109

divine attributes 65–6, 67–8, 70–2, 75

divine causality 203

divine economy 16, 46, 47, 85

   and fellowship with God 48–9

   grounded in perfection of Holy Trinity
     48, 133

   and history of redemption 49

   and reason 47

   as revelatory 49–50

divine and human action, asymmetry
   of 177

divine identity 67

divine missions 48, 108

   follow divine processions 133

divine nature, and divine identity 67–8

divine perfection 16, 70, 74, 83n. 19

divine presence 65

   and eschatology 142

divine processions 48, 108, 111, 115

   as principle in economic missions 132–3

divinity. *See* theology in the university

docility 208

dogmatic reasoning 44, 61, 64n. 34

dogmatics 145

   as ascetical discipline 61

   attentiveness to biblical testimony 146

   boundaries of 145

   as conceptual representation 44, 61

   precedence of definition of description over
     definition by analysis 72

   on presence of God 11

   and Scripture 12

Dorner, Isaak 85, 100

double predestination 122

'economics' of space 80

ecumenical movement 164

Edwards, Jonathan 122, 130, 133, 139n. 36

election 128, 163, 172–3

Emery, Gilles 134

endurance 204

enhypostatsis 137–8

Enlightenment 43

enquiry 31, 33, 37

epistemology 35

eschatological language, and prayer 154

eschatology 142

   and dissolution of teleology 149–55

   and divine presence 142

   and ethics 159–60

   and selfhood 155–8

   and metaphysics 143

   and moral-political action 157

   and teleology 146

essentia dei 67

evangelical freedom 182, 191–4

   and human sexuality 183

exegetical reasoning 44, 60–1, 64n. 33

extra Calvinisticum 66

'facing' (as soteriological theme) 126

fallenness, and necessity of patience 196

Father

   eternal purpose 128

   freedom 190

   paternity 115, 132

fellowship with God 46, 48–9, 54, 105, 182

   breached by sin 127

   as freedom-granting 190, 191–4

Fichte, Johann Gottlieb 29

finitude, and necessity of patience 196

First Commandment, and soteriology
   122–3, 126

forbearance 204–5

Ford, David 179n. 24

forgiveness, as gift of God 176

formation 27

   of desire 200

   of intellectual character 200

Foucault, Michel 33, 158

freedom

   as autonomy 183, 191

   from care of self 193

   gospel-derived account of 189

   as self-constitution 182, 184, 185–6

   as self-government 191

   set over against nature 186

set over against situation 186–7
within situations 192
Frei, Hans 103
futurism 152–3

generic theism 21, 29, 187
generosity 13–14, 208
German idealism 29
God
    absolute otherness 111–12
    as agent who makes himself known 22
    as aloof 77n.
    aseity 73, 74, 191
    as author of patience 203
    communication of moral good to human
        creatures 196
    effortlessness 67, 73
    essence 189
    forbearance 203, 209
    freedom 182, 187, 189–91
    and human freedom 184, 187
    immensity 68, 71–5, 79, 82–3n. 19, 83n. 25
    immutability 111
    infinity 71
    life complete in itself 126
    love for creatures 56, 117
    metaphysics *in se* 68, 72, 128, 130, 132
    mission of, in nature and grace 108
    as *non aliud* 112
    as object of inquiry 22
    omnipresence 69, 72, 75–81, 83n. 25
    as ontological principle of Christian
        theology 44, 59
    patience 196, 203, 207n.
    perfect life in divine processions 132
    plenitude in life 111
    presence 75, 76, 80–81
    prevenience 30
    as principium 117
    pro nobis 72, 119
    purposes for creatures 47
    richness of trinitarian life 129
    self-sufficiency 91, 111
    simplicity 111–12, 117

singularity 67, 70
transcendence 65–6, 188n.
    as 'uncontainable' 76
    ubiquity 68, 69
    works *ad extra* 48, 74, 91–2, 94, 98, 108,
        109, 115
    works *ad intra* 48, 85, 91, 108, 115,
        116n., 133
    see also Father; Son; Spirit; Trinity
God and all things in God, as double theme of
    Christian theology 29n., 55, 124
God and creatures, as 'mixed' relation 105, 107,
    108, 115–16, 117
Goodwin, Thomas 202
Gorringe, Timothy 169–70
gospel 124
    biblical reasoning on 121–2
    and freedom 184
grand narratives 151
Grant, George 26
gratitude 13–14, 201
Gregory the Great 201–2, 211n. 22
Guillory, J. 33
Gunton, Colin 3

habits 195
Hartshorne, Charles 116
Hauerwas, Stanley 163, 195
Hegel, G. W. F. 5–6, 8
hermeneutical ontology 10, 13
Hilary of Poitiers 64n. 34
historical Jesus 97n.
historicism 11
history of redemption 49, 110
Hodge, Charles 71
Holy Spirit
    consummation of purpose of God 128
    freedom 190–1
    and reconciliation 174–5
    spiration 115, 132, 133
Horton, Michael S. 140n. 48
'hospitality' (as soteriological theme) 126
human fellowship 127, 194
human freedom 182, 192

human identity 145, 147
human sexuality 183
humility 201, 208
Hütter, Reinhard 63n. 9, 163
hypostatic union 136

identity politics 14
idolatry, in eschatology 154
imitatio 171
impartiality 201
impatience 205
incarnation 98, 171, 175
    and divine immensity 74
    and eternal inner-triune persons and
        relations 92
    instrumental character of human
        nature 94n.
    redemption of reason 43, 58
intellectual benevolence 201
intellectual courage 201, 206
intellectual faculties 199–200
intellectual goods, as gifts 208
intellectual inquiry 195, 198, 199–200
intellectual ontology 13, 35–36
intellectual patience 196, 201, 206–9
intellectual practices 199–200
intellectual repentance 12
intellectual virtues 196
intelligence 49
interiority 26
International Journal of Systematic Theology 3

Janz, Paul 43, 58
Jenson, Robert 130–1, 163
Jesus Christ
    coming 152–3
    exalted 9, 76, 163, 164
    lordship 9
    patience 203
    resurrection 9–10
    saving history as commissioned
        history 135–6
    as servant 124
    transcendence of moral community 177–8

    see also incarnation; Son
Jones, Greg 176
Jüngel, Eberhard 1, 3, 29, 66, 97n., 181
justification 171

Kant, Immanuel 38, 101, 155, 160
Kantian epistemology 43
Kantzer Lectures (2007) 4, 65, 86, 88n.
Käsemann, E. 179n. 30
kataphatic theology of mediation 175
Kingdom of God 177
knowledge
    acquired over time 207
    love of 200, 201
knowledge of God 50
koinonia ecclesiologies 163, 164, 167, 169

Lacoste, Jean-Yves 154
learning
    as generic human enterprise 26
    patience in 207
    and reading 28
Lindbeck, George 195
long-suffering 203
Lord's Supper 52, 171
Lubac, Henri de 163
Lutheran Christology 99n., 129
Lyotard, Jean-François 142, 149

MacKenzie, Ian 72
MacKinnon, Donald 135
Macquarrie, John 35, 79
magnanimity 201
martyrdom 204
material order 131–2
mediation 175–6
metaphysics of God *in se* 128, 130
metaphysics of presence 176
modernity 22, 28, 33, 149–50
modern theology
    crisis of 8
    excessive devotion to divine economy 99–
        100, 108, 121, 128
modesty 201

Moltmann, Jürgen 117n., 122

monastic vocation 204

Montaigne, M. de 155

moral ontology 10, 181–2

moral theology 13, 195–6

moral virtues 199

Morris, Thomas 66

mortification and vivification 58, 61–2, 118

Musil, Robert 155

mystery, as God's self-disclosing act 129–30

narrative theology 70n., 142

naturalism 51

natural theology 69

nature, order of 186

neo-Platonism 78

new creation 168, 174

Newtonianism 79

Nietzsche, Friedrich 148, 150

nominalism 126, 158, 177, 185

non-local public 38

non-reciprocal relations, between God
    and creatures 105–6, 107, 108,
    115–16, 117

non-theological theology 11

nouvelle théologie 105, 163

Nussbaum, Martha 32

objectivity, modern notions of 46n.

omnipraesentia generalis 76

ontology 43

ontology of indication 176

onto-theology 59, 142, 148, 150, 156

order 186

order of nature 186

orthodoxy, as 'shared attention' 37–8

Owen, John 202

Oxford Handbook of Systematic Theology 3–4

Oxford University 3, 5

panentheism 73

Pannenberg, Wolfhart 70, 122, 137n. 6, 174

pantheism 73

participation 57–8, 105, 175n.

patience 196, 201–2, 210

penultimate 48, 58

persecution 204

philosophical theology 69

pluralism 7, 36

polemical task of theology 8, 184

post-critical, pragmatic epistemology 54

postliberalism 3, 12, 164, 167n.

postmodernism 44, 141–2, 147–9, 192n.
    abandonment of eschatology 150, 152
    apophaticism of 153
    and history 149–55
    on selfhood 142, 155–6

post-Reformation Protestants. *See* Reformed
    scholastics

power, as disorder of sin 62

praise 81

prayer
    act of evangelical freedom 193–4
    and eschatology 154
    and intellectual patience 208

pre-critical exegesis 52

presence of God 11

process philosophy 77

process theology 156

prophetic and apostolic speech 51–2, 61

providence 13–14, 155

Pusey, E. B. 36

rationalism 33, 36

rationality, and social practice 38

reading 28

reason
    as created reality 54–5
    and divine economy 47
    and divine self-communication 57
    as fallen 55–6
    and fellowship with God 54
    as instrumental 26–7
    pilgrim state of 59
    redemption of 53, 56, 58, 60
    as sphere of grace 62

reconciliation 49, 125, 131, 137, 160, 164,
    166, 169

action of God in Christ 169–72

and church's moral action 166–7, 169

and Holy Spirit 174–5

and patience 202

priority over liberation 170

retrospective and prospective 170

as speech 173

reflective self 26

Reformed incarnational teaching 129

Reformed scholastics 30, 31, 45, 53

relation 114

repentance 171

restlessness 205

resurrection

as apologetic 21

from object to ground of belief 30

retrieval 16

revelation

revelation in modern Protestant theology 30

as incarnation 99

Ritschl, Albrecht 85, 101, 102, 177–8

Rorty, Richard 157

Schillebeeckx, Edward 168

Schleiermacher, Friedrich 29, 83n. 20, 99

schooling, as transformation 27

Schrag, Calvin 142, 156, 157–8, 161n. 42

Schwöbel, Christoph 129

Scripture

ambassadorial 51n., 52

authority of 53

cognitive principle of theology 59

in divine economy 51–3

as divine speech 57

and dogmatics 12

inspiration 51n 52

metaphysics 9, 46

prophetic and apostolic testimony 51–2, 61

reading 'against itself' 7

reception of 53

rhetoric of 32, 61, 86

servant of divine Word 52

teleology of 46

Second Vatican Council 105, 167n.

selfhood 142, 184, 185

servant, affliction of 124

sin

bondage to 184, 193

trespass against creatureliness 127

social trinitarianism 163

solus Deus 176

Son

agent of creation 98

aseity 10

deity and relations 89, 95

earthly ministry 89, 98, 128

exaltation 98

filiation 95, 115, 132, 133

freedom 190

names and title 98

offices 98

procession precedes mission 95–6, 132–3

restores covenant between God and

creatures 190

states of humiliation and exaltation 98

soteriology 124–37

derivative doctrine 125

divine self-exposition 129

in systematic theology 121–2, 125

and Trinity 129

space 11, 71–4, 79–81, 158

Spence, A. 140n. 48

Stoicism 77

studiousness 201

suffering, and patience 209

suffering God 77n., 117n., 122

Swinburne, Richard 137n. 8

systematic natural theology 68–9

systematic theology

cognitive order 92

criticisms of 89

end and purpose 90

low-level 61, 86

mutual reference of procession and

mission 96

nature 85, 89

order of exposition and material order 90–2,

100, 131n., 132

practitioners 90
settings 90
sources 90

talk about God 34–5
Tanner, Kathryn 3
Taylor, Mark 150, 156
teachableness 201, 208
teleology 43
    dissolution in postmodern era 142
temporal processions, divine missions as 133
Tertullian 196, 201, 203, 206
theological anthropology 141, 143, 145–9
theological asceticism 12
theological Christology 86
theological education 7
theological inquiry, looks backward and
        forward 13
theological metaphysics 134, 142
theological theology 30, 108n.
theological writing, genres 31
theology
    alert to the challenge of the gospel 7
    as ascetical discipline 44
    and context 148
    as disturbing 24
    as exegetical and dogmatic, not apologetic
        or revisionary 148
    and faithfulness to the gospel 6–7
    as fellowship with God 46
    literary forms of 31
    misreadings of 1
    as positive science 8
    primacy over economy 91–2, 93
    reading of 5–8
    severed from economy 99–100, 101
theology in the university 21, 34–9, 195,
        198–9, 209–10
    conforms to norms of neighboring
        disciplines 23–33, 44
    defined by neighboring disciplines 44
    de-regionalized 32
    marginalization of 8, 29
'theology of embrace' 170–1

Thiemann, Ronald 30
Thomas Aquinas 68, 78, 122
    Christology of 94
    on God's perfections 113–14
    on material order 132
    misreading of 1
    non-reciprocal relation between God and
        creatures 105, 116
    on patience 202, 207
    on Trinity and incarnation 93, 130
time 11
tolerance 208
Torrance, Iain 3
Torrance, T. F. 64n. 34
tradition 6, 26–7, 31, 38, 48
Traherne, T. 81
Trinity 16
    and Christology 88, 103
    and creation 111
    distributed doctrine 106, 109
    and divine attributes 75
    drifted toward margins of theology 187
    immanent prior to economic 169
    mystery of 129–30
    no subordination in 132
    priority of subsistence in 132
    and soteriology 122, 126, 129
    and space 79–80
Turretin, Francis 55, 56, 59

ubivolpraesentia 76–7
universal reason 43
universities
    contain conflict 24
    conventions of 25–6
    texts 28
    threats faced by 209
University of Aberdeen 3
University of Berlin model 29
University Reform Commission (1850) 36
University of St Andrews 3, 195

verbum externum 50
verbum internum 50

'violence' (as soteriological theme) 126
virtues 195–6, 199
    and hope 159n.
    presupposes human nature 209
    required of the systematic theologian 90
    and skills 199
vocation 192
Volf, Miroslav 170–1

will 182, 185–6
Williams, Anna 54
Williams, Rowan 24, 99n.
Williams, Stephen 166
wisdom of the world 56

Wissenschaft 21, 25, 27, 28, 36
Wollebius, Johannes 22, 35
Word
    cognitive principle of Christian
        theology 35, 44
    enacts covenant fidelity of God 128
    terminus ad quem 93
    terminus a quo 92–3
work of grace 13–14, 86, 98, 105, 108,
    109–10
work of nature 13–14, 86, 98, 108, 110
Wycliffe College (Toronto) 3, 5

Yale School 195

CPSIA information can be obtained
at www.ICGtesting.com
Printed in the USA
LVHW020037050822
725201LV00005B/206